AF439743

INVENTING
STEREOTYPE

INVENTING STEREOTYPE

Race, Representation, and Interwar America

MARTIN A. BERGER

The University of Chicago Press
Chicago and London

The University of Chicago Press, Chicago 60637
The University of Chicago Press, Ltd., London
© 2025 by The University of Chicago
All rights reserved. No part of this book may be used or reproduced in any
manner whatsoever without written permission, except in the case of brief
quotations in critical articles and reviews. For more information, contact
the University of Chicago Press, 1427 E. 60th St., Chicago, IL 60637.
Published 2025
Printed in the United States of America

34 33 32 31 30 29 28 27 26 25   1 2 3 4 5

ISBN-13: 978-0-226-84367-4 (cloth)
ISBN-13: 978-0-226-84368-1 (e-book)
DOI: https://doi.org/10.7208/chicago/9780226843681.001.0001

Library of Congress Cataloging-in-Publication Data

Names: Berger, Martin A., author.
Title: Inventing stereotype : race, representation, and interwar America /
Martin A. Berger.
Description: Chicago : The University of Chicago Press, 2025 | Includes
bibliographical references and index.
Identifiers: LCCN 2025004984 | ISBN 9780226843674 (cloth) | ISBN 9780226843681
(ebook)
Subjects: LCSH: Stereotypes (Social psychology) in art. | Minorities in art. | Arts
and society—United States—History—20th century. | Ethnicity—United States—
History—20th century.
Classification: LCC NX651.8 .B47 2025 | DDC 704.0300973/09042—dc23/eng/20250429
LC record available at https://lccn.loc.gov/2025004984

∞ This paper meets the requirements of ANSI/NISO Z39.48-1992
(Permanence of Paper).

Authorized Representative for EU General Product Safety Regulation (GPSR)
queries: **Easy Access System Europe**—Mustamäe tee 50, 10621 Tallinn, Estonia,
gpsr.requests@easproject.com
Any other queries: https://press.uchicago.edu/press/contact.html

*In memory of Judith Mayer
(1921–2015)*

Contents

THE RELATIVISM OF STEREOTYPES

Inventing Stereotype is inspired by a basic question that has troubled my research and teaching on race for thirty years: How does one know if a character in a painting, play, or novel is stereotyped? There exists no agreed-upon methodology. Most of us simply proceed in the belief that we recognize stereotyped figures when we see them. But the issue is more complex. My research has highlighted the degree to which the perception of stereotypes in representations varies over time and among audiences from different backgrounds. Numerous nineteenth-century reviews describe stereotyped figures in paintings or plays that appear nonstereotyped to me; and many twentieth-century studies laud artworks for offering "truthful," "real," or "naturalistic" depictions that I see as littered with stereotypes.

Consider the significant distance between the interpretations of J. G. Brown's painting *A Card Trick* (ca. 1891–92, plate 1) by contemporary scholars and its first critics. The painting illustrates three white bootblacks sitting or leaning against shoeshine boxes on a sidewalk as they smile at a card trick performed by a Black shoeshine boy. Art historians today have provided positive assessments of *A Card Trick*'s racial politics, with one noting that Brown highlighted both the "individuality" and "skill" of the Black bootblack and that the canvas moved past the nineteenth century's "stereotype of the darkey minstrel"; a second claims that the artist "ascribes streetsmarts and a gamesman's skill to this clever character" and that the painting avoids "the most offensive racial stereotypes" of its era.[1] When the painting was exhibited at the 1893 World's Columbian Exposition in Chicago, it was reproduced in several commemorative guidebooks, two of which captioned their reproductions with a lengthy description that read, in part:

> Humor is, in this picture, everything. We laugh with those who laugh. The artist represents a group of four bootblacks in a resting-spell of their professional duties, and devoting their quickening intelligence to the mysteries of cards. Africa, on his knees, is instructing the three descendants of Japheth in a trick which he has learned. . . . The humor of the thing is delicious. . . . Jefferson, for his part, black as the blackest of cards, understands that his professional reputation is at stake in the presence of his white brethren. His otherwise sluggish mind is preternaturally sharpened with the trial, and his face becomes almost luminous with pride as he holds forth the impossible card.[2]

To my eye, the scene is not obviously humorous. The Black child's features do not appear stereotyped, nor do I see legible signs that the white children sit in judgment of the boy's "professional reputation." There are no narrative or physiological clues to the unequal intelligence of the white and Black children. And there is nothing that indicates to me that the characters are anything but individuals, unlike the racial signifiers "Africa" and "Jefferson" (Black) and "Japheth" (white) perceived by the critic.[3] In contrast to those contemporary art historians who see a depiction highlighting the Black character's "individuality," "skill," and "cleverness," the nineteenth-century reviewer interpreted the boy as a generic representative of his race who possessed a "sluggish mind" and is placed "on his knees" to entertain his white betters. We are left to puzzle over whether the painting "avoided the most offensive racial stereotypes" of its era or reproduced them.

The assessments of past critics can be jarringly discordant with modern views even when the critics were deeply informed on race. Take the writings of Alain Locke, a philosopher trained at Harvard, Oxford, and Berlin Universities, who was one of the most sophisticated theorists of race at work in the first decades of the twentieth century.[4] In 1936, he published *Negro Art: Past and Present*. The work offered a primer on the depiction of Black figures in fine art painting and sculpture from the colonial period to the mid-1930s. In the chapter "American Art Re-Discovers the Negro," Locke surveyed the evolving treatment of Black subjects by white artists from the 1880s to the 1930s. He described what he took as the improving state of depictions, beginning with Winslow Homer's rediscovery of Black Americans as worthy subjects of fine art, through Robert Henri's deepening understanding of Black character, up to George Bellows's success in accurately representing Black people as they are. With reference to a string of stereotypes that Locke saw hindering representations of Black Americans, he expressed admiration for Bellows's artwork, writing: "No more Uncle Remuses, Aunt Chloe's or Jemimas or pickaninnies for Bellows, or through his influence, for progressive American art. After this Negroes were individuals not mere types." Locke deemed Bellows's art the catalyst for white progressives to abandon the stereotypes that had dominated depictions of Black Americans since the era of chattel slavery, writing of the canvases' "revolutionary effect and influence." And he cheered that in Bellows's artwork viewers were presented with "fidelity to fact."[5]

Present-day historians have noted that Bellows and his Ashcan colleagues infrequently illustrated Black subjects and that their rare depictions "often conformed to the stereotypes of the era." In analyzing the artist's *Tin Can Battle, San Juan Hill, New York* (1907, plate 2), which pictures a poor and crowded Black neighborhood in early twentieth-century Manhattan, one art historian explained that Bellows modeled the figures on the illustrator E. W. Kemble's "stereotyped and grossly racist cartoons of black" people, while a second observed that "the faces of the children . . . are apelike." Locke's claim that Bellows initiated a new progressive model for the depiction of Black Americans fails to resonate with art historians today who see in the artist's paintings, lithographs, and drawings the unconscious biases typical of the era's left-leaning whites.[6] The Black figures in *Tin Can Battle* are either "individuals not mere types" or "racist" types, depending on who is looking.

Readers are likely to form their own opinions on the artworks' links to stereotypes, but whether they present a new interpretation or support a position advanced by one of the cited critics, my larger argument holds. The diversity of interpretations among audiences and across time highlights the interpretive challenges posed to viewers in assessing the presence of stereotyped figures in artworks. The nineteenth-century description of Brown's painting makes clear that the critic saw things that are unapparent to audiences today. Since we typically assume that stereotypes exist in works of art and literature, is his description evidence that our racial context is so different that we can no longer see what is pictured in the painting? Or is it rather an indication that stereotypes exist in viewers and that the painting's 1890s audiences saw the painting through a racialized filter that distorted its true appearance and meaning? With Bellows's drawing, do we see stereotypes today because we possess a more sophisticated understanding of race and Black identity than did Locke? If a scholar of Locke's erudition missed the stereotypes, does that raise the likelihood that we are surrounded today by art deemed nonstereotyped that future viewers will conclude is laden with stereotypes? And what are the implications if artworks can shift over time from stereotyped to nonstereotyped and vice versa? These are just a few of the knotty issues raised by the disparate receptions of these two artworks.

In an effort to grapple with the complexities of the question with which I began my introduction, *Inventing Stereotype* opens by tracing the emergence of our present-day concept of stereotype in the early 1920s. My interest is not with stereotype's cognitive processes, but with its social and cultural functions in making sense of art and identities during the interwar period. Chapter 1 unpacks the genealogy of the stereotype concept, illustrating how it was uniquely shaped by visuality and race. The chapter fleshes out the concept's intellectual debts to philosophy, psychology, political science, and, most importantly, art history, before illustrating how it was conditioned by racial science in the 1920s, including eugenics, genetics, and social Darwinism. While the stereotype concept was applied to a vast range of topics, its governing logic was rooted in early twentieth-century theories of race. Chapter 2 moves from the theory of stereotype to its application. Within months of its invention, stereotype was a widely embraced concept that had attained currency with both scholarly and popular audiences. The chapter explores the ways in which the concept was transformed by critics, historians, and members of the public as it moved from an abstract idea to a concrete tool. And it explains why the hunt for stereotypes in novels, plays, and the visual arts became a dominant approach to culture among those invested in race.

Chapter 3 studies the reception of elite and popular theatrical productions, and chapter 4 analyzes fine art paintings, all of which were created during the 1920s and 1930s. Both chapters foreground stereotypes associated with Black Americans, given Blackness's centrality to structuring race in America. Chapter 3 also gives significant attention to the era's stereotypes of Jews. In the 1920s, American Jews were deemed less secure in their whiteness than either Protestant immigrants or native-born Christians whose ancestors hailed from western Europe. In addition, the physical signs of their racial difference were understood to be less legible than those of nonwhite groups. The indeterminacy of Jews during the interwar period provides useful context for deepening the understanding of stereotype's function during decades in which social models of race challenged biological ones and white Americans expressed growing fear over the illegibility of racial difference.

The selected plays and paintings in chapters 3 and 4 fall into one of two categories: they stirred debate among their first audiences as to whether or not they employed stereotypes in the depiction of Black,

Jewish, or white Americans; or were deemed nonstereotyped in the interwar period but came to be seen as stereotyped in later decades. Through careful attention to the responses of discrete subsets of the artworks' audiences—parsed by race and political leanings and, at times, by religion and class—the chapters illustrate the relative nature of stereotypes. Readers will come to see that artworks deemed free of stereotypes look naturalistic to viewers for one of two reasons. When the stereotypes embedded within artworks accord with viewer expectations, or when audiences project their internalized stereotypes onto artworks, the artworks appear to represent the world as it is. Artworks also register as naturalistic when they break from dominant narrative or stylistic conventions that viewers understand to be arbitrarily associated with the depicted race. In other words, viewers who accept a particular stereotype as accurate interpret artworks that activate or reflect that stereotype as true; and audiences who are sensitized to a particular stereotype being a stereotype regard artworks that refute or complicate that stereotype as true. Nonstereotyped artworks are so categorized relative to representational norms, not relative to their success in conveying the authentic identities of individuals or racial groups. *Inventing Stereotype* illustrates that the act of categorizing a representation as either stereotyped or nonstereotyped reveals the values of viewers at discrete moments in time. Both seeing and not seeing stereotypes stem from social and psychological processes only loosely linked to what is depicted in works of literature and fine art.

CHAPTER 1

THE WORLD OUTSIDE AND THE PICTURES IN OUR HEADS

What each man does is based not on direct and certain knowledge, but on pictures made by [him] or given to him.—WALTER LIPPMANN, *Public Opinion* (1922)

Whether he will it or no, every individual is a race product,—a wavelet of a great race-ocean.—MONTGOMERY GREGORY, "Race in Art" (1915)

Stereotype was invented in 1921. In December of that year the journalist and public intellectual Walter Lippmann first described stereotype in its modern sense. The description appeared in the second installment of a five-part serial that reproduced the core of Lippmann's forthcoming book, *Public Opinion* (1922).[1] It addressed the seemingly straightforward question of how the public arrived at its beliefs. Convinced of public opinion's great power to influence elected officials, Lippmann expressed concern that citizens routinely arrived at ill-informed opinions of people and events far removed from their day-to-day experiences and expertise. He hoped that his analysis would spur debate on the best means of producing an informed citizenry, which he deemed of paramount importance to democracies. At the heart of his thesis was a new definition of stereotype as a tool used by the public to simplify and order the complexities of the modern world.

The word *stereotype* predates Lippmann. It is a neologism from the turn of the nineteenth century that combined the Greek words for "firm" or "solid" (*stereos*) and "impression" (*typos*). It was coined as a specialized term to describe an advance in printing technology. Prior to the advent of stereotype printing, printers arranged individual movable-type letters to form lines of text. The new process of stereotyping allowed them to cast a single metal plate that contained all the letters required to print a page of text. The technology saved time and allowed for the rapid and consistent reproduction of texts. The fixed nature of the letters on the plate, which ensured identical results with each pressing, allowed for the word to take on a metaphoric meaning sometime after 1850. *Webster's Revised Unabridged Dictionary* (1913) defined this secondary meaning as "to make firm or permanent; to fix."[2]

In *Public Opinion* Lippmann transformed the secondary definition of *stereotype* from anything that was "fixed" into a vastly more complex concept. A stereotype was a shared mental picture (of a person, group, event, thing, or social system) that simplified the thing represented so that it might be easily grasped. Given the impossibility of individuals gaining knowledge of everything in the world through direct experience, stereotypes provided a way of making sense of complicated and often distant things by translating them into digestible images. As Lippmann explained, "The only feeling that anyone can have about an event he does not experience is the feeling aroused by his mental image of the event." And he went on to note: "What each man [thinks and] does is based not on direct and certain knowledge, but on pictures made by himself or given to him." According to Lippmann, thinking with stereotypes was an essential feature of modern life in a hyperconnected world.[3]

In formulating his concept of the stereotype, Lippmann consciously chose to make use of a preexisting word that possessed neutral associations. The "fixing" of something was neither good nor bad in the 1920s; it was simply a factual description of consistency. Lippmann carefully considered the word choice. He explained to readers that he chose to write of stereotypes, rather than "ideals," because the latter "is usually reserved for what we consider the good, the true and the beautiful. Thus it carries the hint that there is something to be copied or attained." He wanted a word that was as apt in describing unvalued as valued qualities. The largely negative associations that stereotypes hold for readers today were not a feature of Lippmann's original conception. In his description, stereotypes could convey either positive or negative attributes at the level of content. And as a mental shortcut, they were simply an unavoidable feature of modern society, which offered both advantages and disadvantages. In providing an efficient means of coping with otherwise overwhelming quantities of information, they distanced one from the complexities of the things represented. As he made clear, stereotypes did not offer a picture of either an ideal or an imperfect world, but rather "the kind of world we expect it to be."[4]

In 1920 the words *caricature* and *type* both came closer than *stereotype* did to approximating Lippmann's new definition, though each carried baggage that would have limited period readers' understanding of the concept. *Caricature* was then defined as "a picture or other figure or description in which the peculiarities of a person or thing are so exaggerated as to appear ridiculous; a burlesque; a parody."[5] Use of the word by Lippmann would have posed two problems. First, caricature was rooted in the "peculiarities" of the person represented. It exaggerated traits that existed. Lippmann hoped to insulate stereotype from any hint that it necessarily captured the essence of things. And second, both burlesque and parody held negative connotations.

Type was then understood as "that which possesses or exemplifies characteristic qualities; the representative. Specifically: (a) (Biol.) A general form or structure common to a number of individuals; hence, the ideal representation of a species, genus, or other group, combining the essential characteristics."[6] The word had the advantage of representing things whether they were valued or not. But as with *caricature*, *type* was problematic for presenting the lowest common denominator of the thing represented. It had the additional complication of being used extensively by eugenicists and physical anthropologists in the 1920s. The word was then strongly associated with a racial discourse and its hierarchy of races. *Type* came with too much baggage to serve Lippmann's need of applying broadly to people, objects, and concepts across society.

Lippmann did reference types in *Public Opinion*, but only as a foundation for the more complex stereotype. In explaining the current conditions that make stereotypes a necessity, he wrote: "Modern life is hurried and multifarious. . . . There is neither time nor opportunity for intimate acquaintance. Instead we notice a trait which marks a well-known type, and fill in the rest of the picture by means of the stereotypes we carry about in our heads."[7] The passage acknowledges our capacity to discern actual traits, while suggesting how stereotypes distance us from the person they purport to represent. Traits conjure up a type, and that, in turn, invokes a series of stereotypes. In this way the observation of a real attribute is quickly subsumed under stereotypical pictures arbitrarily associated with the type and removed from the original trait. Lippmann offers the example of a man perceived to be an agitator. The picture people see when they think about him is based less on the one observed trait than on the multiple stereotyped pictures that the type conjures up. Fixed pictures of unionists, foreigners, and communists are but a sampling of the kinds of images likely to cloud one's understanding of anyone deemed to be an agitator.

Lippmann's consistent reference to "images" and "pictures" in describing the workings of stereotypes was more than evocative prose. He wrote of pictures' critical role in embodying stereotypes. "Pictures," he maintained, "have always been the surest way of conveying an idea, and next in order, words that call up pictures in memory." Graham Wallas, Lippmann's Harvard College professor and, later, close colleague, likely suggested the linkage of pictures and stereotypes. Wallas was an English social psychologist and political scientist who taught at the London School of Economics and helped found the Fabian Society, an organization devoted to socialist economic reform. He offered a course in politics at Harvard during Lippmann's final year, which exposed the young student to the idea that human psychology must be taken into account in order to understand the workings of political systems in practice. Lippmann found Wallas's approach to politics a revelation.[8]

As early as 1899 Wallas described a precursor to Lippmann's modern stereotype using art metaphors, though he gave it no name and explained its operation in vague terms.[9] Concerned to illuminate how citizens gained conceptions of things outside of their direct experience (and, at times, beyond their mental and emotional capacities), Wallas hypothesized that people must employ "some acquired entity of the mind." As he groped for a metaphor to explain this "entity," he first suggested: "Each of us walks through life with his head locked within a lighted box painted with the picture of the world by which he guides his steps." In this evocative vignette, Plato's prisoners are unchained, though each is fitted with a personal cave. But immediately after describing the painted box model, Wallas lists its limitations, noting its inability to account for how direct sensations of our immediate surroundings provide "at least the foreground of [our] mental picture."[10]

After discarding the painted box as a metaphor for how we visualize things beyond our experience, Wallas considered panoramic displays as an alternative model. Panoramas offered an advantage in that they often included real objects in the foreground, which viewers experience firsthand, before their eyes drift back into the illusionistic world of a painted background that conveys a simplified picture of the things depicted. Wallas found satisfying the panoramic model's ability to account for his sense that human beings combine concrete knowledge of material things within their immediate environment with abstract understandings of distant events that are beyond their firsthand experience. Describing a panorama of the Battle of Waterloo that he saw at a country fair as a child, Wallas cautioned that when we act in the world based on an understanding of things that are beyond our sensory perceptions, "we are often like an excited rustic at the fair who should fire a gun at the painted French army on the panorama-canvas and kill a real market woman across the square." As he did with the painted box model, Wallas ultimately concluded that the panoramic metaphor was imperfect. He laments that the static nature of the display, which is arranged to look naturalistic from a single vantage, cannot account for how our mental pictures evolve over time.[11]

Following Wallas, Lippmann introduced stereotypes to his readers by asking how it is that we come to understand things beyond our daily experience. Lippmann did so because the epistemological issues raised by the question were so weighty, not because he shared Wallas's faith in our capacity to clearly see and understand the people and things around us. Lippmann rejected the fundamental distinction Wallas described—between the mental picture of the foreground that we form through direct experience with the material world and those of the background that we acquire through a simplified image of a distant and complex event. He believed our foreground and background pictures were equally likely to be structured by stereotypes. As a result, Lippmann was not compelled to find an art metaphor that accounted for different ways of comprehending near and distant things. He found in conventional prints and paintings an apt model for illustrating to readers how stereotypes functioned in practice.

Public Opinion turned to Sinclair Lewis's best-selling novel *Main Street: The Story of Carol Kennicott* (1920) to illuminate how art provided the visual raw material through which stereotypes structured thought.[12] The mildly satirical novel, set in the early years of the Great War, followed the ineffectual efforts of its protagonist, Carol Kennicott, to promote culture and liberal thinking in Gopher Prairie, Minnesota, the small town to which she moved after wedding the local physician. Kennicott surrounds herself with the town's most freethinking residents, one of whom is the high school's English and French teacher, Vida Sherman. For much of the novel, Sherman serves as the bridge between Kennicott and the native residents, as she is one of the few characters to understand the perspectives of the newcomer, who prefers big city life, and the townspeople, who are content with Gopher Prairie in its current state.

Using Sherman as an archetypal educated citizen, Lippmann reflects on how someone who "has never been to France, and . . . never been along . . . the battlefront" is likely to understand the world war that was then raging. Lippmann writes: "If you could see what she sees with her mind's eye, the image of [the Great War] in its composition might not be unlike an eighteenth-century engraving of a great soldier. He stands there boldly unruffled and more than life size, with a shadowy army of tiny little figures winding off into the landscape behind." She "knows" the war not as a collection of statistics, dates, and battles either described in the local paper or narrated by veterans, but foremost as an image. Her picture transforms the messiness of the war into a coherent narrative, one that has more to do with nascent conceptions of eighteenth-century nationalism, romanticism, and imperialism, than the modern war that was then tearing Europe apart. At the center of her picture is a strong military leader who meets the viewer's gaze, exudes confidence, and implicitly controls the endless stream of soldiers that disappears into the landscape. Shared by millions of Americans, such pictures of war—whether based on engravings of popular paintings by artists such as John Singleton Copley and John Trumbull (plate 3) or Antoine-Jean Gros and Jacques-Louis David—brought order to a maddeningly complex war without having any necessary connection to the reality of the conflict.[13]

Lest we assume that Sherman thinks in stereotypes merely because of her physical distance from France, consider that Lippmann also explored the propensity to stereotype of the French statesman Georges Clemenceau, who played a major role in guiding his government's prosecution of the First World War. As he did with the fictional Sherman, Lippmann speculated on the pictures through which Clemenceau was likely to have filtered the conflict. If during the negotiations for the 1919 Treaty of Versailles, Lippmann asks, "could anyone have penetrated the mind of M. Clemenceau, would he have found there images of the Europe of 1919, or a great sediment of stereotyped ideas accumulated and hardened in a long and pugnacious existence? Did he see the Germans of 1919, or the German type as he had learned to see it since 1871," in the aftermath of the Franco-Prussian War? Answering his rhetorical questions, Lippmann wrote of Clemenceau: "He saw the type." Stereotypes inevitably help shape one's understanding and experience, whether one is a civilian thousands of miles from the conflict, an elected official responsible for guiding war policy, or a soldier serving in the trenches.

While proximity to the front surely affected the type of mental pictures each group held, it did not diminish a fundamental reliance on stereotyping.[14]

Art played an obvious role in furnishing Sherman with her picture of the war—a mass-produced engraving served as the point of reference by which the veracity of newspaper reports, first-person accounts, and political debates of the conflict was judged. In Lippmann's estimation, art connected to stereotypes in two distinct ways. Art furnished many of the mental images that solidified into stereotypes; it was often the visual source material. Given Lippmann's broad definition of art, he was comfortable seeing the "pictures" drawn from painting, sculpture, prints, motion pictures, plays, cartoons, and literature, but he explained that mental pictures were also generated by "moral codes and our political philosophies and our political agitations."[15] In addition to supplying source material, art supplied a framework for making stereotypes intelligible and, through the discipline of art history, a guide to understanding their operation. Sherman and Clemenceau both held pictures in mind, and their respective pictures adhered to a governing logic that art historians were best positioned to illuminate. It did not matter that one image was likely derived from high art and the other from a political philosophy, since in Lippmann's estimation internalized images functioned in a like manner regardless of their source.

The discipline of art history is introduced into *Public Opinion* through the writing of Bernard Berenson, one of the early twentieth century's most influential art historians. Berenson was then known for putting art history on a more scientific footing. He sought to reform a discipline then dominated by the authentication of masterworks through the often-arbitrary judgments of an expert "eye" by promoting a coherent aesthetic philosophy. Berenson styled himself as a scientific connoisseur—someone deeply invested in making attributions that were systematically verifiable. As Berenson explained in his *Three Essays in Method* (1927), the approach required "average powers of observation, and concentration and reasoning of the kind that the botanist or anatomist is supposed to have. It calls, besides, for training in the historical method, that method which teaches not only how to weigh evidence . . . but how to recognize what is relevant when it appears, and how to look for it when it hides."[16]

Berenson enters *Public Opinion* in a lengthy quote from the art historian's *Central Painters of the Italian Renaissance* (1897), a popular book that was the third volume in his loosely organized series on Italian Renaissance art: "What with the almost numberless shapes assumed by an object. . . . What with our insensitiveness and inattention, things scarcely would have for us features and outlines so determined and clear that we could recall them at will, but for the stereotyped shapes art has lent them."[17] The passage provided backing for several of Lippmann's claims: the complexity of objects in the environment proves to be overwhelming to viewers; human failings make it challenging to see what is before us; and art can bring order to the world by teaching one how to see in standardized ways. As with the previously quoted passage on Berenson's method, it also suggested that what we see is but a partial glimpse of the world; significant aspects of it "hide" from view.[18]

Because Berenson wrote in 1897, he necessarily used "stereotype" in its older sense, referring to a codified type that was fixed, though the lack of context for the quoted passage likely masked disparities between the older and newer definitions. In citing Berenson's earlier use of the term, and by making no effort to clarify its period meaning, Lippmann encouraged readers to imagine that the major redefinition of stereotype in *Public Opinion* was best seen as a modest, evolutionary change. This was important. Lippmann anticipated that *Public Opinion* would prove controversial. In it he took the provocative steps of introducing psychology into political science, questioning the utility of a free press, and raising doubt about the capacity of the public to make the informed judgments needed in a functioning democracy. In John Dewey's 1922 review of *Public Opinion*, the philosopher described the book as "perhaps the most effective indictment of democracy as currently conceived ever penned."[19] Other efforts by Lippmann to soften the book's reception included giving it the blandest possible title, as his biographer Ronald Steel has pointed out, and making extensive use of quotations.[20] While all of Lippmann's writings necessarily built on the work of prior scholarship, *Public Opinion* was then alone among

Lippmann's seven books in including long quotations and detailed footnotes.[21] Each of these choices worked to normalize the claims of this radical text.

Just as Berenson's older use of stereotype was useful to Lippmann, so too was the art historian's novel application of a scientific method to the study of art. In the 1920s and 1930s, Berenson's scholarship was regarded as a model of rigor that helped to legitimize the previously subjective study of high-art painting. For Jewish-born professionals, such as Lippmann and Berenson, who faced unique challenges in having their work accepted as objective, such methodological considerations were weighty. The cultural and literary historian Sander L. Gilman illustrated in *Jewish Self-Hatred: Anti-Semitism and the Hidden Language of the Jews* how Jews in early twentieth-century Europe and America were seen as perpetually alien. A European and American discourse held that even those Jews who adopted the outward trappings of the nations in which they resided (language, customs, food, and clothing) were unable to alter their fundamental otherness. Jews who appeared assimilated were believed to still think in their "native" Yiddish or Hebrew, before translating their thoughts into the local language. This left their thought processes and speech tainted by the underlying logic of their mother tongue and rendered suspect the objectivity of even native-born Jews. Consequently, the pressure to distance oneself from Judaism was intense. Gilman explains that in the early twentieth century, Berenson, Lippmann, and a host of other prominent first- and second-generation American Jews downplayed or rejected their Jewish identities. Berenson falsely claimed that German (not Yiddish) was his mother tongue, converted to Christianity (twice), and pondered the "puzzling character" of the Jews. Lippmann advised Harvard University on how to limit Jewish enrollment, declined to support Jewish immigration to the US even after Nazi atrocities were known, and described himself in 1921 as "one of those assimilated creatures to whom the Jewish past has no very peculiar intimate appeal" and as someone who felt most at home in "classical and Christian heritage." While society's identification and treatment of Lippmann as a Jew surely sensitized him to the issues of stereotyping that would feature prominently in *Public Opinion,* it was paradoxically his distancing from Judaism that smoothed the way for his stereotype concept to be taken seriously by academics and members of the public.[22]

In his effort to make the case for the broad applicability of Berenson's insights on art to society, Lippmann prefaced a lengthy quotation from the art historian with the observation "Substitute in the following passage of Mr. Berenson's the words 'politics,' 'business,' and 'society,' for the word 'art' and the sentences will be no less true." He then quoted the following from *Central Painters*: "Unless years devoted to the study of all schools of art have taught us also to see with our own eyes, we soon fall into the habit of moulding whatever we look at into the forms borrowed from the one art with which we are acquainted. There is our standard of artistic reality. Let anyone give us shapes and colors which we cannot instantly match in our paltry stock of hackneyed forms and tints, and we shake our heads at his failure to reproduce things as we know they certainly are."[23] The novel way in which Lippmann presented Berenson's quotation suggests the utility of applying art historical approaches to a broad range of social constructs that have nothing self-evidently to do with art. For as Lippmann explains, the substitution of "politics, business, and society" for "art" leaves *both* sets of sentences "true." The passage reinforces Lippmann's contention that "we do not first see, and then define, we define first and then see." As he argued, "In the great blooming, buzzing confusion of the outer world we pick out what our culture has already defined for us, and we tend to perceive that which we have picked out in the form stereotyped for us by our culture."[24]

The final quotation Lippmann reproduced from Berenson's *Central Painters* illustrated the stability of stereotypes by pointing out the degree to which turn-of-the-twentieth-century viewers judged male bodies through an ideal forged in the Renaissance. An extended quotation from Berenson explained the historical development of the bodily ideal before asking: "Who had the power to break through this . . . standard of vision and, out of the chaos of things, to select shapes more definitely expressive of reality than those fixed by men of genius? No one had such power."[25] The passage appears to argue for the impossibility of transcending fixed types. We are told that "no one" has the power to break through the "standard of vision." But recall that the previous Berenson quotation contained the line "Years devoted to the study of all schools of art [can] teach us to see with our own eyes." The art historian maintained that conversance with art's myriad styles loosened one from the strictures of any single point of view, thus permitting one to see the world with an innocent eye unclouded by types.

Berenson's argument on the Renaissance bodily ideal is that no one had the power to discard this *particular* ideal. He understood that types were continually developed, circulated, and discarded, but was convinced that a select group of types was beyond the capacity of individuals to displace. Taken in the context of its chapter, the quote makes clear that the ideal male type was fashioned by the separate but complementary efforts of two artistic "geniuses," Donatello and Masaccio. In Berenson's telling, both men were inspired by the scientific age and the desire to depict things as "research was discovering them to be." This put art on the road to naturalism, which Berenson believed would have eventually led to artworks that replicated the "chaos" of nature. To preserve the individuality and idiosyncrasies of all people and things was, for Berenson, to paint outside of social systems and reproduce the raw confusion of the natural world. Italian art avoided this undesirable end because Donatello's move toward naturalism was tempered by his personal interest in "movement and action," and Masaccio's was checked by his concern for "tactile values." Additionally, we are told that Masaccio curbed Donatello's push toward action, and Donatello, in turn, helped place limits on Masaccio's move toward monumentality. The ideal male form emerged when each of these efforts and counterforces combined with the Italian humanists' contemporaneous promotion of the antique.[26]

Berenson held that the ideal was unassailable in the fifteenth century because it was a perfect expression of Italian Renaissance character, and that it remained dominant in the nineteenth century because Europe still retained the essential character it acquired during the Renaissance.[27] The type was durable because it captured the ethos of both the quattrocento and modern era. Berenson knew that both artists of genius and second-rate hacks produced images laden with fixed types. His concern was not with the use of types but with their quality. "Great art" was "the reproduction of the visual images haunting great minds," which necessarily embodied the spirit of the age in which it was created.[28] Lippmann of course did not hold Berenson's belief in the possibility of naive looking. He maintained that a given stereotype's staying power with artists, politicians, and members of the public was a function of its imbrication in social systems. The durable types that Berenson took as expressions of artistic geniuses who captured the essence of their societies were, for Lippmann, simply those stereotypes most firmly entrenched in systems (such as laws of political economy or principles of politics) that effectively impressed "upon the world . . . our own sense of our value, our own position and our own rights." As Lippmann explained, instead of offering "a complete picture of the world, [stereotypes] are a picture of a possible world to which we are adapted. In that world people and things have their well-known places, and do certain expected things. We feel at home there. We fit in. We are members."[29]

Berenson believed that types capturing the spirit of an era could be dislodged only after society's "essential character" had been altered. Types that lost their correspondence to society were susceptible to replacement by newer types that expressed more relevant social truths.[30] Lippmann, in contrast, maintained that any stereotype could, in theory, be eliminated. He posited that individual stereotypes could be excised through careful study of both the things being stereotyped and the psychological state of the viewer who read it in stereotypical terms. Through study of the multifaceted attributes of things stereotyped and the psychology of the person seeing, simple pictures could give way to complex understandings.[31] Lippmann cautioned that stereotypes were only theoretically disposable because their elimination required considerable labor. It was no easy task to replace a simple picture with a complex understanding and so jettison a picture "to which we are adapted" in favor of an understanding that feels foreign. Lippmann was careful to distinguish between our capacity to reject individual stereotypes and our continuing dependence on the process of stereotyping.

It is this distinction that he likely had in mind when reproducing Berenson's passage on the durability of the ideal male type. In quoting the art historian's insistence that the "standard of vision" was resilient, Lippmann contrasted idealized types, which resisted change but were ultimately alterable, with what he termed—again quoting Berenson—"our manner of visualizing," which was the fixed process of seeing in the modern world.[32]

What and how people saw was consistently of interest to Lippmann. But his attention to the links between images and knowledge—including the role of pictures in the creation and perpetuation of stereotypes—is not evidence that he privileged the visible field. It is simply a reflection of his belief that we must grapple with the dominant manner in which meaning gets made in order to expand the scope of what can be seen. If anything, Lippmann showed in *Public Opinion* his abiding interest in the unseen. Early in the introduction he declared: "The world that we have to deal with politically is out of reach, out of sight, out of mind. It has to be explored, reported, and imagined. Man . . . has invented ways of seeing what no naked eye could see, of hearing what no ear could hear, of weighing immense masses and infinitesimal ones, of counting and separating more items than he can individually remember. He is learning to see with his mind vast portions of the world that he could never see, touch, smell, hear, or remember. Gradually he makes for himself a trustworthy picture inside his head of the world beyond his reach."[33] Most obviously, the passage helped lay the groundwork for Lippmann's first mention of "stereotype" on the page that followed by noting how readers' internal pictures bring coherence to the environment without regard for the appearance of the material world. But the passage simultaneously referenced our ability to give visual form to that which is beyond human vision. Objects too immense or minute to be seen with the naked eye, along with nonvisual phenomena, are also made visible by social systems. Stereotypes, of course, made the invisible world selectively visible. What Lippmann desired was the formation of political theory and systems that could "come to grips with the problem of how to make the invisible world visible to the citizens of a modern state."[34] He advocated a radical project to visualize for citizens those truths that did not support their preexisting pictures of the world.

In the decades since the invention of stereotype, scholars in a diverse array of fields—from psychology to history and sociology to media studies—have significantly expanded and enriched our understanding of the concept. They have collectively produced many thousands of articles and hundreds of books that explore the operation and consequences of stereotyping. Their work addresses its cognitive and social functions, means of formation and maintenance, modes of transmission, and social, economic, legal, racial, and political repercussions. While Lippmann described stereotype as a product of his hyperconnected era, the research of social scientists and historians offers abundant evidence that the process of simplification and categorization he described and named is innate to human beings.[35]

Modern research on stereotype implies that Lippmann's main accomplishment was making visible to his readers an aspect of our mental process that had previously been obscured. What I have labeled an invention appears more accurately characterized as a discovery. Yet regardless of whether he revealed a fixed mental process, or described a social adaption unique to the modern era, his particular formulation of the concept taught Americans to see stereotype in a historically specific way. Lippmann invented stereotype in the sense that *Public Opinion* offered the first primer for how Americans in the 1920s would think about their simplified pictures of the world. Simply put, the description and structure of the stereotype concept introduced by Lippmann has played a significant role in shaping how stereotypes are understood.

We have seen how Lippmann self-consciously developed his concept with ideas borrowed from philosophy, psychology, political science, and art history. The established ideas on which he drew made the new concept feel familiar to readers, as these ideas offered an intellectual armature for thinking about how stereotypes of the Great War, agitators, or Black Americans worked. But at the same time that Americans thought *about* stereotypes using Lippmann's armature, they thought *with* stereotypes, using the constellation of ideas that each stereotype's theme invoked. Stereotypes of a war or activists or race each triggered in viewers a discourse—or set of discourses—specific to its theme. The human predisposition to categorize found particularized outlets that varied depending on the discursive systems invoked.

Stereotypes of Black Americans, Jews, or Native Americans, naturally enough, prompted audiences to process such pictures through the animating discourse of race. This played out in three interrelated ways. First, the stereotypes' potential meanings were delimited by the particular ways in which race was defined in a given era. The period definition of race set the parameters for what could and could not be part of the debate. Second, the discourse established those racial binaries (uncivilized-civilized, emotional-cerebral, unrestrained-controlled, stingy-generous, open-inscrutable, etc.) over which period audiences tussled in their assessment of individual groups. The discourse did not so much define what it meant to be Black or Jewish—though it pushed toward a dominant reading—as lay out the sets of attributes around which the identities of particular groups supposedly revolved. In both these regards, racial stereotypes operated much as other kinds of stereotype; the discourses to which they were thematically linked shaped how audiences processed the issues at stake. And, third, racial stereotypes were unique for being linked to their thematic discourse by the construction of the stereotype itself. Notwithstanding Lippmann's efforts to articulate a neutral concept, unencumbered by prior associations and equally applicable to all simplified pictures, readers will come to see how the governing logic of the stereotype was linked to the early twentieth-century assumptions of race.

To surface the structural linkage of race and stereotype, I turn now from a consideration of those discourses Lippmann consciously invoked to analyze how race haunted Lippmann's invention in the decade of the 1920s. The period was awash with vigorous arguments over evolution, genetics, and lingering social Darwinism, but I enter the conversation through an analysis of the history and assumptions of eugenics, a field of study then at the peak of its influence, which every racial stereotype necessarily called forth.

∷

The English scientist Francis Galton developed the discipline of eugenics in the 1860s. It was tirelessly promoted in the US by the biologist Charles Davenport from the platform of his Eugenics Record Office on Long Island at Cold Spring Harbor, New York. Eugenics was a program for improving the quality of the human stock, through one or more of the following means: environmental alteration, selective mating, and elimination of inferior genes.[36] Whereas Darwin, and the social Darwinists who followed, had made general pronouncements on an organism's inherited physical fitness, Galton's eugenics made the more specific claim that talent and character were also hereditary.[37] Eugenicists believed in the importance of heredity, with their ranks cleaving over the role played by the environment in human development. Mainline proponents, who were invested in "biology as destiny," are infamous for supporting "negative" eugenic policies, which subjected those deemed feebleminded, criminal, or racially inferior to sterilization, marriage restrictions, capital punishment, colonization, and restrictive immigration controls, while reform eugenicists, who accorded the environment a major role in human development, are more closely associated with "positive" policies that worked to improve nutrition, sanitary regulations, education, and labor opportunities for the disadvantaged.[38]

Today eugenics is overwhelmingly remembered for the excesses of negative eugenics. In the popular imagination it is equated with the genocidal programs of Nazi Germany and with a host of early twentieth-century US scientists and politicians who promoted restrictions on the procreation and immigration of "unfit" populations.[39] But in the 1920s its appeal was broad, uniting scientists, politicians, and members of the public across the political spectrum.[40] The historian Daniel J. Kevles has documented the wide acceptance of eugenic thought in America during the first two decades of the twentieth century. He notes that it was then a frequent topic of popular magazine and newspaper articles and lectures at philosophical societies, schools and universities, women's clubs, medical and nursing associations, and YMCAs. Eugenic societies sprang up in many states, most notably Illinois, Missouri, Wisconsin, Minnesota, Utah, and California; major eugenics organizations were founded, including the Galton Society, Race Betterment Foundation, American Eugenics Society, which was funded by John D. Rockefeller Jr. and George Eastman, and the Eugenic Records Office, supported by the Carnegie Foundation. Prominent advocates of eugenics during the period included Theodore Roosevelt; Alexander Graham Bell; Charles W. Eliot, president of Harvard University; Charles R. Van Hise, president of the University of Wisconsin; David Starr Jordan, president of Stanford University; Herman J. Muller, future Nobel laureate in genetics; Emma Goldman; and Margaret Sanger.[41]

Eugenics proceeded along different tracks in different countries, depending on the symbolic threat that loomed largest in the popular imagination. Eugenicists in the United Kingdom addressed the danger posed to the nation by the inferior stock of the working class, while their US counterparts overwhelmingly attended to the threat nonwhites posed to the country's racial fitness. In the 1920s, mainline eugenicists in the US held that there was no more important work for improving the nation's fitness than staunching the epidemic of miscegenation. They feared that the country's mulatto population was rapidly expanding as a result of interracial sex and that such unions would lead inexorably to the dilution of white bloodlines and the gradual decline of the white race. While sexual relations between Black and white Americans had steadily declined since the Civil War, reaching a low point in the first decades of the twentieth century, eugenicists saw in miscegenation a growing threat to the Caucasian race.[42] In order to protect the purity of white blood, mainline eugenicists supported efforts to bar Asian immigration and limit European immigration from eastern and southern Europe. Some even sought to resurrect the nineteenth-century dream of Black colonization. In addition, they advocated for laws that regulated relations between white and Black people, including bars to interracial marriage, mandatory sterilization of the "unfit," and tightened legal definitions of who was Black or white. As a host of historians have documented, the desire to police a strict boundary between white and Black led to the legal and social ascendancy of the "one-drop rule" for defining racial identity. The rule held that a single drop of Black blood was sufficient for classifying an individual as Black.

The one-drop rule sought to provide a clearly delineated test of one's racial identity that kept the white bloodline untainted by defining as Black all mixed-race people. The rule replaced more relaxed and fluid conventions for Black racial classification that had existed in many pockets of the country in the antebellum period. Historians have described a number of factors that contributed to the rise of more rigid racial definitions of Black identity in the aftermath of the Civil War. In the nineteenth century, the one-drop rule was spurred by Southern white resentment of the solidarity that mulattoes showed toward darker Black Americans during and after the Civil War and by the psychological need of whites in the North and South to clearly demarcate their differences from an "other."[43] With the collapse of the free-slave binary, which had helped give European Americans their identity prior to emancipation, whites invested more heavily in the divide between white and Black. In the early twentieth century, acceptance of the rule was accelerated by passage of a highly restrictive immigration act in 1924, the Johnson-Reed Act. The act was spurred by fear of Japanese and Korean immigrants from east Asia and Jewish and Catholic immigrants from eastern and southeastern Europe. It was assumed that such immigrants had higher rates of "defects" (insanity, crime, feeblemindedness, dependency, tuberculosis, and epilepsy) than did native-born whites and that such immigrants posed a threat to both the quality of white racial stock and republican institutions of governance. Once the symbolic threat posed by inferior races was diminished by the bar of Asian immigrants and the severe restriction of undesirable Europeans, whites placed even greater emphasis on Black Americans as the most significant other against which whiteness was defined.[44]

The one-drop rule brought legal clarity and social confusion. It had the unintended effect of creating a large pool of white-looking people who were legally Black and, in the context of a discriminatory system that accorded social and economic benefits to whites, encouraged Black Americans with sufficiently light skin pigmentation to "pass" as white. As the historian Joel Williamson has famously explained in his study of racial mixing in the South, this gave rise in the 1920s to white fears of "invisible Blackness." The specter of white-looking Black people mingling freely in polite society and intermarrying with whites destabilized the white-Black border that gave coherence to whiteness. This led whites to deem invisible Blackness as a grave threat to the biological and cultural purity of their race.[45] While Williamson analyzed invisible Blackness in the South, it was a national concern during the first decades of the twentieth century.

One of the 1920s' most influential voices on the dangers posed by race mixing was that of Earnest Sevier Cox, a Southern Methodist preacher, amateur ethnographer, political activist, and committed eugenicist. The itinerant Cox studied at an unaccredited college in Tennessee, received a business certificate from a school in Georgia, ran a loan company in Louisiana, worked as a reporter in Oklahoma, taught school in Tennessee and Oklahoma, and attended a religious school in Illinois before stints studying theology at Vanderbilt University and then sociology at the University of Chicago.[46] Between 1910 and 1915 he meandered throughout Africa, Southeast Asia, and South America before returning to the United States to write and revise *White America* (1923), his self-published polemic on the dangers posed to white racial purity by the presence of Black people in the United States.[47] The book held that the cultural achievements of human populations were the product of each race's particular biological attributes acting on their environments. In Cox's estimation, "the higher culture of the world today is originated and sustained by peoples of the North American breed of Caucasians," while the "[Negro] has no cultural possessions save those which he has received from the white man."[48] In order to protect white society, Cox advocated the repatriation of Black Americans to Africa, the exclusion of Asian immigrants, and restrictive European immigration policies to prevent Jews and other "inferior" Caucasians from entering the United States.[49] Cox pointed out that segregation had historically offered few protections against race mixing and that the only way of safeguarding the purity of Caucasian blood was to physically separate superior from inferior races.

White America made clear the unique danger posed to the racial order by mixed-race people. As Cox wrote, "It is this mixbreed element in the United States . . . who constitute the immediate peril to the white race and the institutions of civilization. The near-whites are bucking the color-line and making good in every state in the American Union. The North, the South, the East, and the West are suffering these aggressive negroids to enter white society and to inject the blood of Africa into Caucasian circles. . . . The near-white is a cancer that will eat deeper and deeper into the heart of the white race."[50] Numerous white anthropologists, ethnologists, and mainline eugenicists of the era echoed this fear of racial mixing, cautioning that "the mulatto . . . constitutes the most serious feature of the race problem today" and that "the presence of a considerable number of people of mixed and colored blood presents one of the genuine problems remaining in race relations."[51] Writing in 1926, Cox hammered home the unique dangers of invisible Blackness: "We [whites] dwell with 3,000,000 mixbreeds, and we are just becoming conscious that the offspring of an illegal union of the [white and Black] races is, racially, not to be distinguished from the product of a legal union [of whites]."[52]

While whites in the United States had long deemed miscegenation a damaging and immoral practice, the specific dangers it posed evolved over the early decades of the twentieth century. Earlier warnings on racial mixing typically addressed its deleterious effects on both the Black and white races. For much of the nineteenth century, conventional wisdom held that mulattoes were an intermediate race that, because of their white blood, had greater abilities and social expectations and, because of their Black blood, had no hope of enjoying the benefits of white society. White blood brought mulattoes both benefits and drawbacks. As a prominent white sociologist explained, "The members of the primitive [pure Black] group, recognizing the hopelessness of measuring up to the standards of the white race, are generally content and satisfied with their lower status and happy among their own race. It is the mixed-blood man who is dissatisfied and ambitious."[53] The dangers to whites were summed up by the journalist and popular historian of race Lothrop Stoddard: "Unless man erects and maintains artificial barriers, the various races will increasingly mingle, and the inevitable result will be the supplanting or absorption of the higher by the lower type."[54] Stoddard worried about Black people displacing whites and whites becoming Black. And, crucially, he saw the threat as an external one to whiteness.

In the twentieth century, white Americans continued to believe that miscegenation left mulattoes ill fitted for society and that it would eventually overwhelm the white race, though their main concern now centered on what they saw as a more immediate threat to whites. Rather than describing the distant danger of a disappearing white race, they raised alarm over the daily darkening of contemporary whites, as attention shifted from miscegenation, in general, to mulattoes, in particular. White Americans had long imagined that even minute quantities of Black blood were visible in the physiognomies of mixed-race people. Yet the one-drop rule, and the consequent increase in the number of white-looking Black people, made white belief in the legibility of Blackness untenable. Whites were compelled to reconceptualize the racial threat. What had once been a lamentable, but conscious *choice* to mix with someone of another race became a chance *accident* of marrying, siring, or fraternizing with Black people that was outside of one's control. What began as the mainline eugenicists' crusade to encourage whites to make racially correct choices descended into a helpless fear of one's racial stock being undermined by an unseen enemy lurking within the white community. Miscegenation transformed from an external to an internal threat.[55]

Readers of mainline eugenic and ethnographic texts in the 1920s were confronted with many examples of the damage invisible Blackness wrought. Authors raised the specter of "full-blooded Caucasians . . . put under suspicion as mulattoes" and whites unknowingly taking "up into [their] blood a race of human flesh-eaters." White readers were shaken by stories of light-skinned Black people accepted inadvertently into marriages with both members of the First Families of Virginia and the San Francisco elite. Several authors detailed stories of unnamed white couples from respectable families giving birth to babies "black as coal, and with hair as kinky as the veriest young Congo that a Negress of that race ever gave birth to in America." Such births were explained as a normal "reversion to type" of the unsuspecting parent whose line traced back to a distant female slave.[56]

Southerners are famous for raising the alarm over invisible Blackness, but their concerns were shared and amplified by prominent voices in the North. When Cox failed to find a commercial publisher for *White America,* he turned for advice to Madison Grant, a patrician New Yorker, lawyer, and ardent eugenicist. Grant was the author of the influential *The Passing of the Great Race* (1916), which read European history as a monumental racial struggle and was written, in part, to help promote US federal restrictions on immigration from southern and eastern Europe and state sterilization laws for "criminals, the diseased, and the insane, and extending gradually to types which may be called weaklings rather than defectives, and perhaps ultimately worthless race types." Cox sought out Grant because *The Passing of the Great Race* spurred him to write *White America.* He was struck by the truth in Grant's observation that when races live side by side "but one of two things can happen; either one race drives the other out . . . or else they amalgamate and form a population of race bastards." While Grant did a better job than Cox in cloaking his racial animosity toward nonwhite people in the language of science, he was clear in his belief that miscegenation was "a frightful disgrace to the dominant race."[57]

Grant helped Cox update his manuscript by pointing him toward current scholarship that aligned with their shared racial outlook and, subsequently, wrote a glowing book review of *White America* for the *Richmond News Leader.* Cox also found a sympathetic audience in Charles Davenport, a Harvard-trained biologist and the most prominent US scientist who advocated for mainline eugenics in the first half of the twentieth century. Davenport's research paid considerable attention to the genetic consequences of mating between white and Black populations. His best-known published work is the coauthored study *Race Crossing in Jamaica* (1929), which analyzed "the relative capacity of the negro and the hybrid to play a part in carrying forward the white man's civilization."[58] Reviewing Cox's *White America* in the *Eugenical News,* he called it a "stirring volume" by a man who hopes to save his country from the fate of Haiti.[59] Grant and Davenport were establishment figures who offered Cox's book an imprimatur of social and scientific respectability that significantly increased its reach in the North.

We know that Grant supplied the general inspiration for Cox to write *White America*, and it is likely that a second New Yorker, Dr. Robert Wilson Shufeldt, introduced Cox to the particular dangers of invisible Blackness. Shufeldt was an ornithologist, ethnographer, and retired army surgeon whom Cox acknowledged in *White America* as a naturalist with knowledge of Black Americans "second to none."[60] As early as the 1890s, Shufeldt began publishing academic journal articles that laid out his fears of invisible Blackness.[61] In the twentieth century his views found a mass audience with the publication of his two books: *The Negro: A Menace to American Civilization* (1907) and *America's Greatest Problem: The Negro* (1915). Noting that some Black residents of Washington, DC, "are so white that it takes a very keen eye to detect the Ethiopian blood in them," Shufeldt warned his readers: "They are dangerous from whatever point man may elect to view them, as they may possess all the vicious and sensual traits of the negro, without the color of the latter's skin as a warning flag to the unwary." And he went on to caution that mulattoes "have better opportunities to contract white alliances in marriage, and thus insidiously pass savage Ethiopian blood into the veins of the Anglo-Saxon American." Shufeldt scorned white progressives who, he claimed, are standing by as "the entire white race [is] rotted by heroic injections into their veins of all the savagery and criminality there is in the negro."[62] In the imagination of those who feared invisible Blackness, whites' absorption of inferior social and cultural Black traits was both the cause and the product of Black Americans' increasingly white appearance. As Black people looked more white, white people acted more Black.

In their efforts to understand the mechanism by which organisms inherited character traits, twentieth-century eugenicists moved away from correlating physical signs of difference (such as skin color, cranial shape and volume, skull proportions, etc.) with specific behavioral and intellectual characteristics to focus on how "blood" and, later, genes controlled the inheritance of traits.[63] In modern parlance, they shifted from the study of phenotypes (an organism's physical expression of genes) to attend to genotypes (its fixed arrangement of genetic material). This shift from external to internal evidence accelerated, first, as invisible Blackness threw into question the value of physiognomic evidence, and second, as reform eugenics and the science of genetics began to displace mainline eugenics toward the end of the 1920s. The move away from reading visible traits cleared the way for more evidence-based approaches to studying human differences, but before the broad acceptance of the scientific advances developed by geneticists—including the understanding of complex gene interactions and sophisticated mathematical models for calculating genetic probability—the shift from visible traits to invisible chemical codes allowed long-standing racial prejudices to flow unchecked. As one prominent geneticist observed in 1930, even scientists find it "distressing" when firmly held beliefs are contradicted by scientific observation. The result is often that "the old ideas persist along with the new [scientific] observations; they form the basis—often unconsciously—for many of the conclusions that are drawn."[64]

The racial conclusions and policy prescriptions of mainline eugenicists were widely embraced in the interwar period, though they were by no means met with universal acceptance. By the turn of the twentieth century, a handful of anthropologists and sociologists had begun to chip away at the biological basis for race, which posed a significant challenge to the assumptions of eugenicists. And in the 1920s, a few nascent reform eugenicists consciously rid their work of the social biases of their mainline colleagues and decoupled studies of innate ability from both racial and class identity.[65] The former group problematized the link between physical signs and racial identity by arguing that racial categories owed as much to nurture as nature, while the latter argued that while race might exist, there was no reason to assume that its physiognomic signs were connected to talent or character.

No one did more to unsettle the links between race and its visual signs than the cultural anthropologist Franz Boas. Through his research, publications, and lectures, Boas illustrated the sloppy deductive reasoning and unchecked biases that tainted the majority of scholarly and popular studies of race up through the 1920s. His systematic study of the methodological shortcomings of academic research called into question more than a century of study of "primitive" peoples, which invariably found nonwhite groups physically and intellectually inferior. Boas knew that ethnologists, physical anthropologists, and popular writers made pronouncements absent knowledge of local cultures or facility with their languages; and that they judged their subjects through the lens of Christian religious values, racialized biases against nonwhites, and reductive theories on the evolutionary "stages" of human development.[66] He devoted significant energy to exploring how the ideological baggage that scientists brought with them to work tainted physical anthropology.

Boas cautioned that unexamined beliefs led scientists and members of the public to internalize simple pictures of groups that short-circuited efforts to observe, analyze, and understand individuals. He laid out the problem in terms that would have been familiar to readers of *Public Opinion*. Writing in "The Problem of the American Negro" in 1921, he observed that the accumulated biases of observers ensured that "when we talk about the characteristics of a race . . . we are dealing with an abstraction which has no existence in nature. . . . We form the picture of an ideal personage who combines in himself the striking traits of the race." Keenly aware of how individuals were trapped within idealized pictures, so losing their unique attributes and identities, he noted that in "the popular mind, the negro appears as a class . . . generalized by the white man and . . . combined with dogmatic beliefs regarding the physical and hereditary mental make-up of the race."[67] By drawing attention to biases that observers projected onto their subjects, Boas brought to anthropology a new methodological rigor and scientific dispassion.

But his most consequential contribution to the understanding of race was his insistence that we account for the role of the environment in human development. Politically progressive eugenicists had, of course, long advised that even the best racial stock could not hope to attain its full potential under poor environmental conditions. Boas agreed on the point, but his argument went much farther. Over several decades, in dozens of scholarly talks and published articles, he made the radical case that the environment played a significant role in producing racial difference. In an 1894 address, given for the American

Association for the Advancement of Science, Boas noted the twin assumptions of European and European American researchers: that whites embodied the pinnacle of intellectual and cultural achievement and that physiological distinctions between races were necessarily signs of difference in aptitude and character. Armed with these assumptions, whites consistently read any physical deviation from the norm of whiteness as a sign of inferiority—physical, psychological, and cultural. In the address, Boas conceded: "There is no doubt that great differences exist in the physical characteristics of the races of man." But he went on to argue: "The question is not if differences exist, but if any one race is anatomically considered superior to others." Nutrition, occupation, climate, and childhood environment were all social factors Boas enumerated that played significant roles in producing physiological variations in human populations and whose effects were routinely mistaken for biological differences. He ultimately concluded that those physical variations separating Black from white people that could not be explained by environmental factors "are few in number and . . . not of such a character as to stamp one race as lower than the other."[68] Boas's environmentalist arguments acknowledged visible racial differences (including skin pigmentation, brain weight, head shape, and facial features), but in cleaving such differences from long-standing racialized valuations, he helped problematize both biological determinism and the visibility of race. Black skin for Boas was a footnote of evolution that said little about one's ability or potential.

The impact of Boas's work on race rippled out slowly through academic and public circles. In the first decade of the twentieth century his insights helped spur the rise of cultural anthropology in the United States, particularly once his graduate students at Columbia University began to secure academic and curatorial jobs. By the second half of the 1920s his former students chaired every significant department of anthropology in the country.[69] During these decades Black artists and intellectuals also embraced his work, finding in it reassurance that the conditions of Black Americans were better explained by structural inequities than genes. Boas's research would go on to play a major role in consolidating the sociohistorical theory of race in the 1930s and 1940s, but in the decades prior it remained vigorously contested.[70] Critics attacked cultural anthropology for forsaking what many saw as its responsibility to help clarify the connections between biology and race. Rising fears of Japanese imperialist expansion abroad, and the influx of undesirable Europeans and growth of a "mulatto" population at home, convinced many anthropologists of the need to keep their discipline open to racial psychology.

Boas is rightly credited for his role in revolutionizing the study of race in the United States by questioning the significance of the differences separating white from Black people. But his efforts to strip from race its hierarchical associations nonetheless allowed it to remain tethered to biology. Boas did not question race as a division of human populations, nor that its physical signs had psychological implications. He repeatedly observed: "Differences of structure must be accompanied by differences of function, physiological as well as psychological; and, as we found clear evidence of difference in structure between the races, so we must anticipate that differences in mental character will be found."[71] In the early twentieth century virtually everyone agreed that racial differences were real and at least partially linked to biology; the tussle was over their significance. In allowing the link between race and biology to linger, Boas provided his detractors an opening to attack cultural anthropology. James Bardin, a professor at the University of Virginia, spoke for many defenders of physical anthropology in 1915 when he scoffed at the beliefs of those who "are certain that we cannot change the Negro's facial angle, [and] are equally certain that we can change his mental angle and make it like our own; while we consider it absurd to think that we can do anything to make the Negro's physical skin become white, we believe firmly that we can make the physical analogue of his skin exactly like our own. But is this a fact? Racial psychology says no."[72] Bardin held that since the physiological differences separating races were biological, and hence immutable, the psychological and intellectual differences that sprung from them could not be subject to environmental change.

In the 1910s and 1920s many of the most vociferous supporters of white racial supremacy found in Boas's work support for their arguments. When Cox submitted the manuscript for *White America* to Madison Grant for comment in the early 1920s, it contained multiple references to Boas's work. Cox's selective reading of Boas provided backing for his argument on the inherent differences between the races and, by extension, for the biological dangers mulattoes posed. The citations were removed at the urging of Grant, who counseled Cox that Boas's work had been "discredited," but even Grant's fourth revised edition of *The Passing of the Great Race* (1921) footnoted Boas's publications as supporting sources.[73] In conducting research for his book *America's Greatest Problem: The Negro* in 1914, Shufeldt wrote to Boas in the hope of obtaining research results that supported his thesis. Boas replied: "You would not wish to include an expression of my opinion in your book, because I am not at all convinced that the miscegenation of races is a bad thing from a biological point of view."[74] Boas had published *The Mind of Primitive Man* (1911) three years earlier, which brought his social constructivist view of race and positive assessment of racial mixing to a wide reading public. How revealing, then, that Shufeldt nonetheless felt it worthwhile to solicit his input and that he lauded Boas in *America's Greatest Problem* as "an eminent anthropologist." Twenty-first-century readers are likely to see the racial beliefs of Cox, Grant, and Shufeldt as antithetical to those of Boas, but the ideological lines of affinity were clearly more complex in the 1910s and 1920s.

The sociologist W. E. B. Du Bois waded into these early twentieth-century racial debates to articulate a powerful social theory of race. Throughout his long career—which stretched from the turn of the twentieth century to the early 1960s—Du Bois repeatedly returned to the consideration of race's origin and significance. Writing in "The Conservation of Races" in 1897, he acknowledged the understandable desire of Black people to downplay racial differences, given how such differences had historically been used to question their "natural abilities." While insisting that "purely physical characteristics . . . between men do not explain all the differences of their history," he nonetheless conceded that "in our calmer moments we must acknowledge that human beings are divided into races." At the turn of the century, Du Bois explained that race was produced "first, [by a group's] race identity and common blood; secondly, and more important, [by] a common history, common laws and religion, similar habits of thought and a conscious striving together for certain ideals of life." Race may have had a biological component but, as Du Bois maintained, "no mere physical distinctions would really define or explain the deeper differences" that separated groups.[75]

Du Bois's philosophy of race found confirmation in his quantitative research. His exhaustive sociological study of Black life in Philadelphia, *The Philadelphia Negro* (1899), provided a detailed, statistically grounded analysis of life in the city based on surveys he conducted with 2,500 Black households and his examination of census records and government archives.[76] The study corroborated prevailing white expectations by producing evidence that Philadelphia's Black residents exhibited greater criminality, disease, unemployment, and illiteracy than their white neighbors. But whereas most whites took such failings as proof of the innate inferiority of Black Americans, Du Bois explained them as the legacy of slavery, structural impediments, and the ongoing racial prejudice of whites. *The Philadelphia Negro* offered compelling evidence that the secondary traits Americans consistently took as signs of racial identity and worth were socially produced. His analysis pointed to the "Negro problem" as fundamentally social, not biological.

In the early decades of the twentieth century, Du Bois avidly consumed and promoted the limited corpus of sociological and anthropological research that supported his position on race. In 1897 he assumed responsibility for organizing the annual Atlanta Conference of Negro Problems at Atlanta University. He transformed the conference from one focused on the telltale signs of the "Negro problem" into one that delved rigorously into its social roots. With attention to the lingering repercussions of slavery, economic exploitation, and racism, annual conference topics offered detailed sociological considerations of the Black church, crime, health, economic cooperation, and the family. Du Bois turned a regional conference into one that attracted international attention with a roster of distinguished speakers that included Max Weber, Franz Boas, and Jane Addams.

Under his guidance, the 1906 delegates adopted then-radical resolutions, including "The Conference does not find any adequate scientific warrant for the assumption that the Negro race is inferior to other races."[77] Reporting on the First Universal Races Congress, which took place at the University of London in 1911, Du Bois granted the "tremendous differences in the present conditions of men," but added approvingly: "Practically every anthropologist present laid the chief stress on environment in explaining these differences; not simply physical environment but the even more important social environment."[78]

Du Bois, like Boas, never fully severed race from biology. He argued that research had yet to adequately account for the powerful effect exerted by the social sphere on race and that it was ultimately of much greater consequence than biology. As late as 1940, he observed: "The mark of [African] heritage is upon me in color and hair. These are obvious things, but of little meaning in themselves; only important as they stand for real and more subtle differences from other men. Whether they do or not, I do not know nor does science know today." No matter how forcefully he argued for attending to the social sphere, his writings consistently noted physical racial differences and acknowledged the possibility that they stood for "real and more subtle differences" in psychology and aptitude.[79]

The philosopher and cultural theorist Kwame Anthony Appiah has argued that even if Du Bois himself never fully made the move from "thinking of the Negro race as a natural, biological kind to thinking of it as composed of people who share a socially made identity," his writings provided Americans a roadmap "to make this move without him." By carefully reading Du Bois's work within the intellectual currents of his era, Appiah makes a convincing case for how Du Bois's description of race showed alignment with modern identity theory.[80] But because Du Bois's theories of race were complex, ambivalent, and evolving, a case can also be made for their alignment with a range of twentieth-century perspectives on race. During the same years in which his writings opened the door to race as a social process, they provided support for its biological grounding.

In 1925, Du Bois provided Margaret Sanger with a supportive statement to be read at an international birth control conference. It opened with the line "Next [in importance] to the abolition of war in modern civilization comes the regulation of birth by reason and common sense instead of by chance and ignorance." That he saw a specific role for birth control in improving the quality of individual races was made explicit in his 1932 essay, "Black Folk and Birth Control." In it he claimed: "The mass of ignorant Negroes still breed carelessly and disastrously, so that the increase among Negroes, even more than the increase among whites, is from that part of the population least intelligent and fit, and least able to rear their children properly." He concluded the essay by urging Black people to appreciate that "among human races and groups, as among vegetables, quality and not mere quantity really count." And in a 1922 essay on interracial marriage he urged: "It is . . . undoubtedly a great human duty to improve the human stock by rational breeding and by eliminating the unfit and dangerous."[81]

Du Bois was cognizant of the potential for the birth control movement to be misused in order to advance a racialized agenda, according to the historian Herbert Aptheker, but the dangers did not dampen his faith in eugenic science.[82] He maintained that selective mating would reduce the incidence of inherited disorders and diseases and improve physical and intellectual fitness, as did all eugenic proponents in the 1910s and 1920s. Believing that society was the primary cause of Black American's physical, intellectual, and cultural shortcomings, Du Bois, however, was unique in advocating a biological solution to a social problem. Despite his forceful promotion of racial uplift through social reforms, he nonetheless saw eugenics as a needed tool for improving the quality of Black stock. The unintended result was that the eugenic program he described was barely distinguishable from that of mainline eugenicists. Du Bois joined with his eugenicist peers in advocating that the reproduction of the "mass of ignorant Negroes" be restrained. That he attributed their condition to a different cause did not diminish the extent to which his approach to eugenics neatly replicated the racialized outcomes of his mainline peers.[83] Du Bois's revolutionary philosophy of race coexisted with his support for mainstream racial programs.

At the same moment that a select group of advanced anthropologists and sociologists cast light on the links between race and society, a nascent group of geneticists developed a more scientific approach to the study of biological heredity. The geneticists aimed to detach eugenics from the racial and class prejudices that infected the work of mainline practitioners, fully account for the role of the environment in an organism's development, and verify the links between genes and expressed traits. Unlike the majority of their mainline eugenicist colleagues, the geneticists knew from their research that the expression of human traits was contingent on multiple genes acting in particular environments. By the first decades of the twentieth century there existed a growing body of research illustrating that genetically identical organisms could follow dramatically distinctive developmental paths depending on the environments to which they were subjected. Genes set the outside boundaries for potential development, but within those boundaries there was significant room for variation. As the Harvard-trained geneticist Herbert Spencer Jennings explained, "Every creature has many inheritances; which one shall be realized depending on the [environmental] conditions under which it develops. . . . What their parents leave them are certain packets of chemicals which under one set of conditions produce one set of characters, under other conditions produce other sets."[84]

Jennings took direct aim at the ways in which genetics was then employed to advance nativist immigration policy. He attacked what he called the "false biology" that illustrated higher rates of "defects," such as insanity, crime, feeblemindedness, dependency, tuberculosis, and epilepsy, among recent immigrants than among native-born whites. In his testimony before the House Committee on Immigration and Naturalization, prior to the passage of the Johnson-Reed Act of 1924, Jennings cautioned that "under the heavy handicap of ignorance of the language, customs and laws of the country in which they arrive, often also under the handicaps of poverty and lack of education, [immigrants] have tried to make their way in our fierce competitive life. Will not mental, moral and physical breakdown occur more frequently in that class than in [native-born whites]—even if the [biological] inheritance in the two cases be equal? Beyond question; the immigrant class are bound to show a greater proportion of defects due to environmental pressure than the native class."[85]

Jennings's political commitment to derail legislation intended to preclude Asian and limit Jewish and Catholic immigration to the United States coexisted with a bedrock belief in racial essentialism shared by his more conservative compatriots. In the final paragraph of a long 1924 article in which he attacked the spurious use of science to restrict immigration, and patiently laid out the importance of environmental factors in the expression of genetic traits, Jennings asked: "Are the differences between men due more to heredity or to environment? If we compare ourselves with our [European] ancestors of 10,000 years ago, they are due mainly to environment. . . . If the comparison is of ourselves with the Bushmen of South Africa, possibly the differences are mainly due to heredity." While a lack of scientific evidence did not dissuade Jennings from hazarding a guess that the differences between white and Black peoples were genetic, he declined to speculate as to the root of evident differences separating whites. He concluded the paragraph by urging further study to determine if the physiological distinctions evident among the "diverse races" of Europe (and American whites) were hereditary or environmental.[86]

In *The Biological Basis of Human Nature* (1930), Jennings provided a more sustained consideration of the gulf separating white from Black. In a chapter titled "Race Mixture and Its Consequences" he wrote: "It might well be anticipated that the European whites and the African bushmen would differ in mentality as they do in physical characteristics. . . . On genetic grounds the presumption is that such differences will be found." He went on to cite research conducted by the eugenicist Charles Davenport, which demonstrated the superior musical abilities of Black people and the superior intellectual abilities of white people. Nowhere in *The Biological Basis* did Jennings make claims that these were qualitative differences. He maintained a veneer of scientific disinterest by noting: "Judgments of [racial] superiority and inferiority must of course rest on relative fitness for certain purposes." But he left no doubt that a racial hierarchy existed, writing: "To the superior race, admixture with the inferior one is adulteration; it means a lowering of quality."[87] Because Jennings wrote in an era when the majority of European and European American historians of race consistently ranked African Bushmen (and Aboriginal Australians) at the bottom rung of the evolutionary ladder and racial differences were consistently read in hierarchical terms, the racial valence of the passage was clear to readers.[88]

Lippmann—much like Boas, Du Bois, and Jennings—argued for greater consideration of environmental forces in the production of race. He definitively rejected the anti-immigrant and anti-Black strain of mainline eugenics exemplified by the writings and advocacy of men such as Cox and Grant.[89] In the same year that *Public Opinion* was published, Lippmann wrote a six-part series in *The New Republic* that mounted a spirited attack on the popular idea that IQ tests offered proof of innate intelligence. The tests gained prominence during World War I when, under the auspices of the National Academy of Sciences, Robert M. Yerkes, president of the American Psychological Association, led a team of psychologists, which included Lewis M. Terman of Stanford University, to design and implement a test that allowed the army to quickly sort the inductees who were flooding its ranks in the US buildup to the war. With the conclusion of the war, schools, universities, and corporations embraced the test as a scientific means of ranking their students, employees, and applicants. Yerkes and his colleagues promoted the tests as a reliable gauge of innate intelligence that cut through differences in age, educational background, race, and class. In the 1920s the tests were frequently proffered as evidence that native-born Black Americans and recently arrived European immigrants lacked the innate potential of native-born whites. Lippmann was unconvinced. In *The New Republic*, he cautioned: "The claim that we have learned how to measure hereditary intelligence has no scientific foundation." He noted several glaring problems: the tests were designed without intelligence ever being defined, intelligence was in any case too multifaceted an entity to be tested in a fifty-minute sitting, and there was no evidence that what was tested was innate, rather than a product of the environment. Disdainful of those who used the tests to advance a racialized agenda—such as Terman, Lothrop Stoddard, and Harvard professor of psychology William McDougall—Lippmann wrote: "I hate the abuse of scientific method which it involves. I hate the sense of superiority which it creates, and the sense of inferiority which it imposes."[90]

Lippmann's distaste for sloppy and dishonest research was strong, as was his disinclination to see racial or class hierarchies conflated with an individual's potential for achievement. His faith in individuality and aversion to social stratification made him reluctant to consign people to broad categories that supposedly set the parameters of their worth. In *Public Opinion* he explained that because the social differences among men are vastly greater than the biological distinctions, those of us interested in understanding the unique attributes and predisposition of human populations must first "fix our attention upon the extraordinary differences in what men know of the world." Only after accounting for the considerable variations in how diverse groups interpret the world is it possible to make claims about innate differences separating such groups. In a later passage he warned of the dangers in speaking of "collective minds, national souls, and race psychology," admonishing readers to consider how patterns of values or morals that unite groups are sustained across generations by the instruction of "parents, teachers, priests, and uncles," rather than by "germ plasm."[91]

In making the case that differences among groups are better explained by examining social rather than biological factors, Lippmann left open the door to biology's role. In this, too, his thinking resembled that of Boas, Du Bois, and Jennings. He wrote: "I do not doubt that there are important biological differences [among human populations]. Since man is an animal it would be strange if it were not." Believing simply that there was greater variety in human social conditions than in human biology, he urged his readers to *begin* the study of human differences with the social realm. Lippmann cautioned that we not generalize "about comparative behavior until there is a measurable similarity between the environments to which behavior is a response." Rather than taking biology off the table, Lippmann instead pushed off its study until the time when we can control for the changes induced by the social sphere.[92] His reticence to attribute specific traits and aptitudes to biology must not be equated with a belief in the ultimate power of nurture.

In his advocacy of eugenics Lippmann made clear that biology mattered. His *An Inquiry into the Principles of the Good Society* (1937) lists the various factors that had left some Americans handicapped in their capacity to attain success, including childhood malnutrition and neglect, substandard home lives, poverty and squalor, and "the deterioration of the stock from which they spring." And he went on to argue that for the sake of an efficient economy and to meet our moral obligations in a liberal society, we need to ensure "not only that the quality of the human stock, the equipment of men for life, shall be maintained at some minimum of efficiency, but that the quality should be progressively improved." To achieve this end, Lippmann repeatedly urged "public investment in the eugenic and educational improvement of the people." Lippmann's support for eugenics was even more remarkable given his clear-eyed understanding of its excesses as then practiced in fascist Germany and Italy. *The Good Society* advocated for the compatibility of eugenics and liberal democracies, even as it expressed disapproval of eugenic policies practiced by the National Socialists and National Fascist Party.[93]

In addition to his advocacy for an active eugenic program, Lippmann advanced the intriguing claim in *Public Opinion* that the social sphere was inadvertently influencing human evolution. He made the breathtaking assertion that stereotypes could catalyze changes in human biology. Lippmann observed: "A stereotype may be so consistently and authoritatively transmitted in each generation from parent to child that it seems almost like a biological fact." This sentiment is obviously in keeping with his argument for how stereotypes become naturalized in culture. But his next sentence pushed farther: "In some respects, we may indeed have become, as Mr. Wallas says, biologically parasitic upon our social heritage."[94] "Mr. Wallas" was of course Graham Wallas, the aforementioned social psychologist and political scientist, who was also an advocate of positive eugenics.[95]

In the passage to which Lippmann alluded, Wallas wrote: "Man has been increasingly dependent on his social heritage since the beginning of conventional language and of the art of flint-chipping, that is to say, for perhaps half a million years." Wallas described "social heritage," or what he sometimes called "social inheritance," as the vast body of knowledge and habits that individuals acquire over time and that groups pass down to each generation through formal and informal education. He explained that it is such heritage that makes possible the technological and cultural advances enjoyed by citizens in advanced societies. After noting our dependence on social heritage, he went on to write: "This fact has brought about important modifications in our biologically inherited nature. We have become biologically more fitted to live with the help of our social heritage, and biologically less fitted to live without it." In a footnote, Wallas clarified the point: "This statement does not, of course, involve any Lamarckian assumptions of the biological inheritability of acquired characteristics. It is only necessary to assume (a) that those families which were more able to acquire and hand down social heritage would tend to survive, and (b) that those parts of our bodily and nervous structure which the existence of social heritage rendered unnecessary or less necessary for survival would tend to degenerate."[96]

Wallas did not believe that traits acquired over a lifetime could be biologically transmitted to offspring. It was clear to him that biological changes in human beings occurred only over many generations. The passage claimed that those families, groups, and races with the greatest quantities of useful social heritage were more likely to see their offspring flourish, reproduce, and, in time, raise their own successful children. The biological traits of groups with copious social heritage were thus likely to become overrepresented in the population over time. As an example, Wallas suggested that the burgeoning European social knowledge of applied sciences over the past two centuries was linked to the disproportionate growth in "European breeding-stocks" over those years. At the same time that social knowledge gave certain biological traits a reproductive advantage, it also stripped from other biological features their utility, and that, over time, led features without function to disappear.

Wallas held that "man has evolved, and is still evolving, certain modifications of structure and instinct" in response to social knowledge.[97] His text offered revealing examples of how the social realm had altered the racial fitness of human populations. In explaining the importance of social heritage to highly developed societies, he claimed that if a catastrophe wiped out all social knowledge in the world, "nine tenths of the inhabitants of London or New York would be dead in a month and 99 per cent of the remaining tenth would be dead in six months." Lest we think that this dire prediction is based solely on the density of urban environments, which would complicate efforts to feed, clothe, and house large populations absent social knowledge, Wallas made much the same argument for residents of "country districts," reasoning that they would not "invent, in time to preserve their lives, methods of growing food, or taming animals, or making fire, or so clothing themselves as to endure a northern winter." And he concluded: "The white races would probably become extinct everywhere," but "a few primitive races might live on fruit and small animals in those fertile tropical regions where the human species was originally evolved."[98]

If pressed to consider the racial implications of his assessment, Wallas may well have noted that his prediction turned more on climactic conditions than racial fitness. After all, the survivors in his doomsday scenario were those living in the tropical regions of the world where the climate and resources required for subsistence are present throughout the year. Considering, however, that significant numbers of European colonists lived in tropical climates when he penned his book, his decision to frame the issue in terms of "white" versus "primitive" races is of note. It seems evident from his example that in a world devoid of social heritage, the biology of "primitive" peoples left them better fitted to survive off of the land than did the biology of whites. Whether this was because whites responded to their social heritage by shedding those original biological traits that allowed early man to flourish, because primitive peoples' social heritage allowed them to adapt their biology more perfectly to the natural world, or some combination of the two, it is not possible to conclude from his text.

Wallas's *Our Social Heritage* raises the specter of socially produced racial distinctions becoming biologically rooted over time. In the book's logic, people separated arbitrarily into "races" would acquire distinctive social heritages based on the disparate conditions they experienced, including varying access to resources and their treatment within the broader society. A discriminatory society would necessarily lead different groups to develop different social heritages, which would, according to Wallas, eventually result in each group "evolving . . . modifications of structure and instinct." Traits that fitted groups more perfectly to their social conditions would, in a society invested in the construct of race, be interpreted as evidence of the immutability of racial difference. In articulating how social knowledge could influence biology, Wallas made it easier for his contemporaries to confuse social with biological distinctions, since social difference was now the gateway to biological evolution.[99]

Wallas's attention to the relation between the social and the biological was an outgrowth of efforts to cure what he understood as the great psychological strain endemic to the modern world.[100] He shared the common late nineteenth-century concern that the unprecedented pace of urban growth and industrial development in the West had stripped from people the comfort of communal life enjoyed in small towns and villages in the preindustrial era. In the so-called Great Society, people fended for themselves as atomized individuals in impersonal, large-scale metropolises.[101] Wallas appreciated that the rise of this new social order brought many material benefits (and appeared irreversible), but also that it caused great psychological strain to individuals unmoored from older networks of support and identification. Convinced of Darwin's central insight that human beings' slow evolution was the result of their interaction with the environment, Wallas maintained that human beings were necessarily fitted for an environment that had passed. While it had always been the case that the glacial pace of evolutionary change ensured that our psychological and physical states were perennially out of sync with current social conditions, the problem grew as the pace of environmental change accelerated. With each passing year, human beings in advanced societies found themselves less and less perfectly fitted to their worlds.[102]

In Wallas's estimation the psychological distress caused by the gap between human nature and human society could not be eliminated. At best, one could reduce it through social engineering. His novel argument was that useful social engineering required the introduction of reforms that proceeded from biological realities, rather than ideological beliefs. Tailoring society to better address the psychological needs of human beings would reduce the strain they experienced. That is to say, instead of creating a society that embodied abstract utopian principles, one needed to modify the current environment to better address people's current evolutionary state. That this state was tethered to a society that no longer existed did not make it any less real. Even during Wallas's lifetime, his approach was controversial with progressives. Fellow reformers worried that his emphasis on the rigidity of human nature would play into the hands of conservatives by providing support for the supposed immutability of human biology. For those inclined to dismiss the role played by the environment in human development, Wallas's attention to human qualities embedded in the distant past would have proven to be validating. In making a case for reform programs that begin with biology, and imagining the ways in which various racial groups remained biologically distinct, Wallas clung to a nineteenth-century worldview, even as he crafted nuanced arguments on the imperative of social reform in the twentieth century.[103]

When Lippmann made passing reference to Wallas's idea that human beings had become "biologically parasitic upon [their] social heritage" it was little more than an intriguing aside. Lippmann did not explore the idea, and it is unlikely that many of *Public Opinion*'s first readers puzzled over the remark for any length of time. After all, it was tangential to Lippmann's overarching thesis and just one suggestive line in a book filled with insights. I do not believe that Lippmann's citation led readers of *Public Opinion* to ponder the ways in which his new definition of stereotype, as a socially malleable and simplified mental picture, retained links to biological conceptions of identity; nor do I think that it sold them on an essentialist understanding of race. Lippmann's reference is better seen as a symptom of the idea's ubiquity, rather than a catalyst for change.[104]

In sifting through the complex racial terrain of the early twentieth century, there is a temptation to make order by grouping period actors at one of two poles of racial belief—labeling them either social constructivists or biological determinists. The opposition was frequently described by historians, politicians, and scientists in the first decades of the twentieth century and is one that retains currency today. Yet histories of the period so structured run the risk of distorting our understanding of the era, given that the opposition is unrepresentative of the significant divide that separated Americans in the 1920s. It is not that the opposition is false, but that it was not the dominant one that divided period beliefs. Notwithstanding what they wrote and said about race, the overwhelming majority of Americans acted as if race had a biological root. Virtually everyone weighed the degree to which the environment played a role in the expression of biological traits, not whether or not race was the product of nurture. As we saw, the big tent of eugenics contained those who perceived no role for the environment in influencing development as well as those who believed that it was a major factor in determining the expression of biological traits. At the time *Public Opinion* was published, the vast majority of its readers—spanning political divides and racial identifications—conceived of race as both biological and environmental.

Lippmann invented stereotype to illustrate the distance between the simplicity of public opinion and the complexity of the modern world. In so doing, he highlighted our propensity to project simplified meanings and identities onto the things and people around us. The stereotype concept was linked to Lippmann's interest in accounting for the role of the environment in identity formation, but it was born into a discursive context in which identity and biology were firmly linked. Rather than seeing stereotype resolving this apparent contradiction in 1920s culture, I attribute its power to its capacity to allow for both. Since stereotypes were taken as simplified pictures of the real world, they could coexist with a biological model of race. For many Americans, stereotypes hid biological realities behind their artificial pictures. And because society's racial stereotypes collectively captured the worldviews of those invested in biological identity, their definition as simplified pictures also supported social constructivist views of race. That is to say, the perfect ideological alignment between society's racial stereotypes and the definitions of race espoused by biological determinists made it easy for those so disposed to see the artificiality of stereotypes offering evidence of the artificiality of race. In bundling together physiological signs, aptitudes, and traits, stereotype at once reified race and acknowledged its environmental production. This ideological flexibility was ideally suited to accommodate a category of identity as fluid as race. At the moment when Americans remarked on the visual illegibility of race, stereotype gave to race a new visuality that expressed what was then broadly taken as its biological base and social superstructure. Lippmann's invention helped explain how race operated and, by giving it its particular visual form, allowed it to perform a dizzying range of cultural work.

CHAPTER 2

STEREOTYPING STEREOTYPE

It's the way people look at things, not what they look at, that needs to be changed.—LANGSTON HUGHES, *The Crisis* (1926)

The stereotype is everything except what the Negro is in truth.—*Philadelphia Tribune* (1928)

In the winter of 1932, the *Chicago Daily Tribune* ran an entertaining column that poked fun at US undergraduates' glaring lack of common knowledge. The paper published a list of erroneous test answers submitted to professors at Boston University during the school's recent midterm exams. According to the newspaper, students claimed: "An optimist is an eye doctor," "Theodore Dreiser is a probable candidate for President and the author of *Main Street*," "The death of Socrates was caused by an overdose of wedlock," and "A stereotype is an instrument with two peep holes and a slot between. Look through one hole with one eye and through the other hole with the other eye, you see something."[1]

Rather than correctly defining the concept of the stereotype, an undergraduate student offered an inelegant description of a stereoscope—an optical device invented in the nineteenth century that simulated a three-dimensional scene when a pair of identical photographs mounted side by side on cardboard was examined through a viewer. The reporter saw humor in the inability of the undergraduate to distinguish between a physical apparatus for generating optical illusions and a mental shortcut for ordering a complex world. That the stereotype answer was included in the *Tribune*'s column suggests that the newspaper took for granted its readers' understanding of the concept a decade after its introduction. By 1932, newspaper-reading Americans were evidently as familiar with the concept of stereotyping as they were with Sinclair Lewis, Theodore Dreiser, and Socrates.

The dissemination of the term *stereotype* into American society was rapid and broad. Within three years of the publication of *Public Opinion*, the modern concept of stereotype was invoked by Edward Bernays, the founder of modern public relations, who championed how stereotypes could be used to manipulate the attitudes of citizens and consumers in *Crystalizing Public Opinion* (1923); by A. Lawrence Lowell, the political scientist and president of Harvard University, who described them in *Public Opinion in War and Peace* (1923) as a tool used by the public to arrive at rational decisions; by Mary Parker Follett, the pioneer of management theory, who invoked them in *Creative Experience* (1924) to explain why people often disagree in their identification of problems and solutions, even when the facts are not in dispute; and by Alain Locke, the critic and philosopher, along with three of his co-essayists in *The New Negro* (1925), who each used the concept to analyze the representation of Black Americans in US visual arts, drama, and literature.[2] The popular press also embraced the term. Throughout the 1920s, it appeared in newspaper and magazine articles spanning a vast range of topics: architecture, art, business, fashion, film, gender, law, painting, politics, psychology, radio, religion, science, sociology, sports, theater, and, of course, race. By the mid-1920s, the concept was sufficiently entrenched that editors included "stereotype" in newspaper headlines, evidently confident that readers would distinguish it from the early nineteenth-century printing technique and metaphor.[3]

The rapid absorption of stereotype into American culture left it transformed. Lippmann crafted a sophisticated concept, but the various groups who embraced it—academics, artists, critics, intellectuals, and reporters of various races—seized on those elements of the concept that best jibed with their preexisting worldviews. As it entered the popular imagination, the stereotype concept was itself stereotyped. As a complement to the story told in chapter 1, which rooted Lippmann's theory of the stereotype in the racial discourse of his era and so revealed the unspoken assumptions hardwired into the concept, chapter 2 considers the distinctive ways in which racial stereotype was popularly understood and deployed during the 1920s. It moves readers from consideration of stereotype's ideal meaning and field of possibilities at the moment of its invention to contemplate the conflicting and complementary ways in which disparate groups put the concept to use in the third decade of the twentieth century.

Public Opinion enjoyed scores of scholarly and popular book reviews in the months immediately following its publication. The reviews set the initial terms by which the book, and the concept, would be understood. From the start, a significant number of academic reviewers fixated on a true-false binary that they interpreted stereotype establishing. In reviewing *Public Opinion* in 1922, professor of psychology Harry Dexter Kitson summarized the impediments to "wise" governance that Lippmann supposedly listed. They included "the low intelligence of the public, which hinders them from distinguishing between the true and the false." According to Kitson's reading of *Public Opinion*, Americans' acceptance of stereotypes was directly related to their inability to distinguish the falsity of stereotypes from the truth of the real world. A number of early academic reviews labeled stereotypes as "inaccurate" or "unreliable" to highlight the distance between stereotypes and the real things they represented. Reviewing *Public Opinion* in 1922, the Chicago School urban sociologist Robert E. Park went so far as to claim that Lippmann possessed a naive understanding of truth. After quoting Lippmann's claim that "news and truth are not the same thing, and must be clearly distinguished," Park went on to assert: "Lippmann is still absolutist enough to assume that there is, somewhere, a Fact with a capital *F*, a fact in other words that can be so completely and accurately stated as to have for every individual, at any time and under all circumstances, one and only one meaning."[4]

The view that stereotypes were by definition false, and that they stood in opposition to truth, became pronounced once the popular press latched onto Lippmann's concept. Newspaper accounts regularly praised novels that got "down beneath the surface of stereotype," theatrical productions that presented "real and un-stereotyped" characters, and motion pictures that "eliminated" stereotype and were consequently "accurate to human nature."[5] Popular writers contrasted the "falsity" of "distorted" stereotypes with "honesty," "real" people, and "uncompromising facts."[6] And they criticized stereotyped pictures of people who "never did exist." A feminist critic asserted: "Nobody knows what women are really like because our minds are so filled with the stereotype of the woman." One observer of race relations explained of ethnic stereotypes: they display "a hint of truth in externals but a great deal of falsity in essentials"; a second contrasted literary stereotyping of Black characters with the "honest treatment . . . of Negro life."[7]

Lost was Lippmann's assertion that stereotypes lacked complexity, for the "honest" and "real" pictures advanced by popular writers tended to swap one set of simple (negative) pictures for another (positive) set, which the writers deemed better at capturing the essence of the stereotyped person or group. By the end of the 1920s, it was increasingly common to find even academic writers who contrasted stereotypes with more naturalistic pictures, but missing was Lippmann's admonition that we reduce our reliance on stereotypes by gaining more complex understandings of the represented thing and viewers' psychologies. One prominent historian writing in 1929 explained that "we retain this stereotype unless we are forced by some unusual circumstance to abandon old imagery and approach the matter at issue in a direct and realistic manner." What constituted an "unusual circumstance" was left unexplained.[8]

During the same years, a minority of writers who took up the concept of stereotype wrote of its reflection of truths, prominent among them A. Lawrence Lowell, the nativist and pro-segregationist president of Harvard University (1909–33). He penned *Public Opinion in War and Peace* to push back against what he took as the damaging inroads social psychology had made into the study of politics. He lamented: "In reading some recent discussions one would almost gather that human beings hold no opinions and perform no acts by means of reasoning faculties." Offered as an antidote to the work of such reformers as Wallas and Lippmann, Lowell's book optimistically described the formation of public opinion as an orderly and rational process in which citizens carefully weighed issues to arrive at mutually beneficial compromises. He incorporated reference to Lippmann's stereotypes only to highlight society's inexorable progress. In Lowell's view, "Man can advance no other way than by a series of approximations; and he habitually does so . . . by substituting an entirely new [stereotype] which comes nearer to [fact]." In his telling, new stereotypes were continually invented to move society incrementally closer to the understanding of a truth. Lowell offered his readers examples of what he labeled "imperfect stereotypes" as a foil for those stereotypes that more accurately captured the world.[9]

As an exemplar of Brahmin privilege, Lowell's view of stereotypes as ever-improving representations of truth was unremarkable. Lippmann described stereotypes as "the core of our personal tradition, the defenses of our position in society," "an ordered, more or less consistent picture of the world, to which our habits, our tastes, our capacities, our comforts and our hopes have adjusted themselves"; and noted that for the disempowered, the pictures presented were "unrecognizable."[10] Invested as Lowell was in his unearned advantages and the status quo that undergirded them, he was perfectly fitted for the dominant stereotypes of US society; he consequently took Lippmann's concept of stereotypes, as simplistic and ideological pictures, as an assault on his worldview. Even as Lowell was an outlier for seeing stereotypes as largely true, his concern for assessing their truthfulness was broadly shared. Virtually all those who assumed that stereotypes contained truths were united with those who labeled them as false in their tacit acceptance of a reality that could be discerned and against which stereotypes could be assessed.

Public Opinion provided fodder for those inclined to judge representations based on their fealty to the truth. Lippmann knew that stereotypes worked only to the extent that audiences failed to distinguish between them and the people or things they represented. The most powerful stereotypes were those least seen. To make stereotypes visible *as* stereotypes, Lippmann needed to demonstrate the distance between their simplified pictures and a complex understanding of the people or things for which they stood. He typically did so by providing readers with the exhaustive context that news media outlets were not designed to supply. By illustrating the arbitrary relationship between a stereotype and its referent, Lippmann sought to highlight the dangers inherent in basing public opinion, and government policy, on so flimsy a foundation. Lippmann did not view stereotypes as false or invest in truth as a stable, knowable entity. He refrained from labeling the stereotypes he analyzed as untrue, even when they would have struck the majority of readers in the 1920s as being glaringly wrong. As Lippmann explained, a stereotype is "not necessarily false. It might happen to be wholly true. It may happen to be partly true. If it has affected human conduct a long time, it is almost certain to contain much that is profoundly and importantly true." His aim was to expose the "false absolutism of the stereotype," rather than its falsity.[11] Lippmann repeatedly argued that stereotypes had no fixed relation to truth.

When the sociologist Robert Park cited Lippmann's claim that "news and truth are not the same thing" to argue that Lippmann invested in the existence of facts, he wrested the quote from its context. Lippmann's assessment of the news appeared in a chapter that began with the following observation: "If we assume with Mr. [Upton] Sinclair, and most of his opponents, that news and truth are two words for the same thing, we . . . arrive nowhere. We shall prove that on that point the newspaper lied. . . . We shall vent our feelings, but we shall vent them into air." Lippmann sought to discourage the penchant of media critics to point out instances of the press "failing" to capture truth. To his mind, news and truth were distinct, not because the news was false, but because it was never designed to capture truth. In Lippmann's assessment, those on the left who confused it with truth were prone to rail impotently against "lies" and "capitalist conspiracies" in the manner of the socialist muckraker Upton Sinclair. Lippmann maintained that the news was best seen as a different entity. Within the broader context of his arguments on the press, it becomes clear that "the news is not a mirror of social conditions." Its function is merely to "signalize an event" when "people's affairs touch public authority."[12] It registered those moments when individual lives intersected with governmental entities, such as the army, police, legislature, courts, tax authorities, or office of public health.

Lost on many of his readers was Lippmann's admonishment that the press "fight for the extension of reportable truth"—that it work to expand the boundaries of what counted as news. He appreciated that "the truth about distant or complex matters is not self-evident" and took pains to distinguish the evidentiary standards needed to confirm different kinds of truth. Lippmann contrasted the ease with which the press might verify the physical fact of a politician's death as opposed to ascertaining what his constituents "wanted" from their state. Numerous critics missed the subtlety of Lippmann's argument, assuming that a "simplified picture" must be necessarily false and that the truth was a self-evident entity that one could know.[13]

The tendency of Americans in the 1920s to weigh stereotypes based on their understanding of the correspondence between stereotypes and the authentic attributes and qualities of actual individuals and groups had a significant impact on period interpretations of race. For those Americans who wrote about stereotypes as either truthful or partially true, the consequences were obvious. This group saw stereotypes as a near-seamless extension of their preexisting views of whites and nonwhites, and, as such, stereotypes tended to confirm the status quo. For those who held that stereotypes were false, the implications were more varied. This group was superficially united by objection to the ways in which less-empowered people were then depicted and the desire to spur the creation of more accurate representations. Yet the white and Black liberals and Black conservatives who made up this group held a range of political beliefs; the significant ideological differences that separated them ensured that a shared investment in the relationship between stereotype and truth would manifest itself in slightly different ways.

White progressives were surprisingly unreflective on their investment in stereotypes. They showed scant awareness of their reliance on stereotyping; failed to understand how the stereotypes they internalized were often informed by racialized beliefs that they consciously rejected; and were frequently oblivious to how their acceptance of "real" racial identities—obscured by supposedly "false" stereotypes—helped reify race. The complex work that racial stereotype performed for this group is illuminated by the period debates surrounding a widely reported-on speech by the poet, novelist, and social reformer Clement Richardson Wood. On the evening of March 13, 1924, Wood read an invited lecture in Rankin Memorial Chapel on the campus of the historically Black Howard University in Washington, DC. Titled "The Negro, Survey and Forecast," the talk dealt extensively with the need to change what Wood understood as white people's pernicious stereotypes of Black Americans.

Wood was a frequent speaker to Black audiences in the North. He was known as a writer and teacher invested in racial justice who sought to transcend the prejudices of his Southern white heritage. Wood was a self-described radical socialist who advocated for Black suffrage in the South, worked to promote the literary work of African Americans, and published poems and novels that dealt with Black Southern life.[14] Reviewing Wood's 1920 novel, *Nigger*, which chronicled the suffering of three generations of a Black Alabama family from the Civil War to the 1910s, *The New York Times* optimistically deemed it "free of prejudice" and praised the author for his "always sympathetic" treatment of Black characters.[15] In the early 1920s, Wood contributed several essays to national periodicals that advocated for Black rights. In a 1922 article in *The Nation* he asked: "What is the least we must give to the modern Negro?" And answering his own question, he enumerated education, political rights, economic justice, and legal justice. In the same year, he wrote in the Black-owned *Chicago Defender* that his literary and journalistic work was intended to advance nothing less than "full political, economic and social justice" for Black citizens.[16]

In its coverage of the Howard talk, *The Washington Post* reported: "According to Mr. Wood, the mention of the term negro seldom or never suggests the type of negro like James Weldon Johnson, negro poet and author; W. E. B. Du Bois, the Harvard doctor of philosophy; Dr. A. L. Locke, Rhodes scholar and Oxford graduate, or many others of similar cultural development. It is always the 'black brute' type which comes first into the minds of the better class of Caucasians when reference to a negro is made." The *Post* recounted Wood's claim that the duty of the white man is to "be open-minded enough to recognize individual merit wherever it is found" and that "the duty of the educated negro is to break down this degrading group stereotype and force upon the Caucasian American recognition of the fact that the negro is to be appraised on his individual merit."[17] In a speech given in Harlem the year prior, Wood had told his audience that "when a white man thinks of a Negro he has a stereotype in his brain that runs like this: black face, thick lips, poverty, lack of culture, vice, unrestrained passions of every kind. . . . Now what is your job? To change it—to build up a very different stereotype. It is a very hard task but still Negroes will have to do it if they wish the whites to think differently."[18]

The Black journalist and activist Roscoe Simmons responded to Wood's Howard University talk in his weekly *Chicago Defender* column by noting the absurdity of imposing on the victims of stereotypes the obligation to break them down. He went on to claim: "What Mr. Wood should have told the young ladies and gentlemen at Howard is how to go about the performance of this duty and at what point will they begin to 'force the Caucasian'" to change. Simmons caustically concluded: "Shut out here; shut in there; turned down by Tom, Dick and Harry; jim-crowed, disfranchised in one section; beaten off the hotel steps in another—do tell, Mr. Wood, how the Negro will begin his attack."[19] Wood provided little detail on this point. Many published reports of his address concluded by recording Wood's hope "that there may be developed a larger cultural group among negroes," noting that "[as the Negro] has progressed economically he has also progressed culturally," and arguing for the importance of developing a "representative" group of Black exemplars.[20]

Wood's belief that "cultured" Black Americans were the key to dismantling whites' stereotypes emerged over time in response to Black criticism of his work and as his contact with the Black middle class in the North increased. While *The New York Times* had nothing but praise for Wood's aforementioned novel, it was greeted with ambivalent responses from Black America.[21] Black reviewers lauded the novel for having created a humanized portrait of Black life, even as they expressed unease with what they took as character portrayals that reinforced racial stereotypes. Reviews remarked on the novel's exclusive focus on an uneducated underclass that embodied standard "Black" traits. Charles S. Johnson, the editor of the National Urban League's journal, *Opportunity*, praised Wood for picturing the Negro "as a human being capable of some aspirations and standards," but lamented that his Black characters were just human enough "to feel . . . disappointment over failure to attain them." Johnson went on to opine that the novel is weighed "down with . . . stereotyped 'Negro traits' like stealing, crap shooting, immorality, ignorance and vice." The Baltimore *Afro-American* suggested "Futility" as an alternate title for the novel. Observing the absence of successful Black characters, the reviewer lamented that in Wood's narrative "it is futile for a Negro to be educated; it is futile for him to fight for his country; it is futile to attempt to [pass as] white. It is even futile to give up the struggle."[22]

Wood was sensitive to Black criticism. He responded to critics with several letters to the editor of Black periodicals and interviews with Black journals and newspapers that explained his intentions. To *Opportunity* he admitted: "I do leave out the cultured truly educated Negro: I did not meet him, till I came North." To *The Chicago Defender* he clarified: "The Negro reaction to the book is singularly unanimous in one thing: A regret that I have not shown the successful cultured Negro. First, he's scarce in the South; second, I didn't know him."[23] The next year he explained to a Black audience that when he wrote the novel, "I never thought of the Negro readers at all. I wrote for the white people. I painted things as they are in an effort to show my race the great difficulties that beset Negroes when they tried to rise."[24] When the novel was published in 1920, Wood saw the problem of race as one for white

Americans to solve. He wrote exclusively for white readers about the oppressive economic and social conditions facing Black Americans in the hope that they would work to improve the material conditions of Black life. In his estimation, better conditions would, in turn, allow Black people to develop less-stereotypical characteristics. As Wood explained, as long as Black Americans were "kept from wisdom, and in economic, mental, and spiritual poverty," there was little hope of improving their depictions.[25] At this stage of his career, he wrote with no thought for nonwhite readers, imagining that any good that would come from his text would stem from its capacity to change white attitudes and actions toward Black Americans.

During the next few years, Wood shifted from thinking of the race problem as a challenge to be solved by whites to one in which both races had a role to play. Acknowledging that the picture of Black life presented in his novel, which many African American critics deemed unrepresentative, stemmed from his lack of contact with "culturally advanced" Black people, Wood shifted his emphasis from advocating for economic opportunities, which he imagined would allow Black Americans to develop nonstereotypical traits, to focus on the positive changes in stereotypes that would result from whites having more contact with "cultured" Black residents in the North. His emerging approach to racial change was in sync with that of the many white liberals who saw in interracial contact the seeds for greater white regard for nonwhites. Advocates of contact advanced a range of ideas for improving race relations, from Boas's radical recommendation of miscegenation to the more mainstream calls for either an end to segregation or an increase in personal and professional contacts between the races.[26] A subset of those who advocated greater contact made the more specific argument that it was incumbent on Black Americans to present a truer picture of their racial group through personal example and for whites to remain open to nonstereotypical ways of seeing. The white poet Vachel Lindsay echoed Wood in declaring: "The Negro should make every effort to put before the public a true picture of the race, in totality; and white folk of sufficient intelligence and courage to recognize the issue as it stands should be enlisted as an auxiliary force to the same end."[27]

Wood's assertion that he did not depict "successful, cultured Negroes" because he had yet to meet them, coupled with his claim that he "painted things as they are," strongly suggests that the traits he ascribed to his characters were, from his vantage in 1920, true to life. In a letter Wood sent to the editor of *The Messenger* in 1923, in which he praised NAACP field secretary William Pickens's recently published essay on Black life in Arkansas, he encouraged Black Americans to "labor in every way to wipe out the current stereotype of white thinking that the Negro is an uncivilized brute, and replace it by the truer stereotype that the Negroes are a race rapidly acquiring culture."[28] Note that Wood referred in *The Messenger* to a "truer stereotype," and recall that to a Black audience in Harlem he outlined their obligation "to build up a . . . different stereotype." The suggestion that exposure to "cultured" and "educated" Black people would "wipe out" less-positive stereotypes credited audiences with the capacity to objectively assess the correspondence of stereotypes to human beings. Lippmann had argued that one could shed stereotypes only by replacing them with more complex understandings. Since stereotypes were internal, mental pictures that existed prior to observation, no amount of looking was capable of dislodging them. Wood's reference to "truer stereotypes" assumed a correlation between stereotypes and reality, and to his acceptance of "more" and "less" accurate representations of truth. He advocated for "truer" and "different" stereotypes to better capture what Black Americans were really like.

Despite their periodic claims to the contrary, many progressive whites acted as if a link existed between racial stereotypes and the real attributes of nonwhites. While Wood maintained that men such as Johnson, Du Bois, and Locke were too few to overthrow dominant white attitudes by their examples, he effectively argued that a critical mass of culturally sophisticated Black Americans would compel whites to jettison their racial stereotypes. In his circular argument, negative stereotypes would disappear once they were no longer characteristic of the people for whom they stood. This was then a common belief among literary whites. DuBose Heyward, author of the 1925 novel *Porgy* (the inspiration for George Gershwin's *Porgy and Bess* opera), reassured readers of *The Crisis* that "educated Negroes are rapidly arriving at a point where they are their own best refutation of this [stereotyped] portrayal." The novelist and Yale professor of English William Lyon Phelps advised that in order to counter negative depictions Black Americans "must hope that by setting a good example in their lives they can correct the false impression."[29]

When seen in conjunction with Wood's avowal that his novel captured "things as they are," and his characterization of Black Americans as "easy going, happy souled optimist[s]" who possess a "religious life [that] is deep and primitive," it is evident that the author held racialized views broadly shared by his race.[30] Even as he advocated for various ways of diminishing negative stereotypes of Black people—through increased economic opportunity or growing the pool of educated Black Americans—Wood continued to believe in a host of racial stereotypes. Both prior to 1923 and after, his solution to negative stereotypes was to swamp them with positive ones, driven by the implicit assumption that "truer" stereotypes are those exhibited by a larger percentage of the population. Despite the liberal credentials of whites such as Wood, Heyward, and Phelps, their advice neatly jibed with that of the conservative political scientist A. Lawrence Lowell. All of them expressed faith in the capacity of the public to distinguish more- from less-accurate stereotypes and in the existence of legible, racial attributes against which the verity of stereotypes might be judged. And, to varying degrees, they thought feasible the project of producing truer stereotypes, which came closer to representing the actual attributes of Black Americans.

African Americans shared with liberal whites the desire to see, in Wood's terms, "full political, economic and social justice" for Black citizens. But this common endpoint masked a range of differences in how the races conceived of America's racial problems and solutions. Most Black Americans saw racial stereotype as an issue of white perception, not Black conduct. There were certainly Black academics who conceded to truths in stereotypes, claiming, as did poet and Howard University professor Sterling A. Brown, that "there is no stereotype without some basis in actuality," but they tended to use the observation to emphasize the dangers of generalizations. In contrast to the common white assessment that Black people needed to change before the stereotypes about them could improve, the Black author and activist James Weldon Johnson declared: "The problem for the Negro is . . . less a matter of dealing with what he is and more a matter of dealing with what America thinks he is." Writing in 1923, Charles S. Johnson expressed satisfaction that a growing number of scholars were shifting their explanations of racial prejudice from being rooted in the failures of its victims to those of its perpetrators. What had once been explained as an outcome of biological failings were increasingly understood to result from limitations in our "thinking processes." With explicit reference to Lippmann's "excellent" work on stereotype, Johnson described them as mental pictures that "build up and crystalize a fictitious being unlike any Negro."[31]

Since Black Americans were less likely to see a correspondence between themselves and the "Negro stereotype," they tended not to share the white belief that economic and cultural advancement would lead to a restructuring of stereotypes. In "Race Prejudice and the Negro Artist" (1928), James Weldon Johnson explained that the "race problem" was "not at all the problem of a moribund people sinking into a slough of ignorance, poverty, and decay in the very midst of our civilization." It was "more a question of national mental attitudes toward the Negro than a question of his actual condition." Locke praised the accomplishments of the New Negro in 1928, before lamenting that few whites would know of his achievements given that "many minds still halt at the wall of prejudice." The director of research at the Chicago Urban League, Jacob Milton Sampson, believed that Black economic and social advancement was actually a provocation to whites. To rebut the common "conviction that with growing [Black] success, the whites will have greater respect for the Negroes and will concede them fair and equitable treatment," Sampson reminded his readers: "If history means anything at all . . . success would call forth increasing measures of repression, for fear that this . . . supposedly inferior group would reach equality with or superiority to the dominant group." This was a point conceded by even a subset of liberal whites. The executive director of the New York Joint Committee on Methods of Preventing Delinquency, Graham Romeyn Taylor, observed: "Higher standards of education and life among the Negroes create . . . the most intense prejudice on the part of many whites."[32] Johnson, Locke, and Sampson each promoted Black advancement, though not as a corrective to the racial stereotypes held by whites.

Black Americans were also considerably less sanguine than liberal whites about the potential of interracial contact to alter stereotypes. This is partly explained by their aforementioned belief that white attitudes toward them were both at the root of stereotypes and unconnected to Black conduct. In this regard, Black observers adhered closely to Lippmann's original formulation of stereotype as mental shortcut than preceded experience. Their interactions with whites provided evidence that whites were more likely to see cultured Black people as exceptions, rather than proof of the simplicity of racial stereotypes. Roscoe Simmons's commentary on Wood's Howard University speech made clear his view that Black Americans were in no position to "force" white relinquishment of stereotypes through their conduct. The Black-owned *Philadelphia Tribune* argued in 1928 that interracial contact had little impact on whites' attitudes toward Black Americans, since whites had their racial outlooks "fixed" in segregated schools during early childhood. The editors claimed: "Only in rare instances do Negroes have the opportunity of changing the impressions formed in the minds of white people during [whites'] early life." And Alain Locke wrote plainly in 1925: "It does not follow that if the Negro were better known, he would be better liked or better treated."[33]

In many respects, Black Americans in the 1920s held a more complex understanding of stereotype than did whites. We have seen how they interpreted stereotype as a problem of perception, not identity, and discounted the possibility of either racial uplift or interracial contact offering a ready solution. Black artists and academics of the period also expressed greater understanding than whites of the broad penetration of stereotype throughout American society. Whereas whites tended to view stereotypes as the province of those with "low intelligence," Black observers wrote about their hold on people with a range of political beliefs and from all strata of society. Locke explained in *The New Negro* (1925) that the Black American had historically navigated between "the unjust stereotypes of his oppressors and traducers," on the one hand, and those "of his liberators, friends, and benefactors," on the other.[34] Wood was an obvious example of a "friend" who clung to stereotypes; even as he fretted over the harm that the picture of the "black brute" inflicted, he unselfconsciously attributed a series of "primitive" traits to Black Americans that were broadly shared within white culture.

Black intellectuals were at least as vigorous in monitoring the stereotypes deployed by members of their race as they were of those used by white artists, whether such simplified pictures were tied to positive or negative associations. Writing in "Dilemma of the Negro Author" (1928), James Weldon Johnson surveyed the social pressures faced by Black novelists and poets. He began by explaining their need to grapple with the white expectation that Black writers confine themselves to a limited range of subjects deemed appropriate and craft characters that conformed to racial type. But Johnson went on to argue that when a Black author "turns from the conventions of white America" he frequently "runs afoul of the taboos of black America." He remarked that for years the defects and limitations of Black Americans had been "exploited to produce exaggerated effects" in the depiction of Black characters in painting, literature, and drama. The Black public consequently developed "a strong feeling against exhibiting to the world anything but their best points." Negative depictions were "not for the ears or eyes of white America." In a similar vein, the novelist Claude McKay noted the censorship that Black cultural leaders imposed on authors of their race through insistence that representations of "Negroes in literature and art . . . be decorous and decorative." In "Criteria of Negro Art" (1926), W. E. B. Du Bois explained that "the white public today demands from its artists, literary and pictorial, racial pre-judgement which deliberately distorts Truth and Justice, as far as colored races are concerned." He went on to declare: "The young and slowly growing Black public still wants its prophets almost equally unfree," given that "our worst side has been so shamelessly emphasized." And, finally, Langston Hughes lamented that the Black artist was pressed by his own people to "be respectable, write about nice people, show how good we are."[35]

Art threatened to codify and circulate racial stereotypes, but during the 1920s, it also struck many Black Americans (and some of their white compatriots) as a powerful tool for their dismantlement. James Weldon Johnson noted the limited progress to date in solving the "race problem" through traditional reforms, be they "religious, educational, political, industrial, ethical, economic, [or] sociological." Johnson trumpeted a new course, which he termed "the art approach to the Negro problem." It called for the conscious Negro artist to attack "the inner walls of race prejudice" through the creation of artworks that displayed the "intellectual and artistic achievement [of] Negroes." In *Black Manhattan* (1930), Johnson went further, writing: "Through his artistic efforts the Negro is smashing this immemorial stereotype faster than he has ever done through any method he has been able to use." In a similar vein, Alain Locke counseled Black readers: "One of the soundest and most constructive ways out of the distortions of social prejudice will be through [the] correction of its reflected distortions in the conventions of the arts." And George S. Schuyler credited Black literature with the power "of destroying . . . racial stereotypes." Most Black intellectuals did not seek to replace negative with positive stereotypes, but rather, in the words of Sterling A. Brown, to transform a stereotyped race into a "people with the same blunders, the same triumphs, the same farces, the same tragedies, the same ignorance and the same aspirations as the rest of humanity." As we will see in chapter 3, while virtually all Black critics wished to see more positive representations, most Black intellectuals were insistent that they remain grounded in reality, to show, in Brown's words, how Black people were of "humanity." The civil rights activist Joel Elias Spingarn cast art's power in dramatic terms, labeling the novels and plays of activist Black authors "instruments of progress as real as the ballot-box, the school-house, or a stick of dynamite." Such admonitions were in keeping with Lippmann's description of stereotypes as being replaceable with more complex understandings and with his belief in the capacity of art to alter one's perspective. As he wrote, "Sometimes an artist of compelling skill will force us to enter into lives altogether unlike our own, lives that seem at first glance dull, repulsive, or eccentric."[36]

Art's power to advance racially progressive politics was then understood to operate in one of two mutually reinforcing ways. The mere existence of poetry, novels, music, plays, and paintings produced by Black artists held out the promise of chipping away at the white belief that Black Americans were less-civilized people who consumed, but could not produce, culture. Writing in 1921 about Black contributions to US society, W. E. B. Du Bois noted that most Americans "assume that the place of the Negro in American culture is not that of a contributor, but rather of a passive victim or brute fact." Du Bois sought to dispel this impression by cataloging Black accomplishments in arts and industry from the colonial era to the early twentieth century. No one can write about US history, art, literature, or industry, Du Bois cautioned, without addressing the contributions of Black Americans. James Weldon Johnson, in his *Second Book of Negro Spirituals* (1926), celebrated spirituals for "softening down of some of the hard edges of prejudice against the Negro." He credited them with "breaking down the immemorial stereotype" that the Black American is "intellectually and morally" empty and is "here to be filled . . . with education, filled with religion, filled with morality, filled with culture, in a word, to be made into what is considered a civilized human being." Negro spirituals served as irrefutable evidence of Black achievement and influence, according to Johnson, proving that the Black American "has long been a generous giver to America; that he has helped to shape and mold it; that he has put an indelible imprint upon it; that America is the exact America it is today because of his influence."[37]

Black art was also thought to challenge stereotypes through its depiction of a more diverse array of Black characters. Varied representations, it was imagined, held the potential to expand whites' horizons for what constituted Black identity. It was not simply that a popular novel or play showcasing complicated Black characters could reach exponentially more white Americans than its creator could through interpersonal contacts alone, but that art was assumed to be a uniquely powerful catalyst of change. Montgomery Gregory wrote approvingly of Jessie Redmon Fauset's handling of the middle-class Black characters in her debut novel, *There Is Confusion* (1924). He praised her for presenting "to white America a milieu of its civilization of which it has been totally ignorant" and imagined that whites would "gladly welcome this opportunity of 'looking in' on the actual life of the more cultured class of Negroes. Here lies the great value of this novel, in interpreting the better elements of our life to those who know us only as domestic servants, 'uncles,' or criminals."[38]

Lippmann's close linkage of stereotypes to pictures may have heightened the interest of Black intellectuals in promoting art as a tool for combating skewed and simplified pictures of identity, though such interest predated *Public Opinion*. More than half a century prior to the invention of stereotype, Frederick Douglass outlined the power of pictures in remarkably modern terms: "Granite and iron are not more real supports to things material than are [pictures] to the subtle architecture of the mind." He described pictures as the building blocks through which human beings constructed their internal worlds and deemed the soul "a picture gallery." And he expressly linked the making of pictures to social and racial progress. Douglass laid the groundwork for twentieth-century Black thinking on the power of art by outlining how whites' racial perceptions could be altered both by evidence of nonwhites' picture-making abilities and by the specific ideologies that the artworks advanced. During an era when the humanity of Black people was vigorously debated, Douglass claimed that their demonstrated desire to create pictures offered evidence of their human qualities. He wrote: "The . . . remotest tribes of men manifest this great human [picture-making] power and thus indicate the brotherhood of men." Douglass saw the impulse to create art refuting the claims of "a certain class of ethnologists and archeologists" who drew "an unvarying and definite line separating what they are pleased to call the lowest variety of our species, always meaning the negro," from whites.[39]

Douglass read the project of picture making in explicitly racial terms, regardless of the racial identity of the picture maker. In 1849 he bluntly asserted: "Negroes can never have impartial portraits [made] at the hands of white artists." As he explained, "The reason is obvious.

Artists, like all other white persons have adopted a theory regarding the distinctive features of negro physiognomy. . . . This theory impressed strongly upon the mind of an artist exercises a powerful influence over his pencil. . . . The temptation to make the likeness of the negro, rather than of the man, is very strong." In a later essay he lamented that at the hands of whites "the negro is pictured with features distorted, lips exaggerated—forehead low and depressed—and the whole countenance made to harmonize with the popular idea of negro ignorance, degradation and imbecility." Douglass did not imagine that even well-intentioned white artists could avoid this pitfall, for they held fast to the "prejudice of color which prevails in this country." His solution lay in the Black community investing in picture making to create a critical mass of depictions untainted by racial bias. He described artists, but also poets, prophets, teachers, preachers, and reformers, as "picture makers . . . [who] see what ought to be by the reflection of what is, and endeavor to remove the contradiction." More images meant more "contradictions," which Douglass believed would catalyze social progress by prompting viewers to make more critical judgments. As Douglass explained, "It is the picture of life contrasted with the fact of life, the ideal contrasted with the real, which makes criticism possible. It is thus by looking upon this picture and upon that [one] which enables us to point out the defects of the one and the perfections of the other." Because whites had created a vast pool of images of Black subjects that both expressed and offered confirmation for how Black Americans purportedly looked and acted, Douglass believed that any meaningful effort to disrupt standardized types would need to work through images. Contradictory pictures would necessarily encourage critical thought as viewers tried to reconcile incompatible pictures. While such pictures could not guarantee altered racial perceptions, their disruption of the type represented in the standard image increased the likelihood of unsettling the dominant white view of Black Americans.[40]

A number of Douglass's ideas on the power of art to alter white racial attitudes and perceptions in the middle third of the nineteenth century were remarkably compatible with those of Black intellectuals in first third of the twentieth century. In a 1926 speech honoring Carter

Godwin Woodson, a pioneering historian of Black life, Du Bois echoed Douglass's point on the power of art to humanize Black people in the white imagination. Decades after Douglass first raised the idea, Du Bois lamented: "Until the art of the black folk compels [white] recognition they will not be rated as human." But even as Black intellectuals in the early decades of the twentieth century continued to champion the power of art, they defined its power in more expansive terms.[41]

At the same time that Locke promoted Black art as a corrective to false pictures, explaining that younger modernists "aim at hard realism . . . [that] breaks through the compensatory idealization and achieves objectivity," a number of Black critics pushed beyond a model of art that saw it simply mirroring the world in all of its complexities. Even as they continued to believe that art could help correct the visual distortions common to representations of Black Americans, they showed greater interest in art's capacity to picture conditions and relations that did not currently exist. Du Bois, for example, believed that Black Americans' unique experiences in the US allowed them to "see America in a way white Americans can not." Black observers consequently held "a vision of what the world could be," beyond its deeply flawed, racialized state. Along similar lines, the poet and editor Madeline G. Allison wrote: "It is, perhaps, unfortunate that beauty or those representations of it coaxed from stone or molded from metal need to be taken seriously as having racial importance." Allison yearned for an art that was free from political concerns, even as she believed that the "peculiar cultural environment by which Negroes are surrounded" made that impossible. "In the sense that art is idealization," she wrote, it holds the potential to improve the lot of Black Americans by confronting whites with alternate narratives of race.[42]

Black intellectuals from the early decades of the twentieth century routinely advised that in order for whites to shed their racial stereotypes, they needed to gain exposure to and internalize more complex pictures of Black identity. It is consequently noteworthy that they imagined such exposure was best achieved through greater contact with *representations,* rather than with living human beings. The diminishment of whites' internalized stereotypes would come through their exposure to complex depictions of Black characters, which, it was hoped, would lay bare the shortcomings of their simplistic mental pictures. Representations were credited with the power to make the complexity of racial identity apparent to whites and so improve how they thought about and treated their Black compatriots.

The Black American response to the stereotype concept was nuanced and considered, though it was ultimately no less fractured and contradictory than that of whites. The shared investment of racially conservative and progressive Black observers in the existence of a relation between stereotype and truth ensured that each group responded to race in ways antithetical to their stated beliefs. The distance between their written words and unconscious investments is encapsulated by the famous exchange on "Negro art" commissioned by *The Nation* in 1926 from two prominent Black intellectuals. The periodical aimed to spark public debate by soliciting back-to-back opinion pieces from George S. Schuyler, the conservative chief editorial writer for *The Pittsburgh Courier*, and Langston Hughes, the socialist poet, novelist, and playwright.[43]

Schuyler's June 16 essay, "The Negro-Art Hokum," was followed a week later by Hughes's article, "The Negro Artist and the Racial Mountain." Schuyler began with the provocative assertion that "Negro art 'made in America' is . . . non-existent." After conceding that Black Americans had created spirituals, blues, ragtime, jazz, and the Charleston, the author argued that these were regional art forms created by a Southern peasantry that only "happen[ed] to be a darker hue than the other inhabitants of the land." Schuyler maintained that these regional products were not representative of Black Americans as a whole and said nothing about Black people in the North, the West Indies, or Africa. Schuyler's overarching thesis was that white and Black Americans were culturally alike after having lived for generations under similar social conditions. The same schools, jobs, politics, advertising, consumer products, moral crusades, and restaurants had united them into an undifferentiated people. In his estimation, the superior writing of Du Bois, sculpture of Meta Warrick Fuller, and painting of Henry

Ossawa Tanner were therefore not "expressive of the Negro soul," but of the deracialized American nation.[44]

Schuyler discounted the existence of meaningful racial differences, either biological or social. But when it came to his explanation of stereotypes, his message showed inconsistencies. He observed: "Mere mention of the word 'Negro' conjures up in the average white American's mind a composite stereotype of Bert Williams, Aunt Jemima, Uncle Tom, Jack Johnson, Florian Slappey, and the various monstrosities scrawled by the cartoonists." The "composite" stereotype united fictional characters with living people in the white imagination. Schuyler saw such stereotypes built "upon the imbecilities of the Negro rustics and clowns and palmed . . . off as authentic and characteristic Afra-merican behavior." The newspaperman was unequivocal in his belief that the white stereotypes of Black people were false, but instead of dismissing them as simplified pictures that originated in the white imagination, and had no necessary relation of Black life, Schuyler pointed to their genesis in the real traits of rural Black Americans. With an undergirding logic shared with Clement Wood, Schuyler argued that the stereotype was false because its ascribed traits were uncharacteristic of a Black majority (whose traits were indistinguishable from its white neighbors); the traits society ascribed to Black residents of the rural South were stereotypical because they were unrepresentative of those exhibited by the millions of Black inhabitants of the urban North.[45]

Hughes's "The Negro Artist and the Racial Mountain" did not directly cite Schuyler's essay, even as it offered a tacit refutation of its thesis. Hughes began by conceding that the art of many Black Americans was indistinguishable from that of their white peers, though he attributed this sameness to the unhealthy "urge within the race toward whiteness." Whereas Schuyler described such sameness as "the impress of nationality rather than race," Hughes saw it in decidedly racialized terms, explaining that the major obstacle standing in the way of a "true Negro art" was the desire on the part of many economically secure Black Americans "to pour racial individuality into the mold of American standardization, and to be as little Negro and as much American as possible." For Hughes, the Black desire to be American was synonymous with its desire to be white.[46] Hughes believed that the Black artist was pressured by his own people to create respectable representations of Black life and by whites to create comforting images that did not disturb their fantasies of Black life. While each race expected a different kind of image, their shared desire for reassuring pictures pushed both toward stereotypes.

Hughes's prescription was for the Black artist to ignore the criticism and misapprehension exhibited by both Black and white audiences in order to "discover himself and his people." He sought a Black art that offered "honest" and "true" pictures of Black life, which he acknowledged few white or Black audiences were eager to see. In his estimation, true pictures were the antithesis of the stereotyped artwork Black novelists, poets, and painters were pressured by both camps to create.[47] Hughes's position on an authentic Black culture (and identity), which he saw masked by stereotypes, was in alignment with many Black critics and intellectuals in the 1920s. Walter White, the civil rights activist and future executive director of the NAACP, similarly read stereotypes as the antithesis of the real. Writing in "The Paradox of Color," White contrasted the "falsely painted" pictures of Black Americans created by Thomas Dixon, Octavus Roy Cohen, and Irvin Cobb in their popular films, novels, and short stories with the "real Negro" of New York City. An editorial in the Black *Philadelphia Tribune* put this view succinctly: "The stereotype is everything except what the Negro is in truth."[48]

White liberals and Black conservatives saw links between stereotype and truth, which invariably led them to make determinations about "more"- and "less"-accurate stereotypes. The wall they erected in theory between real identities and false stereotypes crumbled as they worked in practice to account for the fact that some stereotypes came closer to articulating their internalized picture of a given race than others. An intellectual belief in stereotypes' falsity bumped up against an experiential feeling of stereotypes' truth. While white liberals and Black conservatives tended not to see truth in the same stereotypes, each group played a role in maintaining the essential link between stereotypes and racial identities, which had the collateral result of reinforcing stereotypes' power.

The most progressive Black observers saw no truth in stereotypes of their race; as a group, they came closest to preserving the complexity of Lippmann's original stereotype concept. But through their understandable desire to cast stereotypes as wholly false, and their corresponding aim to proffer true depictions, they preserved a bedrock assumption that racial identity could be defined and its qualities parsed. In their estimation, Black people had discernible attributes that could be visualized. This also delimited Black identity. Black progressives effectively codified Blackness as a particular range of appearances and behaviors, thus restricting the representational (and real-life) attributes that they could comfortably inhabit. In the 1920s, Americans of all political outlooks and racial identifications united in the search for the "real" attributes of race.

We saw in chapter 1 how Lippman's definition of stereotype left open the door to race as a biological product and how powerful discursive currents pushed even self-proclaimed social constructivists to act as if race had a biological root. In chapter 2 it has become clear how the stereotype concept that was deployed in the 1920s encouraged the assessment of individual stereotypes based on their capacity to accurately visualize the attributes of racial groups. This necessarily reified race. For conservatives, stereotypes simply mirrored real characteristics. Progressives saw dominant stereotypes as false, but that assessment nonetheless sustained belief in the possibility of creating authentic racial pictures. Every effort to name and attack stereotypes silently advanced the idea that the stereotype stood in contrast to the true picture of how racial and ethnic minorities actually looked or acted. While it remained theoretically possible for that real picture to be a social product, we saw the degree to which period Americans were inclined to link identity to biology. For those wedded to the ties between stereotype and reality, a biological picture of race appeared as the more substantive truth. During the same years in which reformers in genetics, anthropology, sociology, and social psychology pushed Americans toward social constructivist models of race, the stereotyping of the stereotype concept sustained biological models of identity in American thought and life.[49]

CHAPTER 3

HUNTING FOR STEREOTYPES

The identical story is not the same story to all who hear
it. Each will enter it at a slightly different point, since
no two experiences are exactly alike. . . . And so, the
original theme as it circulates, is stressed, twisted, and
embroidered by all the minds through which it goes. It
is as if a play of Shakespeare's were rewritten each time
it is performed with all the changes of emphasis and
meaning that the actors and audience inspired.—WALTER
LIPPMANN, *Public Opinion* (1922)

In making his case for the role of psychology in shaping
public opinion, Lippmann returned again and again to
the example of the Great War to illustrate the challenges
faced by an educated citizenry in developing opinions on
distant and complex events. The war presented Lippmann
with an ideal case study. All of his readers had established
views on the Great War, which was the most discussed and
far-reaching event of the new century. Lippmann's unique
knowledge of the conflict, gained through his wartime

service as an intelligence officer in Europe, engaged in crafting propaganda and interrogating prisoners of war, and, later, as a staff member of the commission charged with negotiating the peace, allowed him to offer readers complex pictures of key events and decisions, which contrasted with their necessarily simplified pictures.[1] The obvious distance between his textured and their rudimentary understandings of the formative events of the day drove home to readers the practical challenges of arriving at informed opinions of world events. The Great War also afforded an unambiguous example of the complex and critical events for which citizens in democracies needed to develop deep understandings in order to effectively participate in public debate and make informed electoral decisions.

In *Public Opinion,* Lippmann augmented his discussions of the war with a diverse array of case studies drawn from more than a thousand years of Western history, all of which illustrated how stereotyping had consistently shaped perceptions of people, groups, events, things, and social systems. Collectively, his examples built a case for the ways in which stereotypes guide public opinion on everything from military leaders to political parties, from philosophical positions to class identities, and from labor unrest to racial groups. The most comprehensive of Lippmann's wide-ranging case studies shared a common formula: simplified pictures that increased legibility and comprehension as they diminished complexity; meaning produced by preexisting mental frameworks that preceded experience; and opinions that were never fully detached from stereotyping. The last point is worth emphasizing. Members of the press, politicians, military leaders, the general public, and, later, historians have debated the causes of the Great War since its outbreak. While analyses over the past century have enriched our understandings of the roots of the conflict, they have not arrived at a definitive explanation of its "causes"; the factors leading to war were ultimately too wide-ranging, multifaceted, and unknowable, and the lenses of its interpreters too varied, for historians to produce a conclusive explanation that transcends simplifications.

Recall that Lippmann explained stereotyping as the only practical way for human beings to digest information and make decisions within the dizzying torrent of stimuli that is endemic to the interconnected, modern world. Gone were the days of preindustrial communities in which citizens knew one another and the major issues of the day were confined to one's town, county, or region. The modern citizen was linked to a world of sufficient complexity, Lippmann explained, and "the need of economizing attention is so inevitable, that the abandonment of all stereotypes for a wholly innocent approach to experience would impoverish human life." *Public Opinion* illustrated stereotypes performing complex psychological work, reducing the clutter of stimuli to which we are subjected in order to speed our analyses and ease our decision-making process; they also cocooned us in ideologies that reinforced our sense of self and our positions within society.[2] In performing their psychological work, stereotypes had the collateral impact of flattening our understanding of the stereotype's object. When individuals are linked to the stereotypes associated with their race, complex human beings are essentialized. As the research of contemporary social scientists has confirmed, stereotyping compacts individuals into a collection of basic group traits, features, and motivations and, in turn, solidifies in- and out-group status, reinforces the status quo, and makes the unequal treatment of the impacted individuals and groups more likely.[3]

Lippmann was keen to convince his readers that given the ubiquity and shortcomings of stereotyping, it was critical for democratic societies to develop what he termed a new "machinery of knowledge." Because even highly informed citizens could not be realistically expected to gather and analyze all of the facts necessary to make educated decisions on the myriad of complex issues that were regularly at issue in elections, he argued for the creation of a professional cadre of public servants organized into "intelligence bureaus," which would take on this vital work and aid legislators and voters in arriving at informed decisions.[4] Lippmann diagnosed the "problem" as more stimuli than modern citizens could effectively process (with stereotypes serving as an imperfect solution), and, yet, contemporary responses to and invocations of *Public Opinion* illustrate that virtually all readers understood stereotypes as the problem to be solved. This approach remains largely true to this day.

As we saw in the previous chapters, debates inspired by Lippmann's text centered on how stereotypes could be eliminated, improved upon, or made true, and with the ideological or perceptual limitations of those who used them or failed to perceive them. Virtually everyone ignored Lippmann's prescription for a new class of civil servants; what they took away from *Public Opinion* was the need to establish whether representations did or did not offer stereotypical depictions of their characters and events. Unbeknownst to those who hunted for stereotypes, their search helped shore up their identities by dividing people into one of two distinctive groups: those on the lookout for stereotypes and attuned to their dangers, on the one hand, and those who either trucked in stereotypes or failed to see them, on the other. Ironically, the maintenance of such hierarchical divisions was a major function of the stereotypes they sought to root out.

A basic question asked by critics and audiences in the 1920s—Is it or isn't it stereotyped?—was ultimately misplaced. Since representations are not the thing they represent, they necessarily simplify the object of their attention through the process of representation. Lippmann paid little attention to stereotypes embedded within social products; his focus was on the process by which viewers projected their stereotypes onto people and objects. Since stereotypes were an unavoidable feature of modern life, resided within viewers, and preceded looking, nonstereotyped art had no relevance within his epistemology. It was only in the postwar period that art historians began to consider the mechanism by which stereotypes were embedded within works of art. The most prominent among these historians was Ernst Gombrich. Building on the insights of Lippmann and the research of the psychologists Jean Piaget and Frederic Charles Bartlett, Gombrich famously illustrated that even those artists who aim to create "truthful" or "naturalistic" renderings of the world produce artworks whose final appearance is as contingent on their media, manner of production, style, and worldviews as on the properties of their subject. In picking up a pencil, the artist looks for elements of the subject that can be rendered in lines; in taking up a brush, the artist looks for masses. The selected artistic media—be it drawing, etching, painting, sculpture, or photography—delimit and enable what can be communicated through representations. The limitations inherent to particular tools and media are compounded by what Gombrich understood as the internalized pictures of the world that artists of specific nations and eras shared. Gombrich argued that in attempting to create a "correct portrait," the artist produces "not a faithful record of a visual experience but the faithful construction of a relational model," representing the artist's best efforts to compare his internalized schema for the sitter (as an intellectual, financier, political leader, union organizer, mother, Native American, etc.) to the live subject sitting before the canvas. The most successful artists, Gombrich argued, are those whose portraits move toward closing the gap between their a priori mental picture and a posteriori visual stimuli. Gombrich did not believe in the possibility of "perfect" representations that captured everything about their subjects. But he did believe that his "relational model" allowed artists and historians to determine those works of art that did better and worse jobs of expressing the identity of their sitters during particular epistemes. His research on the formal and ideological implications of art making points out the futility of making binary determinations as to whether artworks are either stereotyped or nonstereotyped.[5]

Imagine a painting that shows a Black protagonist. How would one determine if the depiction was racially stereotyped? If it was known that the painting was a portrait of a living person, one would have the benefit of actual physical features against which to assess the representation. Viewers would presumably begin by comparing the sitter's physiognomy to her depiction to consider if there existed any variances. If variances were found, they would need to be studied for their fit with tropes of Black stereotype. In addition, one would consider whether the artist's selected style, as well as the sitter's props, pose, or activity, was linked to stereotypes associated with her race. If stereotypes were detected, viewers would also need to discern if they were present in the portrait or instead brought to the canvas by viewers. In the event that the painting depicted a fictional character, the exercise would become more involved. All of the steps described above would be relevant, aside from the first, which would require viewers to begin with a comparison of their mental picture of Black identity against the character's physical features (in light of the style, props, pose and any depicted activity on the part of the sitter). As is likely apparent to readers, these exercises are far from straightforward. Their feasibility rests on a series of dubious assumptions: that racial identity can be quantified, or at least that its borders can be clearly demarcated; that viewers share a common understanding of that identity and its associated stereotypes; that they can objectively catalogue the visual differences between a sitter and her representation and distinguish those that are incidental from those that are racially significant; that they are capable of determining the presence of stereotypes and distinguishing between those stereotypes in the artwork and those in their mental pictures; and, finally, that a social product as amorphous and complex as racial identity is representable. None of these assumptions is true. The insights offered by Lippmann and Gombrich, and a host of subsequent scholars who have studied the conditions of art's production and circulation, lead to the conclusion that stereotypes are an essential component of representational art.

With the acknowledgment of stereotypes' ubiquity, the salient question shifts from "Is it or isn't it stereotyped" to "Why was it seen as stereotyped or not?" The extensive record of artists, critics, and historians who wrestled with the issue of stereotyping in artworks offers a rich source of information on the beliefs of the period. The collective appraisal of viewers, as well as the segmented assessments of those viewers who shared common values (white progressives or Black conservatives, for example), can illuminate both the period's racial norms and the ways in which the idea of stereotype functioned in practice. Debates over the stereotypical nature of artworks both offer evidence of normative racial expectations at a moment in time and shed light on the continuous negotiation of the borders of racial identity.

:::

Months before Eugene O'Neill's drama *All God's Chillun Got Wings* premiered at the Provincetown Playhouse in Greenwich Village on May

15, 1924, it had already received more publicity than many of the productions then running on Broadway. *All God's Chillun Got Wings* began to generate controversy in February 1924, when O'Neill published its script in *The American Mercury*.[6] The drama plumbed the psychologies of a Black man, Jim Harris, and an Irish American woman, Ella Downey, who married and lived in New York. We meet the pair as childhood friends who drift apart, and we are reintroduced to them years later. Jim graduated from law school and is at work studying for the bar exam; he comes from an educated family proud of its racial heritage. The working-class Ella suffered a bruising relationship with a white boxer, who eventually leaves her; she loses a young child to diphtheria. Jim and Ella reconnect, marry, and move to France for two years before returning to New York, where their relationship is torn apart by their internalized racial biases and the hostility of family, friends, and society to their interracial marriage. By the end of the play, Ella experiences a mental breakdown, and Jim has failed his bar exam for the final time. The drama critic John Corbin summed up the malice that the play aroused, stating: "From the moment the Provincetown Players announced the production of Eugene O'Neill's play it was evident that we were in for a campaign of race hatred and bigotry differing in no essentials from the propaganda of the Klansmen."[7]

The storm that swirled around *All God's Chillun Got Wings* largely centered on its depiction of a marriage between a Black man and a white woman and a scene in which the wife tenderly kisses her husband's hands (plate 4). When O'Neill's choice to cast a Black actor, a young Paul Robeson, as Jim Harris, and a white actor, Mary Blair, as Ella Downey, became known, the controversy intensified. In the 1920s, Black people were barred from marrying whites in thirty of forty-eight states, and theatrical convention encouraged the directors of plays populated with white and Black characters to assign the Black roles to white actors in blackface or give the white roles to light-skinned Black actors, in order to avoid interracial casts. In the lead-up to the premiere, outraged articles were produced by newspapers across the country and angry letters sent and petitions circulated by the Society for the Prevention of Vice and Crime, United Daughters of the Confederacy, Authors' League of America, Salvation Army, New York Board of Education, New York City Hall, and various regional and state chapters of the Ku Klux Klan. The play's detractors demanded, variously, that it not be staged; that it not be staged with an interracial cast; that it be revised to remove the offending kisses. Many observers predicted that the opening would be met with violence, and a number recommended it. To the surprise of both O'Neill and Robeson, the play's opening and subsequent run were met with calm. The ferment was confined to print, mostly among those who had not read the script or attended the play.[8]

A few prominent white reviewers defended O'Neill and his play, among them both Edmund Wilson and T. S. Eliot, with the former labeling the play "one of the best things yet written about the race problem."[9] Most whites were either apathetic or critical. The mainstream white reaction to *All God's Chillun Got Wings* was epitomized by two New York City papers that spearheaded a crusade against the play in the weeks between the script's publication in February and its opening in May. *The Morning Telegraph*, which covered New York City theatrical and sporting news, expressed outrage that a "full-blooded negro" would be paid to play the husband of a white woman and reported on the ensuing "storm of criticism, which last night appeared to be gaining dangerous proportions." The paper claimed that the production would "bring about a situation concerning intimacy between a white woman and a negro unparalleled in the history of the American stage." In a subsequent column, the *Telegraph* rehashed the playwright's intention to illustrate a mixed-race marriage before mocking his position "that there is absolutely no difference in the mentality, morality or psychological reactions of a negro and a white man, all of the facts of biology to the contrary notwithstanding." The writer then noted approvingly: "A little further south that would call for the burning cross and the thud of hoofs across the countryside and the appearance of the masked riders." Such an allusion would not have surprised readers of the *Telegraph*, who were accustomed to its frequent front-page references to the rise of the Ku Klux Klan, which coincided with the apogee of the Klan's membership in the North during the mid-1920s.[10]

William Randolph Hearst's *New York American* was similarly aggrieved by the prospect of O'Neill's play being staged. It described *All God's Chillun Got Wings* precipitating "violent discussion" and casting the playwright into "the storm centre of the greatest controversy of his career." Also troubled by the choice to cast a "full-blooded negro" in the lead role, the paper noted with incredulity that within the production "it is accepted that negro players will be used to represent negroes on the stage." And the paper ultimately advised: "They should not put on plays which are, or threaten to become, enemies of the public peace; they should not dramatize dynamite, because, while helping the box office, it may blow up the business. . . . It is hard to imagine a more nauseating and inflammable situation." In describing what he took as the shameful coverage of the play by these two New York dailies, James Weldon Johnson lamented: "The *New York American* and the *Morning Telegraph* . . . appeared to be seeking to provoke violence in order to stop the play."[11]

Time magazine succinctly summarized the overarching concern of many whites: "Mr. O'Neill writes a 'revolting' play. . . . It is a drama of miscegenation." A lengthy review of the play in a South Carolina newspaper fleshed out the perspectives of white detractors. After noting approvingly that animals did not mate outside of their species, the author explained: "The same law of nature applies in the case of distinct races of men and is made none the less imperative by a few violations of it with tragic consequences." The reviewer went on to claim: "Mr. O'Neill is altogether mistaken when he says he at least found an actress willing to hold art above prejudice. What he finally found was an actress willing to hold art above nature. And Mr. O'Neill is pleased only because he has definitively repudiated the long-accepted canon that true art is the mirror of nature."[12] As with many reviews of the play penned by white critics in the 1920s, the focus is on the destabilizing hint of interracial sex, rather than on what Paul Robeson deemed as the essence of the play: "the struggle of a man and a women . . . against forces they could not control."[13] In appealing to Southerners' investment in the higher law of nature, the reviewer denigrates what he sees as the dangerous unnaturalness of a mixed-race marriage. Like the assessments of many period audiences, the review is structured around an artificial-real binary. Both those with progressive and conservative outlooks on race marshaled their disparate interpretations of "the real" to advance their subjective positions on the drama.

The Black reception was equally polarized, though it broke down along more fault lines. A subset of Black detractors joined their white peers in foregrounding the play's depiction of miscegenation. Whereas whites were distressed by the danger miscegenation posed to the purity of white blood, the supremacy of Western civilization, and republican governance, Black observers worried about the social and physical threats posed by whites who had their fears of Black men's sexual desire confirmed. Writing for the Black-owned *Pittsburgh Courier*, a reporter lamented that the play reinforced "the time-worn and absolutely wrong impression that all Black men are attracted to white women simply because they are white. . . . Never was there a more malicious and untruthful insinuation." The "time-worn" picture of the lascivious Black male lusting after white women was frequently invoked by whites to support a range of unjust laws and practices, from commercial, educational, and residential segregation to lynching. Reverend J. W. Brown, who led the oldest Black church in New York City, claimed that the play "portrays the negro in the wrong light," as "no thinking colored man desired to marry outside of his own race." And the powerful Reverend Adam Clayton Powell, who led one of the largest congregations in Harlem, warned that the play endangered racial progress by suggesting that Black men "are desirous of marrying white women. . . . The kissing of a white woman by a big strapping negro is bound to cause bad feelings."[14] Not known for their theatrical reviews, the religious leaders weighed in out of concern for the impact of the play on their congregants. Powell was sufficiently steeped with the white fantasy of Black male carnality that he inadvertently transformed the white character's kiss of her husband's hands in the script into "the kissing of a white woman by a big strapping negro" in his review.

The other major concern voiced by Black critics centered on what was seen as the unequal social positions of the husband and wife. The mass-circulation *Chicago Defender* had its entertainment editor,

Tony Langston, weigh in on the play shortly after the script was published and the cast announced. In his review, "White Actress to Star with Paul Robeson in Eugene O'Neill's Drama," Langston began by labeling the play's white critics "prejudiced" for their objections to an interracial cast. He worked to distinguish the arguments of white from Black critics, writing that many Black New Yorkers "have chosen an entirely different viewpoint," even though their concerns also related to miscegenation. After dismissing white criticism, the editor relayed that Black critics are "voicing their indignation that the story shows the leading male character eloping with, marrying and taking into his home a woman who has been rejected by her own people, the tossed-aside, degenerate concubine of a pug-ugly [boxer], despite [the Black husband's] education and refinement." And he concludes: "They claim this to be an insult to the Race." In giving voice to unnamed New Yorkers, Langston labeled whites as "prejudiced" for objecting to the casting of an interracial couple, given the Black actor's "breeding and education," before explaining Black objections to a fictional interracial couple based on the social distance between the "degenerate concubine" wife and the "education and refinement" of the husband. Three months later, after the play opened, *The Chicago Defender* continued to note white objections to the play, but advised its readers that "any objections to the theme of the play should come logically not from the white but from the colored community," given that the plot "gives to a first[-]rate negro a third[-]rate white woman."[15]

The major points of Black criticism of the play—rooted in the depiction of miscegenation and the disparate class positions of the husband and wife—were the subject of vigorous debate among Black newspaper reporters and academics. The Howard University professor and poet Sterling A. Brown acknowledged both concerns in a lengthy discussion on the formation of Black audiences for art. With specific reference to those Black critics who faulted the depictions of interracial marriage and class relations in *All God's Chillun Got Wings,* Brown wrote: "To what absurdity we may sink in our determination to consider anything said of Negroes as a wholesale indictment or exaltation of all negroes. . . . We should be able to distinguish between individual and race portraiture, i.e., between literature on the one hand and pseudo-science and propaganda on the other." Whereas Black detractors of the play saw it filled with stereotypes, Brown deemed it "a humane . . . observation of the wreck of prejudice" and cautioned that efforts to police playwrights' depictions of Black characters would "hamper the artist, and . . . add to the stereotyping which has unfortunately, been too apparent in books about us." In Brown's judgment, Black audiences exhibited a "natural" but unwise desire to pressure artists to produce affirming stereotypes that showed us at "our 'best.'" In a subsequent article devoted to "Negro drama," Brown listed a series of characters created by progressive white playwrights, including O'Neill's Jim Harris in *All God's Chillun Got Wings* and his Brutus Jones from *The Emperor Jones* (1920), before claiming: "Those who still see nothing but a stereotype in characters as diverse as these lay themselves open as suspect. One fears that for them the dramatic ideal is race glorification, and any portraiture of Negroes means the betrayal of a race."[16]

This was an unease expressed by a number of Black intellectuals. After the production concluded its run, Paul Robeson wrote an article for *Opportunity* to defend the play, its playwright, and his participation in the project to Black audiences. He interpreted the negative Black responses to his role in O'Neill's *All God's Chillun Got Wings*, and before that in *The Emperor Jones*, to "point out one of the most serious drawbacks to the development of a true Negro dramatic literature. We are too self-conscious, too afraid of showing all phases of our life,—especially those phases which are of greatest dramatic value." W. E. B. Du Bois expressed similar sentiments in his essay "The Negro and Our Stage," which O'Neill reprinted in his playbill for *All God's Chillun Got Wings*. The essay outlined the challenges faced by playwrights in getting at the "facts" of Black life, given a "series of concentric shells" that distanced artists from "the inner life of this black group and the contact of black and white." Du Bois described three "shells": society's internalized pictures of Black people; a desire for art to communicate a politically correct message, which resulted in propaganda; and the self-consciousness of the Black community to its portrayal. On this last point, Du Bois sympathetically described the sensitivity of Black

Americans to their depictions, given that they have "been maligned and caricatured and lied about to an extent inconceivable to those who do not know." Du Bois explained: "The Negro today fears any attempt of the artist to paint Negroes. He is not satisfied unless everything is perfect and proper and beautiful and joyful and hopeful. He is afraid to be painted as he is, lest his human foibles and shortcomings be seized by his enemies for the purposes of the ancient and hateful propaganda." Du Bois concluded that "O'Neill is bursting through" the shells, adding: "He has my sympathy. . . . It is work that must be done."[17] A host of lesser-known Black critics and publications also described the play as an antidote to stereotypical depictions. They predicted that *All God's Chillun Got Wings* would not be popular with white audiences, given that "white America does not relish any such assaults on its 'Credo' concerning the negro"; proclaimed that "no better study of the relations of white and colored people in the United States has ever been projected on the American stage"; and lauded its depiction of "authentic negro character," noting that "the effort to look under the old superficial burnt cork is a very recent one."[18]

Black intellectuals understood the desire to see affirming depictions of the race and showed understanding of those who advocated for positive stereotypes. Two years after Du Bois wrote of Black Americans' aversion to unvarnished depictions, given their history of having "been maligned and caricatured and lied about," he noted in 1926 of the Black public: "Our worst side has been so shamelessly emphasized that we are denying we have or ever had a worst side." Sterling A. Brown deemed it "natural that when pictures of us were almost entirely concerned with making us out to be either brutes or docile housedogs . . . we should have replied by making ourselves out superhuman. It is natural that we should insist that the pendulum be swung back to its other extreme."[19] In his analysis, the desire for affirming depictions was an expected reaction to centuries of negative portrayals, heightened by excitement that Black writers and artists now had the training, patronage, and audiences to represent Black people on their own terms.

The Black intellectuals who did not see stereotypes in the characters of *All God's Chillun Got Wings* feared that the pressure exerted by

Black critics who wished to replace negative with positive stereotypes would inadvertently lead to more untruthful depictions of Black life. In a 1926 address, "The Criteria of Negro Art," Du Bois assured his audience that he supported using art as "propaganda" to advance the race, explaining: "Whatever art I have for writing has been used always for propaganda for gaining the right of black folk to love and enjoy." But, as he also made clear, Black propaganda must tell the truth. After centuries of stereotypical depictions produced by whites who refused to see Black humanity, Du Bois argued that the antidote was truthful depictions of Black life. For Du Bois that meant representations that displayed a range of positive and negative traits that, as much as possible, captured the full spectrum of Black identity. While couched in different language, his argument overlapped with Lippmann's belief in complex understandings as the only recourse to stereotypes. As Du Bois wrote, "We can afford the Truth. White folk today cannot."[20]

The "correctness" of Black judgments on the presence or absence of stereotypes in *All God's Chillun Got Wings* cannot be definitively adjudicated. On one level, we can conclude that those who saw stereotypes in the work were technically correct, since all representational artworks make use of established schema to picture the thing they purport to depict, though the conclusion holds no analytic payoff. We need to appreciate that when Du Bois, Brown, Robeson, Locke, and others declared the play's Black characters nonstereotyped, they made a statement that was relative—not to actual Black identity, but to the dominant representational norms for Black characters then in circulation. O'Neill's characters looked to them nonstereotyped because of the specific ways in which the critics interpreted them as breaking from period conventions—showing a diverse array of complicated Black characters who responded to psychological and social forces in ways that appeared less formulaic than dominant representations. For these writers, the major Black characters of *All God's Chillun Got Wings*—Jim Harris, his sister Hattie, and their mother, Mrs. Harris—offered striking contrasts to the shopworn types then dominating American culture in the popular short stories, novels, and films of Octavus Roy Cohen, Thomas Dixon, and Thomas Nelson Page.

Sterling Brown made clear his understanding of stereotype's relative nature through his defense of authors who depicted striving Black characters who suffered tragic fates. He noted in 1930 that among Black audiences today "especially taboo is tragedy. . . . Into these tragedies we read all kinds of fantastic lessons, 'Intended to show that the Negro never wins out, but always loses,' 'Intended to impress upon us the futility of effort on our part.'" He went on to ask why it was not "invigorating" and "inspiring" to see in the Black protagonist of Paul Green's *In Abraham's Bosom* (1927) "man's heroic struggle against great odds, showing the finest virtue man can show in the face of harsh realities?" He concluded with a reminder: "We seem to forget that for the Negro to be conceived as a tragic figure is a great advance in American literature. The aristocratic concept of the lowly as clowns is not so far back. That the tragedy of this 'clown' meets sympathetic reception is a step forward in race relations."[21] Brown saw a universal lesson that transcended race—"man's heroic struggle"—in the suffering of Green's Black protagonist precisely because of the character's distance from the early twentieth century's standard Black depictions. A mix of positive and negative traits, the display of a more complex psychology, the departure from standardized Black tropes (and, ideally, the display of different types of Black characters within the same text), allowed the characters to be read as less stereotyped and even, at times, as universal symbols of "man." Representations deemed to be nonstereotyped do not illustrate a fixed set of attributes, since they are made nonstereotyped by their location relative to other representations and the psychology of the viewers; the "nonstereotyped" attribution is always relational and the depicted qualities of its characters highly fluid.

Black detractors of *All God's Chillun Got Wings* read the negative attributes displayed by Black characters, and the disappointing life outcomes they faced, as expressions of whites' belief in the supposed deficits of the race. Those critical of the play saw the attributes and fate of Jim Harris as part of the long-standing, dehumanizing lineage of Black representations that ran throughout US history. Black supporters of the play were more likely to focus on the Black characters as artistic representations of individuals, rather than as stand-ins for all Black

Americans. And they perceived various ways in which the characters' traits, values, actions, and outcomes pushed beyond dominant depictions of Black protagonists. Virtually all Black critics and proponents of *All God's Chillun Got Wings* were united in their disdain for negative stereotypes and in their desire for representations that improved the social and economic conditions of Black life. Yet they expressed profound disagreements over what constituted a stereotype, which artworks contained them, and the social and racial impact of the growing body of artworks that featured Black protagonists.

Writing in 1927, the theater critic Lillian Krieger noted the unique challenges faced by critics in summarizing the themes of US theatrical productions. Krieger explained that America enjoyed an unprecedentedly large and diversified population with the disposable income required to support theatrical productions. In her estimation, "the critic's natural function . . . to trace tendencies" of the productions staged was thwarted by the diversity of those productions, which resulted from America's "unique . . . possession of a huge stratum of wealthy unsophisticates." She contrasted conditions in the US with those in the UK, "where the theater-element is confined to a homogeneous class," resulting in thematically aligned productions. In highlighting what she took as the thematic "chaos" caused by the diversity of tastes evident among American audiences, Krieger wrote: "I can find no more striking example of the chasms that exist within the ranks of our theater-goers, than the freak of some five years ago, when in almost the same breath the American people acclaimed . . . O'Neill and *Abie's Irish Rose*."[22]

Krieger pointed to 1922, the year in which O'Neill won the Pulitzer Prize for Drama for *Anna Christie* (1920) and staged *The Hairy Ape*, and in which a minor vaudevillian actor and playwright, Anne Nichols, wrote and produced the crowd-pleasing and critically disparaged comedy *Abie's Irish Rose*. The plays of O'Neill and Nichols had little in common: drama versus comedy, high art versus popular entertainment, and avant-garde versus tradition bound. Because of the opportunity that such a "chasm" affords, I have paired my analysis of stereotypes in *All God's Chillun Got Wings* with *Abie's Irish Rose*. The plays were each at the center of debates on stereotypes and, as several period observers commented, shared the theme of miscegenation. Given the large and varied audiences that embraced *Abie's Irish Rose*, the play offers a deeper pool of primary-source material: more reviews, greater diversity in the types of periodicals, and more variety in the identities of the reviewers. As a complement to the critiques of O'Neill's play, which skewed toward intellectual and academic writers and audiences from the Northeast, the reviews of Nichols's play give voice to the outlooks of critics and audiences frequently dismissed by the elite art world.[23]

Anne Nichols's popular comedy portrayed the efforts of two newlyweds, a Jewish veteran of the Great War and his Irish Catholic bride, to gain acceptance of their marriage from their stubborn, prejudiced, and loving fathers. We meet Abraham "Abie" Levy and Rose Mary Murphy in the New York apartment of the groom's father immediately following their offstage marriage by a Methodist minister. The couple wait nervously for Abie's Orthodox Jewish father, Solomon, to enter so that Mary can be presented to him. Afraid to reveal his mixed marriage to a father who is determined to see his son matched with a Jew, Abie presents his bride as his girlfriend and, when pressed as to her religion, as Rosie Murpheski, a name designed to deceive Solomon into believing that she's "a nice Jewish girl."[24] Before the close of the whirlwind second act, the couple is married by a rabbi to please Solomon, while the bride is still thought to be Jewish; Mary Rose's true identity is revealed by the arrival of her Catholic father, Patrick Murphy; the couple is married by a Catholic priest, to force the bride's father to accept the permanence of their union; and there is much bickering between the fathers, both of whom demand that the couple break up, and each of whom holds a fierce antipathy for the other man's race and traditions. In the third and final act of the play, an ecumenical reconciliation is effected through the efforts of an open-minded rabbi and priest, through the birth of twins, and by the fathers, whose desire for grandchildren ultimately surmounts their prejudices. The play features eight major characters: Abie Levy and Rose Mary Murphy (the newlyweds), Solomon Levy and Patrick Murphy (the fathers), Dr. Jacob Samuels and Father Whalen (the rabbi and priest), and Mr. and Mrs. Isaac Cohen (Levy family friends) (plate 5).

Abie's Irish Rose was enormously popular with the public, becoming the longest-running play in US history and supporting multiple touring companies across the US, Canada, UK, and Australia. The Broadway production alone staged 2,327 performances during its run from May 1922 through October 1927. Its critical reception was polarized. A significant number of critics violently disparaged the play, particularly those who considered themselves champions of high art. As one detractor succinctly summed it up, "No play ever produced on the legitimate stage of this country has been so universally 'slammed,' 'panned,' and 'roasted' as *Abie's Irish Rose*." In his one-line theatrical reviews for *Life* magazine each week, the humorist Robert Benchley declared it "something awful" and later cautioned that "it couldn't be much worse."[25] A reviewer for *Billboard* declared it so bad that it "filled me with an almost irresistible impulse to start a pogrom [against] playwrights, managers, actors and critics." And the drama critic George Jean Nathan labeled it "obvious and childish mush."[26]

The New Yorker reminded its readers how the city's intelligentsia explained the popularity of the play: "New York is moron by a two-thirds majority." Unfriendly critics expected the play to close quickly and displayed a mix of confusion and irritation once it became clear that *Abie's Irish Rose* would smash all theatrical records. A year after its first effort to explain the play's popularity, *The New Yorker* published a satirical piece by a "statistician" calculating how long the play would run, based on the Jewish and Irish populations of New York City and taking into account the groups' expected growth over time given their fertility and immigration rates. For elite critics troubled by the play's success, the only reasonable explanation was that it was patronized by less-sophisticated audiences who valued seeing themselves represented on stage. But as an astute observer pointed out, "It didn't seem to make any difference how many Jews or Irishmen a town had or didn't have. The play ran nineteen weeks in Toronto, where eighty percent of the population is straight Protestant."[27]

As *Abie's Irish Rose* continued to draw enthusiastic audiences, a segment of the press accorded it a begrudging acceptance, even as it continued to express confusion over the play's commercial success.

During the second year of the play's run, a *New York Times* reporter wrote: "What makes the thing tick, thus, remains a mystery. There is no question of the fact, however, that it does tick and that it is today the undisputed leader of all New York theatrical attractions in point of length of run." Reviewing the play during its fourth year, *Variety* characterized its longevity as "a miracle" and noted that "like all miracles," it was "to be accepted, bowed to, but not dissected or submitted to scientific diagnosis."[28]

Dismissive reviews were counterbalanced by many paeans to the play that matched the hyperbole of the detractors. A theme that runs through a number of the most supportive assessments is the play's role in stamping out racial intolerance. Anne Nichols advanced this interpretation in her many press interviews, explaining to one reporter that the play's success "is the result of its great message—the spirit of tolerance" and, to a second, that it was due to its ability "to banish bigotry from human hearts." *The Boston Daily Globe* claimed that in *Abie's Irish Rose* "there runs a telling plea for racial and religious tolerance that will not be quickly forgotten"; *The Spur* declared "its spirit of religious tolerance" a significant factor in "the prodigious success of *Abie's Irish Rose*," concluding that the "play might even be called a reactionary force in the age of growing intolerance"; *Collier's* deemed it "a comedy more significant than most acts of Congress" for its ability to prod audiences to question their prejudices; and, writing in *The Messenger*, the Black radical Chandler Owen described it as "calculated to destroy race prejudice."[29]

Linking the play to the racial intolerance of the era, one theater critic claimed that its "message of religious and racial tolerance" was not new, but "in the day of the Ku Klux Klan and William Jennings Bryan, it cannot be repeated too insistently and too often." In the ultimate tribute to the play's power, Arthur Hobson Quinn, Welsh Professor of History and English at the University of Pennsylvania, wrote in his *History of American Drama* (1927) that in *Abie's Irish Rose*, the playwright "not only attacked . . . intolerance indirectly through her revelations of the absurdity of the fathers' prejudice, but she embodied it in the characters" of the rabbi and priest. Quinn argued that by the conclusion of the play, with its familial reconciliations, "the reaction against the germ of race hatred had set in, and if *Uncle Tom's Cabin* was a powerful weapon against slavery, *Abie's Irish Rose* has become important in our social history as a potent force toward sanity and feeling in the Republic."[30]

As such glowing endorsements may suggest, many of the play's supporters saw no stereotypes in the play. A supportive critic for *McCall's* described "characters [that] are as close to their originals in life" as possible; while another for *The American Monthly* wrote: "The character drawing is excellent. There is not a person on the stage whom one cannot recognize in life." In *The Atlanta Constitution*, the theater critic assured readers that "*Abie's Irish Rose* is one of those delightful comedy affairs that picks its characters from every-day life. There is nothing pointing to the author's inclination of getting the audience acquainted with personages which are simply stage figures" and that the characters' authentic "experiences keep the audience in a delirium of laughter." Evidently aware of critics who questioned the naturalism of the characters' renderings, a reviewer wrote: "Some may say that Solomon Levy is caricature and not a real flesh and blood character. [I] can't agree with that." Finally, one supporter of the play turned the tables on the negative critics, deeming them "hopelessly academic and stereotyped in their standards."[31]

Detractors of *Abie's Irish Rose* would have found dubious its linkage to *Uncle Tom's Cabin* as a comparably potent agent of progressive social change. Unsympathetic critics deemed *Abie's Irish Rose* a reactionary play whose success was rooted in the appeal of racial and ethnic stereotypes. The theatrical critic for the *New-York Tribune*, Percy Hammond, championed "drama as an aid to moral betterment," but maintained that the critical consensus held that *Abie's Irish Rose* has "done little to mitigate prejudices and hatreds." J. Brooks Atkinson, a *New York Times* theater critic, regarded as one of the twentieth century's most influential critics, labeled *Abie's Irish Rose* "a rude comedy" featuring "five stage-convention Jews and three Irish." He went on to state: "The character portrayals have no basis in fact; they exhibit only the machine-made types common to the old stage hocus-pocus." And, writing in a specialized journal for insurance agents, a reviewer urged his readers to look elsewhere for entertainment, claiming that audiences of *Abie's Irish Rose* will find themselves "floating on a sea of banality, mawkish sentimentality and stereotyped humor."[32]

The editors of *The Nation* opined: "It would be heartwarming to believe that the playwright's profit of $5,000,000 came wholly out of America's great love and passion for tolerance. During the life of this comedy celebrating denominational democracy the Ku Klux Klan rose and fell. Governor [Albert] Smith wrote his famous letter explaining how one might be both Catholic and patriot. Henry Ford discovered a Jewish conspiracy and recanted. And here and there in minor ways race prejudice was manifest." The editors went on to note that "some who remained to applaud [*Abie's Irish Rose*] no doubt went down to business the next day and advertised for 'Christians only,'" before concluding: "Possibly Miss Nichols is mistaken. It may have been the jokes and not the message" that accounted for the play's popularity. *The Nation* reminded readers of two key points: *Abie's Irish Rose* was not written and performed in a vacuum, but in the context of surging anti-Jewish and anti-Catholic bias; and that claims for causal links between popular entertainments and social change are more often made than proven.[33]

In contrast to the reception of *All God's Chillun Got Wings*, which critics overwhelmingly judged within a binary framework—as either stereotyped or stereotype-free—a number of critics described *Abie's Irish Rose* as mixing both "true" and "exaggerated" depictions. After describing the charm of the play being rooted in its "human touch," a reviewer noted: "All of the characters are drawn true to picture, except perhaps the Cohens, whose idiosyncrasies are exaggerated until they become caricature." A second claimed: "Father Whalen and Rabbi Jacob Samuels play well, as do Abie and his Irish Rose. But the rest of them are vile and stupid caricatures." It is significant that a number of reviewers wrote of "caricatured," rather than "stereotyped" depictions; since "caricatures" were then understood to "exaggerate traits that existed," some in the audience evidently believed that the racial depictions were based on kernels of truth. It is also of note that those critics of *All God's Chillun Got Wings* invested in truthful depictions did not engage in a character-by-character assessment of traits and their degree of naturalism. The reviewers instead concerned themselves with whether the play as a whole was tainted by stereotypes significant enough to impact race relations. The analysis of *Abie's Irish Rose* proceeded along more focused lines because there was more than one minority group for which stereotyping was a potential issue and because there was significant variation in the playwright's development of her main characters.[34]

The perceived mixing of stereotyped and nonstereotyped elements in *Abie's Irish Rose* was broader than assessments of individual character portrayals. A review in *Theatre Magazine* stated: "The comedy of the play runs the gamut from low comic-strip caricature to a satire on intolerance. There is also realism in the comedy, for if you do not believe that there are any such Jews as 'Mr. and Mrs. Isaac Cohen,' 'Rabbi Jacob Samuels,' and 'Solomon Levy,' then you do not know the Jews I know."[35] The reviewer sees the play existing on a representational continuum from "comic-strip caricature" to "realism," with "realism" connected to the naturalistic portrayal of Jews. It is noteworthy that the only Jewish role in the play not included under the critic's "realist" banner is Abie. He is the lone Jewish character who speaks in standard English, never references money (and, in fact, accepts poverty as a consequence of breaking with his father to marry Rose Mary), makes no ethnic or religious references, and shuns wearing a kippah. In the reviewer's estimation, the Jew who is scripted with the fewest signs of Jewishness is the only one not real.

A lengthy and laudatory review of the play in *Collier's* claimed: "Back of her stage Jew, with his trick dress suit and his funny way of talking, and her stage Irishman, with his pugnacity, his brogue, and his wit, [Nichols] has struck to the truth." While acknowledging that the Jews and Irish depicted are artificial "stage" versions and, as such, adhere to conventions, the reviewer nonetheless claims that the characters are backed up by "truth." A review in *McCall's* pushed this idea further: "The characters are as close to their originals in life and in the theatre—for these are both actual and theatrical portraits—as could be possible." In an odd designation, depictions of "actual" people from life and "theatrical" conventions from the stage are deemed "as close to their originals . . . as could be possible." The play, in other words, is "real" because of its mix of real and artificial people, with one set of characters being true to life and the other true to the stage. These various interpretations either naturalized stereotypes as real, by branding characters who slip them as stereotyped, or interpreted the stereotypes of the stage as expressing their own kind of naturalism.[36]

The assessments of Jewish critics and publications, much like those of non-Jews, ranged widely. Writing in one of the era's indisputably highbrow publications, *The Dial*, the Jewish writer and cultural critic Gilbert Seldes wrote of the play: "I was disappointed. Primarily because the humour of it is not at all racial humour, either for the Irish or for the Jewish. It is stage-Irish and stage-Jewish humour. And I was grieved to note that it was not, as I had been led to expect, a sympathetic treatment of both peoples. . . . There is no imaginative touch making any one a real person, Irish or Jew. . . . *Abie's Irish Rose* let me down terribly." A theatrical review commissioned for the *Jewish Exponent* derided the play for its "racial exaggeration and caricature," which it claimed "constitute the appealing elements" for its adoring public.[37] Writing in *The Jewish Advocate*, William Spiegelman contrasted the experience of avowedly antisemitic viewers who found the portrayal of Jews in *Abie's Irish Rose* too sympathetic for their liking, with those of Jewish audiences "grown weary for the past six years of seeing *Abie's Irish Rose* blossom among the bright lights of Broadway." Spiegelman concluded: "[The play] is as far from being complimentary to the Jew as it is far from truth." A number of Jewish critics referred to the characters in the play as "stage Jews" or "imitation Jews."[38] In a letter to the editor of *The American Hebrew* in 1922, a writer lamented the stereotyping in *Abie's Irish Rose*, which he took as typical of productions today. The writer stated: "The Jews—and also the Irish—as presented to a playhouse audience today are a lamentable lot. They have no relation to those members of dignity and discernment of a race that has a background and a tradition. And the public can't dissociate. They make pictures of the easiest picture called to mind."[39]

The Jewish audiences who saw stereotypes in *Abie's Irish Rose* reacted similarly to the Black viewers who saw stereotypes in *All God's Chillun Got Wings*, in that each group deemed the respective plays to offer an untruthful depiction of their race. A few Jewish viewers voiced objections to the play's depiction of miscegenation—it was even denounced in one Upper West Side rabbi's Friday sermon—but in contrast to Black critics of O'Neill's play, it was but a minor complaint on Nichols's plotline.[40] Jews critical of *Abie's Irish Rose* were sensitive to, in the words of one previously quoted writer, the failure of the play to portray Jews as "a race that has a background and a tradition." This was a point that Gilbert Seldes elaborated on in an essay published in *The Menorah Journal*, "Jewish Plays and Jew-Plays in New York." Surveying the New York theatrical landscape, Seldes noted the many productions that took as their subject the Jew and described a divide between those that reflected Jewish thought and culture and linked it meaningfully to "a background larger than itself" (Jewish plays), and those that, with an eye on commerce, "exploit[ed] the more trivial characteristics of the Jews in order to provide a Roman holiday on Broadway" (Jew-Plays). Seldes classified *Abie's Irish Rose* as the latter type. He explained that the Jewish plays for which he advocated highlighted an authentic aspect of Jewish life—beneath the superficial traits commonly associated with Jews—and explored how its expression was complicated within the US context. In discussing recent Jewish plays that he admired, he praised them for illustrating the interaction of Jewish religious beliefs and cultural practices with, for example, the "materialistic elements of American business life" or in relation to struggles of "second generation" Jewish immigrants. The Jewish critics who saw pernicious stereotypes in *Abie's Irish Rose* need not have held a philosophical position as developed as Seldes to have shared his concern for depictions shorn from history and contemporary context.[41]

While the play was routinely promoted in the mainstream press as a comedy that made good-natured fun of Irish and Jewish prejudices, a selection of critics—both Jewish and non-Jewish—held that audiences' enjoyment came primarily from laughing at the Jewish characters. *Time* magazine snidely observed: Nichols "wrote *Abie's Irish Rose,* which she thought would please the Jews because it made fun of the Irish, and please the Irish because it made fun of the Irish, and please the rest of the public because it made fun of the Jews." Writing in *The National Jewish Monthly*, Zelda Popkin deemed it "a shoddy little play—a mixture of slapstick, of stage characterization of the Jew, of sentiment, or tawdry propaganda and hokum," whose success is due to the fact that "the world likes to laugh at the Jew, and in the mispronunciations, the mannerisms and mental processes of his adaption to his American environment it has found cause for abundant mirth. For it is at the Jew they laugh in *Abie's Irish Rose*."[42] The structure of the play supports Popkin's assessment. Of the eight main roles, the only comic characters are Solomon Levy, Mr. and Mrs. Cohen, and Patrick Murphy, and for the first half of the play it is only the Jewish comedians who are onstage. Whereas Patrick Murphy generates laughter with his anti-Jewish quips, Solomon Levy elicits mirth with his Irish put-downs, heavy accent, tortured English grammar, garish suits, and his consistent reference to his desire for "dollars," "savings," and "discounts." Over the course of the play, Solomon's dialogue unselfconsciously exposes the avarice or parsimony of himself or other Jews on twelve occasions. In their more minor roles, the Cohens perform similar functions. An example of Solomon revealing his miserly nature for the bemusement of audiences occurs when Abie remarks on the comically oversized suit his father has donned for the impending (Jewish) wedding:

Abie: Father, I told you to have that suit made smaller.
Solomon: Vot? I paid fifty-nine dollars and ninety-eight cents for this suit. Und den you vont dot I should have some of it out? No, sir. I vant all I paid for.[43]

In such exchanges, Solomon's identity as Jewish was communicated to audiences through his accented and nonstandard English and his preternatural attention to money. Yet these cultural traits were only part of what Nichols imagined coded his otherness, as the playwright's description in the script of Solomon's "round Jewish face" makes clear.[44] Solomon's Jewish identity was a product of both culture and biology. We have evidence that audience members were predisposed to see links between the actors' physical features and their religious identities. In recounting the plot of the play to his readers, a reviewer for the *Boston Daily Globe* noted his incredulity that Abie's father would accept "Rosie Murpheski" as Jewish; using a now-dated term for an ophthalmologist, he wrote: "That Solomon falls for it is conclusive proof that he should consult an oculist." When Rose Mary is first introduced to Solomon, Abie frets that his father will notice her brogue and Irish expressions. The reviewer for the *Globe* makes no mention of these cultural signs, seemingly convinced that the conclusive evidence of her identity is found in her physical features, since a deficiency in Solomon's vision is the only proffered explanation for his failure to identify her as Gentile. The implication that it was impossible for anyone with good eyesight to read her physical features as Jewish indicates the degree to which the reviewer invested in the physical differences of Jews.[45]

A second mainstream press review complimented the playwright for having "universalized certain well-known mental and physical traits of both the Jew and the Irish." In praising Nichols for "universalizing" "mental" and "physical" characteristics of the two groups, the reviewer effectively cheered her creation of accurate stereotypes as he illustrated his belief in the physical differences distinguishing Jews from Irish. A third reviewer, writing for a Jewish periodical, noted approvingly how the rabbi "looks and acts" Jewish, based on his "fine physique and dignified bearing."[46] In both of these reviews, mental and physical characteristics provided key signs of Jewish identity. No reviewers of *All God's Chillun Got Wings* praised the playwright, director, or actors for Robeson's interpretation of a Black man or for Mary Blair's depiction of a white woman. That was unnecessary. Because the play was infamous—months before it opened—for the racial identities of the actors who played husband and wife, and since period Americans did not question the ability of actors to represent the races to which they belonged, there was no need to comment on Robeson's or Blair's depictions of their respective races. In *Abie's Irish Rose*, the context was different. Nichols hired lesser-known actors and rarely included their names in publicity materials. The draw was the play, not the players.

In addition, while many Americans in the 1920s saw Jews as a separate race, with their distinctive racial physiognomies, the visual signs of their Jewishness did not have the same legibility as Blackness. As with Black people who could pass as white, the racial dangers posed by Jews made the identification of physical differences all the more urgent. That is likely why the playwright scripted, and reviewers looked for and commented on, the physical signs of difference that the actors displayed. The comparative elusiveness of Jewish legibility made its "accurate" depiction noteworthy to viewers. While Nichols and her audiences could have focused on cultural traits alone, the addition of physiognomic evidence reinforced the racialization of Jews and, hence, added safely to their distance from white Protestants.

The historian Matthew Frye Jacobson has documented how the huge increase in US immigration beginning around the middle of the nineteenth century complicated the racial identities of American Jews and other European immigrant groups. As immigration from Ireland, Germany, Italy, and Russia surged from a low of thousands to a high of hundreds of thousands per year, the evident foreignness of the European immigrants, who constituted a growing percentage of the population in urban centers, raised fears among native-born whites as to the fitness of the immigrants for republican governance. A selection of Europeans who had been accepted as self-evidently white in the nineteenth century were now increasingly categorized as provisionally or inconclusively white. While the foundational Black-white binary remained, subcategories of racial whiteness emerged that accorded a number of immigrant groups a lower and less-stable assignment on the white racial ladder. Christian Americans had previously distinguished Jews by their religious differences alone, yet by the 1920s they routinely remarked interchangeably on their religious and racial distinctions. It would not be until the 1930s and 1940s that the arguments of American sociologists for Jews constituting an ethnic—rather than a racial—group gained widespread currency and references to the "Jewish race" declined.[47]

The influential racial theorist Madison Grant reminded readers of *The Passing of the Great Race* (1916) "that the specializations which characterize the higher races are of relatively recent development, are highly unstable and when mixed with generalized or primitive characters tend to disappear." He consequently went on warn: "The result of the mixture of two races, in the long run, gives us a race reverting to the more ancient, generalized and lower type. . . . The cross between any of the . . . European races and a Jew is a Jew." The professor of English Francis P. Gaines, who would go on to serve as president of Wake Forest College and, later, as president of Washington and Lee University, described *Abie's Irish Rose* in precisely these terms. In an essay devoted to the "tragedy" of miscegenation as depicted in US literature, Gaines listed a series of novels and plays illustrating disastrous outcomes for couples who mixed white and Black blood. He then added: "Not wholly dissimilar in pattern are the fictional fabrics . . . which commingle threads of Jew and Gentile temperament into effects usually somber but sometimes, as in *Abie's Irish Rose*, gaudy. There is, nevertheless, a peculiar potential woe in the definitely American complication of love between the white and the partly, faintly, Ethiopian, a love that must defy alike inarticulate hereditary convictions and vociferous public opinion." Gaines likened Jews to light-skinned Black people and asserted that the "sociological implication" of Jews' union with whites resulted in the same "tapestry of terror" as did the mixing of Black with white.[48]

With this context in mind, readers may be surprised to learn of the numerous Jewish reviewers who described *Abie's Irish Rose* offering an antidote to intolerance or positive depictions of Jews. *The Jewish Advocate* wrote of "the deep regard the Jewish people of the [Boston] metropolis have for this wonderful play of love and tolerance," before quoting approvingly from a review published in *Variety* that declared: "The art with which Miss Nichols threaded the story of *Abie's Irish Rose* marks her as one of the greatest, if not the greatest, of the world's playwrights."[49] In 1927, Samuel P. Sharron penned a lengthy essay for the *Jewish Exponent* that surveyed the depiction of Jews in contemporary US stage and moving picture productions. Sharron lauded the birth of a golden era "of plays that . . . had as its main object the purpose of glorifying the Jew" and noted that depictions of Jews today are "far different from that low, sordid, despicable character that has been his thus far in the play world." Claiming that the world is "coming to the conclusion that the Jew is a regular fellow—at least a human being," Sharron listed *Abie's Irish Rose* among several plays "that have taken up the cudgel in defense of the long-suffering Jew."[50] *The Jewish Advocate* breathlessly described *Abie's Iris Rose* as "a lesson most valuable in these days of intolerance and strife, which is sadly needed, and has done more for the benefit of mankind than any sermon ever preached." And *The American Israelite* assured its readers that in *Abie's Irish Rose* "there is not the slightest affront to even the most devout adherent in either of the faiths involved in the development of the story," which was a striking claim to make for a play that makes frequent reference to Jews' affinity for money and whose finale includes Orthodox Jews served ham on Christmas Eve. Additional supportive reviews were reproduced in *The American Hebrew*, *The American Israelite*, *The Jewish Advocate*, the *Jewish Exponent*, and *The Menorah Journal*. Jewish reviewers who approved of the play commended its positive portrayals of Jews, which were seen to counterbalance prevailing depictions, and lauded a storyline that advanced racial tolerance for and acceptance of Jews.[51]

Jews who saw no stereotypes in *Abie's Irish Rose* fell into one of two camps: they either praised the play without mentioning the issue of stereotyping or explicitly detailed how the play offered nonstereotyped or truthful depictions. Much as we saw in the reaction of those Black audiences of *All God's Chillun Got Wings* who perceived no stereotypes in O'Neill's play, it is likely that some of the Jews who failed to mention or see stereotypes in *Abie's Irish Rose* understood the play to be performing other useful, racial work. In 1923, a writer for the *Jewish Exponent* praised several contemporary plays for their handling of Jewish characters, among them *Abie's Irish Rose*, stating that they "have presented the Jew in a new light, perhaps not strictly authentic, but still it is encouraging to note the improvement." He went on to celebrate what he interpreted as the "comparatively refined" rendering of Jews in many twentieth-century plays. Implicit in his analysis is an understanding that Jewish stereotypes existed when a given depiction mirrored society's dominant picture of Jews; if the depiction complicated the picture—even if it was not perfectly faithful to the appearance and actions of living Jews—it was less likely to be deemed stereotypical.[52]

Jews not only appreciated improving depictions but also the opportunity to see Jewish actors take leading roles in a Broadway play. While Nichols did little to promote the individual actors she hired for the numerous traveling productions, Jewish publications showed a keen interest in the Jewish actors employed. Reviews of the play in the Jewish press often singled out Jewish performers, particularly those who were veterans of the Yiddish theater, such as Hyman Adler, Jacob Frank, Helen Grossman, and Alfred Wiseman.[53] As theater historians Paul Distler and Harley Erdman have each explored, depictions of Jews onstage declined precipitously in the second decade of the twentieth century. In the 1910s, effective letter-writing campaigns, public forums, and theater boycotts organized by the Anti-Stage Jew Ridicule Committee, Associated Rabbis of America, and Anti-Defamation League attacked depictions of Jews that relied on facial prosthetics, exaggerated accents, scruffy beards, and garish, shabby, and ill-fitting clothing and that illustrated them "as sly, conniving, and ethically reprehensible" characters. Since this was the dominant manner in which Jews were then represented, the success of the campaigns led to the virtual disappearance of Jewish characters from the stage by the 1920s.[54] For some Jewish audiences, *Abie's Irish Rose* offered the last gasp of the nineteenth-century stage-Jew, updated with respected Jewish actors and fewer of the sartorial, physiological, and psychological tropes that aroused Jewish ire in the previous decades.

The plethora of distinctive reactions to *Abie's Irish Rose* from Jewish audiences makes it challenging to speak in any meaningful way of the "Jewish" response to the play. Yet, if the reactions of Jews are examined in the aggregate, revealing patterns emerge. Jewish observers saw the depictions of the play's various Jewish characters residing on a continuum from least naturalistic (or most stereotyped) to most naturalistic (or least stereotyped). The Cohens' depictions were the most criticized, with viewers sensing that they served no role in driving the plot and existed exclusively for comic effect. They reminded viewers of older stage-Jews from the vaudeville era. Solomon Levy was also a comic figure whom they often linked to older stage traditions. His exaggerated Yiddish accent, oversized suit, malapropisms, and acquisitiveness were, however, leavened by his obvious love for his son and late wife and by his attachment to his grandchildren. Solomon was comic, but never venal or conniving. While the Cohens were interpreted by many Jews as one-dimensional, Solomon appeared to have more depth. Abie, the title character of the play, received strikingly little attention from Jewish viewers. This was likely because, apart from his name, viewers detected nothing recognizably Jewish about him. Many Jewish reviews proceeded as if Abie's character was incidental to the message of the play.

Jewish audiences paid the greatest attention to the character of the rabbi, Dr. Jacob Samuels. He spoke excellent English, was highly educated, served no comic function, and did not reference money, but he wore a kippah and, as is made evident through his exchanges with Father Whalen, was invested in both Judaism and religious tolerance. Samuels appealed to Jewish audiences who interpreted the character as Jewish and American. In a 1922 review, the art critic for *The Jewish Forum* provided evidence of the importance of Samuels's character to Jews. The critic began his review, stating: "I came to laugh. The title of the comedy alone was sufficient to put a smile on my face. The rising of the curtain fulfilled all my expectations. The Jew was to be ridiculed. His speech was to be distinctly 'foreign,' his grimaces funny." He went on to note: "Solomon Levy and Patrick Murphy—the Irish and the Jew; I really cannot laugh any more, for my sides are splitting." The reviewer acknowledges his acceptance—even, embrace—of the play's genre; he knows the kind of play he has selected and finds humor in the comedic characters. But, after recounting how funny he found the opening scene, the reviewer notes a shift in his perspective as the rabbi takes on a larger role, causing his sense of the play to shift. He writes: "As the comedy progressed, I sat up and 'took notice.' . . . The Rabbi speaks English 'English' and speaks it well; . . . he neither grimaces or lacks dignity. I note that the Father shakes the Rabbi's hand and that their theological discourse ends in a perfectly harmonious agreement. . . . Rabbi Samuels and Father Whalen spoke of equality, open-mindedness;

they condemned prejudice." Whipsawed between laughter and reflection, his reaction points to the complexities of American Jews seeing themselves represented in popular entertainments. The reviewer, in Seldes's terms, signed up for a "Jew-play," which he found amusing, but touched by the depiction of the rabbi, he came to experience a performance that—for him—contained elements of a "Jewish play."[55]

Writing in 1927, Stella Heilbrunn described contemporary depictions of the Jew in plays and novels for the Jewish periodical *The Reflex*. Heilbrunn criticized both those Jewish and non-Jewish writers who "romanticize" the Jew with scripts that "play the picturesque, introduce jargon for its color, and embroider with racial custom," rather than striving to depict what she termed the "truth" of Jewish identity. With reference to a series of contemporary plays and novels that adhered to this reductive formula, including *Abie's Irish Rose*, she submitted that they make "one appeal to Jews and another to the rest of their audiences and readers." This was certainly the case with *Abie's Irish Rose*. We have seen evidence that non-Jewish audiences may have patronized the play less for its message of religious tolerance than for affording them a venue for laughing at Jews. Those Jews who enjoyed the play certainly laughed, even as they focused on what they took as its more positive and respectful portrayal of Jews.[56]

As noncomic characters who spoke standard English and valued racial tolerance, both Abie Levy and Jacob Samuels were scripted as respectable figures, but only one of them read as Jewish. This was a critical distinction for US Jews at a time when they struggled to navigate what it meant to be a Jew in America. Historians have documented the unease that gripped American Jews with the passage of the 1924 Johnson-Reed Act, which virtually closed the US to Jewish immigration. The historian Jeffrey Gurock illustrated this unease through the editorials of *The American Hebrew*, which fretted in 1924 over what would become of American Jews without the benefit of a constant stream of European immigrants to renew American Jewry through exposure to Old World culture, religion, and language. With the passage of the Johnson-Reed Act, American Jews were isolated from European Jews, and the editors feared that assimilation would be the inevitable outcome. Gurock goes on to note that the disinterest of second-generation Jews in maintaining the practices of their parents led to a broad decline in Jewish religious life during the interwar years. Jews may not have wished to preserve the religious practices of Europe but that did not necessarily equate with a desire to shed their identity as Jews. What sustained American Jews as a coherent cultural group during the 1920s and 1930s was largely the prejudice of Christian society. Jews experienced residential segregation, due to racial housing covenants that excluded them, and attended many of the same institutions of higher education, because of restrictive quotas imposed on Jewish students at elite universities. In addition, social discrimination against Jews encouraged their creation of unrestricted clubs, hospitals, and professional societies, which had the collateral result of counteracting the decline in religious observance by binding them into secular Jewish communities. The result has been labeled Jewishness without Judaism.[57] For acculturated Jews who both feared the loss of their Jewishness and craved the acceptance of their Christian compatriots, the respectful depiction of Rabbi Samuels interacting with Father Whalen on equal terms was an affirming picture of a forward path.

For Gentile audiences, the play's call for racial tolerance was overtly linked to the assimilation of Jews. For them, the play's protagonist was Abie Levy, not Rabbi Samuels. *Abie's Irish Rose* is named for its most assimilated Jewish character and his Christian bride, culminates in a scene of familial reconciliation on Christmas Eve with the two grandfathers cooing over Abie and Rose Mary's newborn twins in front of a Christmas tree that Abie decorated (plate 6), and ends with Mrs. Cohen serving a ham cooked by Rose Mary to all of the play's main characters. Harmony arrives as Jews set aside religious values from the Old World and partake in the holiday rituals of contemporary American society. Writing of *Abie's Irish Rose* in *The Waterbury Democrat*, a reviewer described the play as "the yeast that is serving to raise the big white loaf of humanity."[58] Whether the newspaper writer described a "white" loaf to directly invoke racial whiteness or not, he clearly understood the play to unite the characters through a homogenizing process that made them less foreign. Writing in *The Smart Set*, George Jean Nathan dismissed the play's theme as "the superficial transmutation of Jews into Americans." In explaining the popularity of the play, an associate editor of *The New Republic* enumerated its appealing qualities: "The Jews are made fun of, their persons on stage are lovable caricatures, they wear skull-caps [and] eat ham." A theatrical review in *The Music News* directly linked Solomon's embrace of ham to racial reconciliation, writing that "the wild effort to reconcile an Irish Family with one of Jews . . . is happily accomplished at the end when Solomon Levy, the most stubborn and racially prejudiced of them all, is heard calling for 'a large slice of ham, with rye bread of [*sic*] plenty of mustard,' as the closing curtain falls."[59]

Published Jewish responses make clear that even some of those who enjoyed the production did not see the appeal of its ending. The previously cited reviewer for *The Jewish Forum*, who laughed at Solomon Levy and the Cohens and took note when Rabbi Samuels was on the stage, concluded his review by expressing upset at the play's "grand finale." He puzzled: "It is Christmas. . . . A big ham is served. I do not laugh anymore. Good ham is good for the Gentile, but is forbidden to the Jew, and why is Rabbi Samuels there? . . . The end is not what I expected. . . . Why, then, is a Jew good only when he eats ham?" For the Jewish reviewer who "came to laugh" and whose sides "split" at the humor, but was moved by the dignity of the rabbi and his respectful reception by the priest and by talk of ending "prejudice," a finale that showed the rabbi served ham was not a satisfying ending to the comedy.[60] In *The National Jewish Monthly*, Zelda Popkin wrote of her disappointment in the ending, noting: "It is the Jew who makes all the compromises—eats ham and celebrates Christmas." And a letter writer to *The American Hebrew* complained bitterly about the ending of *Abie's Irish Rose*, which he claimed prompted a flood of plays and moving pictures that "mention pork very suggestively."[61] In 1926, *The Jewish Advocate* reported on the "many requests from prominent rabbis throughout the country" urging Nichols to revise the last line of the play, given the ways in which it negatively "reflected upon the Jewish religion."[62] While the Christmas ham would have been an obvious affront to religious Jews, it is possible that it held even more symbolic weight for acculturating Jewish

Americans. For religious Jews, the laws of kashrut were one of many elements of their adherence to Judaism, whereas less-observant American Jews saw the eating of pork as a key symbolic barrier separating them from Gentiles.

A thoroughly acculturated Jewish professional explained that even as an adult, she found the sight of nonkosher food nauseating. Writing in 1925, she recalled that at "the sight of ham and bacon . . . some relic of the generations of strictly-observant Jews who preceded me whispers in a still, small voice: 'This far shalt thou go and no further.'" When a group of anarchists (who had rejected the Judaism of their parents) staged an 1889 parade through a Jewish neighborhood to draw attention to what they took as religion's role in preserving the state and the social order, they, as an observer described it, "marched through the streets on Yom Kippur with great audacity, making a terrible racket. . . . Each of them had a lit cigarette in his mouth and a piece of pork in his hand." For acculturated Jews committed to holding onto their identities and for Jewish anarchists equally committed to the overthrow of religion, the eating of pork was their religious Rubicon.[63]

Non-Jewish reviewers expressed no surprise at the ending, Rabbi Samuels's presence, or the dinner menu. The stock characters and plot made the ending unsurprising, if not inevitable. A review in *The New York Times* captured the sentiments of mainstream publications in asserting that "the comedy progresses according to convention, without dramatic surprises, . . . with every cliché of stage conceptions exposed," and noting that "the practiced playgoer can foresee every step in the story." The responses to the play's ending in *The Jewish Forum, The National Jewish Monthly,* and *The American Hebrew* provide evidence that not all Jews saw the consumption of pork as an inevitable conclusion to the play and reveal ways in which Jewish and Gentile audiences found pleasure (and offense) in different aspects of the comedy.[64]

The reactions of Jewish audiences to their portrayals in *Abie's Irish Rose* showed several commonalities with Black viewers' responses to their depictions in *All God's Chillun Got Wings.* Both minority groups had reviewers on each side of the debate as to whether or not the plays offered stereotyped depictions of their respective groups; and both groups assessed the degree to which the plays advanced or hindered race relations. Black and Jewish audiences each showed a keen interest in improved depictions (defined, variously, as either "positive" or "truthful"), convinced that such representations would lead to more equitable treatment of their group by the most empowered whites. But a closer look at the politics of the reviewers arrayed in each camp reveals telling differences as well. In the case of Jewish viewers, politically progressive critics dominated the ranks of those who judged the play as hopelessly stereotyped; in the case of Black audiences, it was overwhelmingly progressive intellectuals who saw the play as free from stereotypes. As these distinctive responses suggest, the detection of stereotypes is not necessarily either a progressive or a reactionary act. Seeing stereotypes has no political valence outside of the specific social and artistic contexts of the artwork being judged.

When Black historians, authors, and actors who spent their lives analyzing race and representation—people such as Du Bois, Brown, Robeson, and Locke—label *All God's Chillun Got Wings* free of stereotypes, scholars are apt to give them the benefit of the doubt and accept their conclusions. After all, their analyses were made from positions of considerable knowledge, study, and thought. When the Jews who see no stereotypes in *Abie's Irish Rose* are an eclectic assortment of theater critics, editorialists, and general news reporters working in the popular press (and the Jews who have thought deeply about race are largely on the other side of the debate), the conclusions reached are more open to question. The impulse to judge mistaken the assessments of those Jews who saw no stereotypes in *Abie's Irish Rose* is heightened by our modern vantage, from which we can hardly imagine a play more shot through with stereotypes. There exists a strong temptation to conclude that the positive assessments are evidence of the Jewish critics having internalized the dominant stereotypes of their era, for the stereotypes one holds are by definition naturalized and, hence, invisible.

The Jewish periodicals from which the chapter's positive assessments of *Abie's Irish Rose* are drawn were founded and largely managed by Jews whose families arrived in the US prior to the massive influx of Jewish immigration that began in the 1880s.[65] Numerous historians have documented that these earlier arrivals saw themselves as distinct from the newer waves of Yiddish-speaking immigrants—the type depicted in the play. The more established Jews were made anxious by the arrival of their coreligionists, whose great numbers and concentration in major cities made them conspicuous in America and whose presence catalyzed a dramatic uptick in antisemitism. As historian Eric Goldstein has described, the new Jewish arrivals "transformed a middle-class, acculturated, and politically conservative Jewish community into one largely working-class, Yiddish-speaking, and committed to a mix of ideologies including socialism, Zionism, and religious orthodoxy." To drive home the distance that more established Jews saw between themselves and the new arrivals, Goldstein quotes from *The Hebrew Standard*, a periodical of establishment Jewry, which judged the "thoroughly acclimated American Jew" to be "closer to the Christian sentiment around him than to the Judaism of these miserable darkened Hebrews."[66]

In a 1922 essay for *The American Hebrew*, Walter Lippmann, the epitome of the establishment Jew, offered his idiosyncratic take on the roots of US antisemitism. After dismissing Henry Ford's promotion of *The Protocols of the Elders of Zion* (1905), theological conflicts, jealousy over Jewish achievements, and economic competition as significant factors in fomenting antisemitism, Lippmann wrote: "The fundamental fact in the situation is that the Jews are fairly distinct in their physical appearance and in the spelling of their names from the run of the American people. They are, therefore, inevitably conspicuous." While maintaining that Jews were no more likely to exhibit undesirable traits or qualities than any other group, he argued that "ordinary anti-Semitism in America is simply the startled recognition of evils that are not so recognizable when they occur in people of less distinct characteristics." And he concluded: "The rich and vulgar and pretentious Jews of our big American cities are perhaps the greatest misfortune that has ever befallen the Jewish people. They are the real fountain of anti-Semitism."[67] Within a context in which establishment Jews saw the physical differences of Jews—whether "darkened" or merely "conspicuous"—and remarked on the visibility of "rich and vulgar and pretentious Jews," it appears plausible that some of the Jewish critics who saw no stereotypes in *Abie's Irish Rose* joined in laughter with their Christian compatriots in distancing themselves from the "dark" and "vulgar" immigrants of the play.

While it is doubtlessly true that some Black and some Jewish audiences in the 1920s had internalized the dominant stereotypes pertaining to their groups, I am discomfited by the ease with which later generations of critics assume that the plays' original audiences simply missed seeing stereotypes. Given that representations can be stereotyped only relative to other representations, and in a specific cultural context, period viewers are vastly better placed to make determinations as to what representations meant in their era than are audiences who look back to interpret works of literature and art from the past. It is my contention that for the majority of those Jews who consciously rejected negative stereotypes of their group, and also failed to detect them in *Abie's Irish Rose*, the play performed other valued cultural work that mitigated against the existence of the stereotypes, notwithstanding how obvious those stereotypes appear to twenty-first-century audiences. Considering the compelling record of nuanced ways in which Jewish audiences explained the play's positive impact, it is vital to take seriously nonstereotyped readings of the play.

My approach explicitly constricts one's latitude to label a work "stereotyped." While it is true that the classification of artworks into the categories of "stereotyped" or "nonstereotyped" has been a dominant feature of art, theatrical, and literary criticism since the publication of *Public Opinion*, I do not believe that much is lost by curtailing this classificatory exercise. It remains both possible and ethically desirable to distinguish how and why particular representations did and did not appear stereotyped to readers of distinct identity positions and political beliefs. Concluding that viewers of *Abie's Irish Rose* or *All God's Chillun Got Wings* failed to detect stereotypes that existed in the productions tells us nothing about how the plays held their audiences, nor of the ways in which the stereotyping of "others" functioned in the broader culture of the 1920s. The determination that readers of the plays missed seeing stereotypes may even cause harm if it diminishes efforts to conduct the more challenging work of analyzing how and why specific depictions of Black and Jewish characters evolved, were naturalized, and were contested in interwar America.

CHAPTER 4

STEREOTYPED AFTER THE FACT

Any vital artistic expression of the Negro theme and subject in art must break through the stereotypes to a new style, a distinctive fresh technique, and some sort of characteristic idiom.—ALAIN LOCKE, "The Legacy of the Ancestral Arts" (1925)

Some of the best attacks upon stereotyping have come from white authors, and from Southerners, just as some of the strongest upholding of the stereotypes has come from Negroes.—STERLING A. BROWN, "Negro Character as Seen by White Authors" (1933)

A decade after the death of the Black painter Archibald J. Motley Jr. (1891–1981), the Chicago Historical Society organized a large retrospective of the artist's work. The exhibition charted the career of an artist regarded as a unique chronicler of Black life. His reputation rested primarily on portraits and scenes of contemporary life created during the 1920s and 1930s, which captured Black leisure in the clubs, bars, streets, and parks of Chicago's South Side. Motley had enjoyed a distinguished career. He graduated from the School of the Art Institute of Chicago in 1918, during an era when few US schools of fine art admitted Black students into integrated class-rooms.[1] After graduation, he won two prestigious prizes in 1925 for paintings shown at the Art Institute of Chicago's annual exhibition. In 1928, he was awarded a gold medal for painting by the Harmon Foundation and shortly thereafter opened a one-artist exhibition at a prominent New York City gallery where twenty-two of his twenty-six exhibited paintings found buyers. The next year, a Guggenheim Fellowship supported a year of study and work in Paris. During the 1930s, Motley's paintings were exhibited at the Century of Progress International Exposition, Art Institute of Chicago, the Baltimore Museum of Art, the Brooklyn Museum, the Carnegie Institute, the Corcoran Gallery of Art, Howard University, the National Gallery of Art, the Toledo Museum of Art, and the Whitney Museum of American Art.

Reviewing Motley's posthumous retrospective at its DC venue in 1992, the longtime *Washington Post* art critic Paul Richard opined:

His champions don't discuss it, but a smug superiority—a dehumanizing distance between the painter and his subject—hollows out his art. He caricatured his people, though the catalogue denies it. "Motley," we are told by Howard University's Floyd Coleman, "was among the artists of the 1920s who consistently depicted African-Americans in a positive manner. . . . He extolled his African ancestry." Motley "hoped to break down stereotypes," adds Jontyle Theresa Robinson of Atlanta's Spelman College, who helped organize the show. The trouble with such claims is that they're often contradicted by the paintings on the walls. . . . His African Americans, especially the males, are exaggerated. . . . Their lips are over-thick, their teeth are over-white. Not always, but too often, they appear to be speaking in Amos 'n' Andy dialect. . . . At this juncture in our history, Motley's vivid mixing of racial imagery and caricature is not easily digested.

The lengthy review went on to lament that "the Africans in his paintings look like those in Tarzan films" and that one of his female figures resembles "Aunt Jemima."[2]

The *Post*'s review, and the twentieth-century art history it quotes, see stereotypes in Motley's paintings, though the respective interpretations of stereotypes' function could not be more distinct. Whereas the newspaper critic contends that Motley is simply trafficking in stereotypes, the art historians perceive a progressive project to dismantle them. The critic knows that the canvases do not depict Black subjects in "a positive manner" or "break down stereotypes" because such claims are "contradicted by the paintings on the walls." These disparate interpretations illustrate a dynamic that has haunted the reception of Motley's art from the late 1960s to the present. In the final third of the twentieth century there was growing consensus that some of his canvases contained obvious stereotypes, and a tussle over what that revealed.[3]

Efforts to understand the racial significance of Motley's artworks in their original contexts are complicated, however, by the paintings' markedly different reception during the 1920s and 1930s. In the interwar period, the vast majority of Black and white critics, reporters, academics, and activists were united in their admiration for Motley's artwork, believing that it offered positive, truthful depictions of Black life. Criticism of his paintings was limited. And, more tellingly, not one of the hundreds of popular and scholarly references to Motley and his art that I have reviewed from these decades saw stereotype (or caricature) in the artist's work. Quite the opposite. In 1928, the art critic for *The Brooklyn Daily Eagle*, Helen Appleton Read, deemed Motley's "portraits . . . notable for their technical excellence and honesty of statement—an honesty governed by the fact that he paints Negroes as fellowmen, not as exotic types." Read's assessment evidently struck a chord with mainstream editors, for it was subsequently quoted in both *The Chicago Daily News* and *The Arts Digest*. The latter publication added that Motley was a chronicler of "modern Negro life" with "crisp authority."[4] The art critic for *The Chicago Daily News* subtitled a review of his artwork "Archibald Motley, Jr., Pictures His Own People in Fearless Fashion" and claimed: "He spares nothing to make his people real." In *The New York Times,* the editor of the *Sunday Magazine* and the paper's art critic wrote that "Motley possessed a genius . . . for visioning and reporting upon the varied existence of black people plunged in the great American crucible of change." The art critic for the *New York Herald Tribune* declared of a Motley exhibition: "The pictures of modern Negro life show keen racial sympathy and understanding."[5]

Prominent Black academics, art critics, and activists were similarly laudatory. Writing in *The Crisis,* W. E. B. Du Bois listed Motley as a "credit" to his race in 1925, and James Weldon Johnson grouped Motley with a selection of Black New York City and Chicago artists in 1931 who were "enriching American culture [and] bringing a new vitality to art forms and giving them his own particular genius." Johnson deemed the "emergence of Negroes in the arts . . . the most significant chapter yet written in the history of the race."[6] Many of the laudatory Black reviews remarked on the artist's realist credentials. The *Negro History Bulletin* deemed Motley's portraits and scenes of Black life "realistic paintings dealing with life as Motley had observed and understood it." An essay in *The Chicago Defender* contrasted paintings of Black subjects by whites that illustrated "exaggerated types" with a Motley painting whose "painted representation is faithful in every detail." An editorial in *The Chicago Defender* described a new generation of Black artists, naming Motley among them, that depicted Black subjects for Black audiences, noting: "This return to their own racial inspirations has resulted in a sincerity and truthfulness which amount to art." In a third article on Motley in the *Defender,* the paper's art editor described that in the artist's paintings "we instinctively feel the truth of his presentation."[7] A review in the *Chicago Bee* gushed over Motley's "realistic compositions," declaring that each of his portraits displays a "very real person." Alain Locke wrote in "The American Negro as Artist" that Motley's artworks "aim at hard realism" and that Motley, along with a young generation of like-minded Black artists, "breaks through the vicious circle of self-pity or contemporary idealization and achieves objectivity." Echoing Locke, the sociologist Charles S. Johnson similarly expressed his admiration for Motley's "hard realism."[8]

The interpretations advanced by critics were in sync with the artist's expressed aims. Throughout much of his career, Motley articulated a desire to produce truthful images of Black life as a counterweight to the country's history of disparaging portrayals. Writing in 1932, he explained: "It is my earnest desire and ambition to express the American Negro honestly and sincerely, neither to add or detract." In 1947, Motley wrote a detailed statement on his painting philosophy for the Harmon Foundation in which he explained: "For years many artists have depicted the Negro as the ignorant southern 'darkey,' to be portrayed on canvas as something humorous. . . . In my paintings I have tried to paint the Negro as I have seen him and as I feel him, in my self without adding or detracting, just being frankly honest." In an unpublished autobiography begun in 1968, Motley asserted: "All my life I have sincerely tried to depict the soul the very heart of colored people by using them almost exclusively in my work." And toward the close of his life, he reported in a 1978 interview: "I've always wanted to paint my people just the way that they were" and agreed with the interviewer's assessment that he had made "a conscious effort . . . to help correct the image of the Negro in American art."[9]

Black activists of the interwar period had a lot invested in Motley's career. The fine arts were a high-prestige field in which only a handful of Black Americans had achieved critical and financial success. Edward M. Bannister (1828–1901), Robert S. Duncanson (1821–72), Edmonia Lewis (1844–1907), and Henry O. Tanner (1859–1937) were often-cited predecessors. In 1921, Du Bois celebrated Lewis and Tanner in an essay, "The Contribution of the Negro to American Life and Culture," for mastering European aesthetic styles, attaining financial success, and winning white recognition. For Du Bois, they were noteworthy artists for having overcome racial roadblocks and for offering clear evidence of Black talent and perseverance. In 1924, the poet, novelist, and editor Jessie Redmon Fauset interviewed Tanner during one of his return trips to the US from France and published a tribute to his "genius" in *The Crisis*. The brief essay devoted less attention to Tanner's art than to the artist's refined manners and the honors bestowed on him by the Third Republic. In keeping with Du Bois's understanding of

Tanner's importance, Fauset celebrated the artist for the recognition he garnered from European and European American patrons and institutions. The Black press demonstrated their attachment to such measures of success, as the majority of their reviews in the interwar period listed Motley's academic training, prizes, fellowships, and prominent white patrons.[10]

During the same decade that Lewis and Tanner were celebrated for attaining mainstream recognition, a rising generation of critics and activists demanded more from Black artists. Recall that, in his 1926 essay "The Negro Artist and the Racial Mountain," Langston Hughes advocated for the emergence of a "true Negro art" and saw as its major obstacle the desire on the part of many economically secure Black people "to pour racial individuality into the mold of American standardization, and to be as little Negro and as much American as possible." He wrote, as well, that he was "ashamed . . . for the colored artist who runs from the painting of Negro faces to the painting of sunsets after the manner of the academicians because he fears the strange un-whiteness of his own features." Hughes's call for "true Negro art" remained at the level of generalities; it entailed Black artists shaking off their inferiority complexes and embracing Black subjects, but it was nonetheless an attack on older notions of Black success that relied on playing by the rules of white America to win accolades and sales. As Hughes boldly declared, "We younger Negro artists who create now intend to express our individual dark-skinned selves without fear or shame. If white people are pleased we are glad. If they are not, it doesn't matter."[11]

A more detailed roadmap was offered in 1931 when Alain Locke published "The American Negro as Artist." In it, Locke labeled Bannister, Duncanson, and Lewis "artists [who] were incidentally Negroes." In contrast, Locke saw Motley's art as inseparable from his race. Locke described Lewis and Tanner as having mastered European and European American aesthetics, while Motley had joined with a critical mass of younger Black artists to forge a new "Negro art" that was uniquely racial. Locke had this to say about the emergence of such art: "Although the Negro artist has been having his occasional say for many generations, sometimes notably, Negro art in the group sense is a comparatively recent development. It dates only from the World War, and a decade later became an important branch of the so-called 'new Negro' movement for cultural and racial self-expression." For Locke, "Negro art" eschewed the imitation of European styles; it instead displayed African or African American aesthetics, typically drew on working-class Black subject matter, and neither perpetuated the negative Black stereotypes that had historically infected American art nor replaced them with equally false idealizations of Black life and identity. Boasting of "a new vitality and maturity among American Negro artists [and] a pronounced trend toward racialism in both style and subject," Locke predicted "the advent of a representatively racial school of expression, and an important new contribution, therefore, to the whole body of American art." He saw Motley as one of the new generation of artists actively building that desired "racial school of art."[12]

Readers may question the degree to which Black critics granted Motley latitude in his depictions of Black subjects because of his race. While the playwrights O'Neill and Nichols depicted groups to which they did not belong, Motley focused almost exclusively on representing members of his race. In addition, Motley was a rare Black artist who had both demonstrated critical and financial success in white America and become internationally known for creating racialized art that chronicled early twentieth-century Black life. He had something to offer Du Bois and Fauset, on the one hand, and Hughes and Locke, on the other. But recall that Black commentators from a range of political vantages read Motley's paintings as "real" and "truthful," and keep in mind that the Black intellectuals of the period were riven by ideological fissures, and that many did not hesitate to attack prominent Black artists and thinkers whenever they perceived their artworks or arguments as harmful.

The Black artist and art historian James A. Porter responded to Locke's *Negro Art: Past and Present* in 1937 with a detailed refutation of its thesis, ultimately branding it a "segregationist" text that he deemed "one of the greatest dangers to the Negro artist to arise in recent years."[13] In *The Negro in American Fiction* (1937), Sterling A. Brown analyzed Paul Lawrence Dunbar's *In Old Plantation Days* (1903) and complained

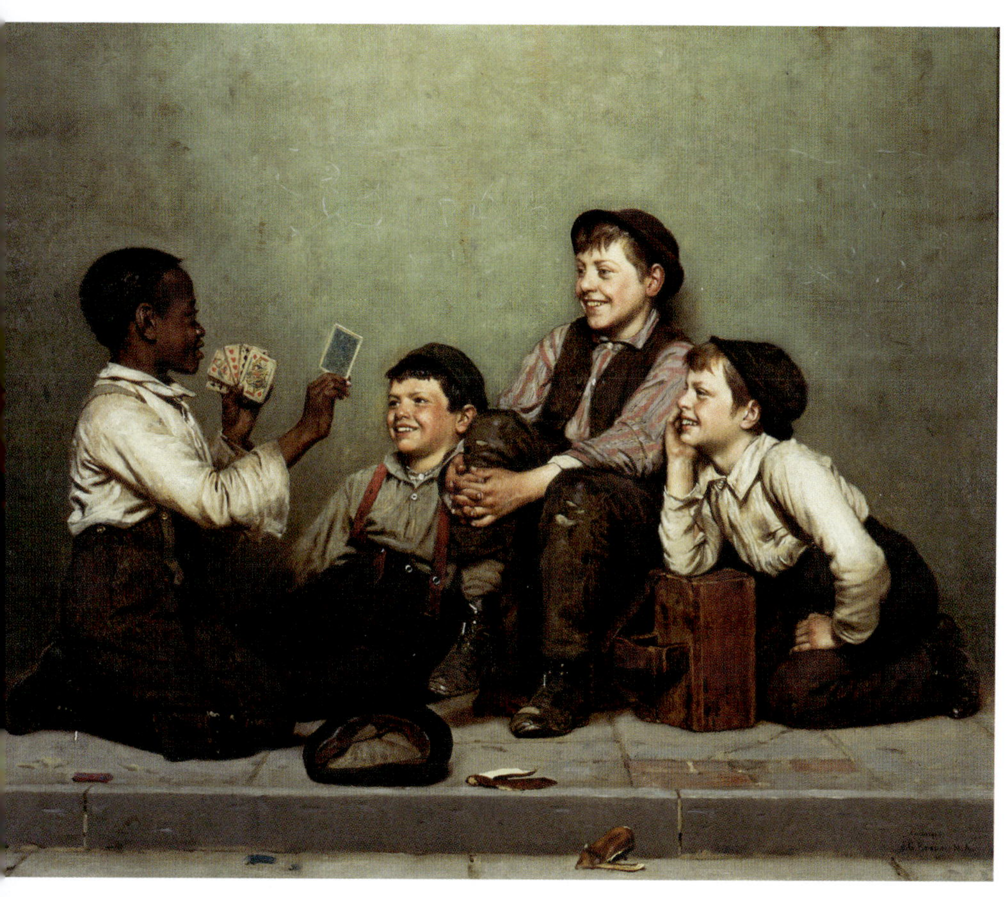

PLATE 1. John George Brown, *A Card Trick*, ca. 1891–92, oil on canvas, 40¼ × 45½ in. Joslyn Art Museum, Omaha, Nebraska. Gift of the Estate of Mrs. Sarah Joslyn, 1944.14.

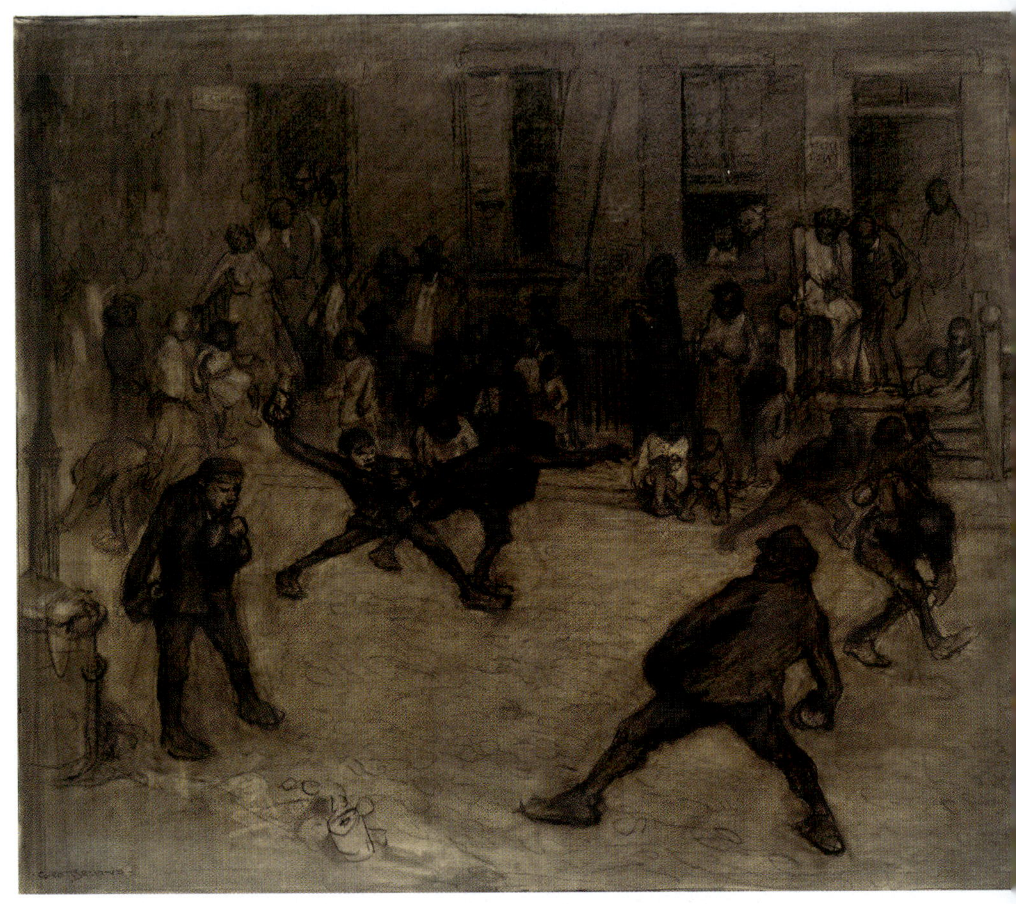

PLATE 2. George Bellows, *Tin Can Battle, San Juan Hill, New York*, 1907, crayon, ink, and charcoal on paper, 20 × 23¾ in. Sheldon Museum of Art, University of Nebraska—Lincoln. Anna R. and Frank M. Hall Charitable Trust.

PLATE 3. Thomas Cheesman, after John Trumbull, *General Washington*, 1796, color-printed stipple engraving and etching with hand coloring in watercolor on paper, 25 × 17¾ in. Yale Center for British Art, Paul Mellon Fund.

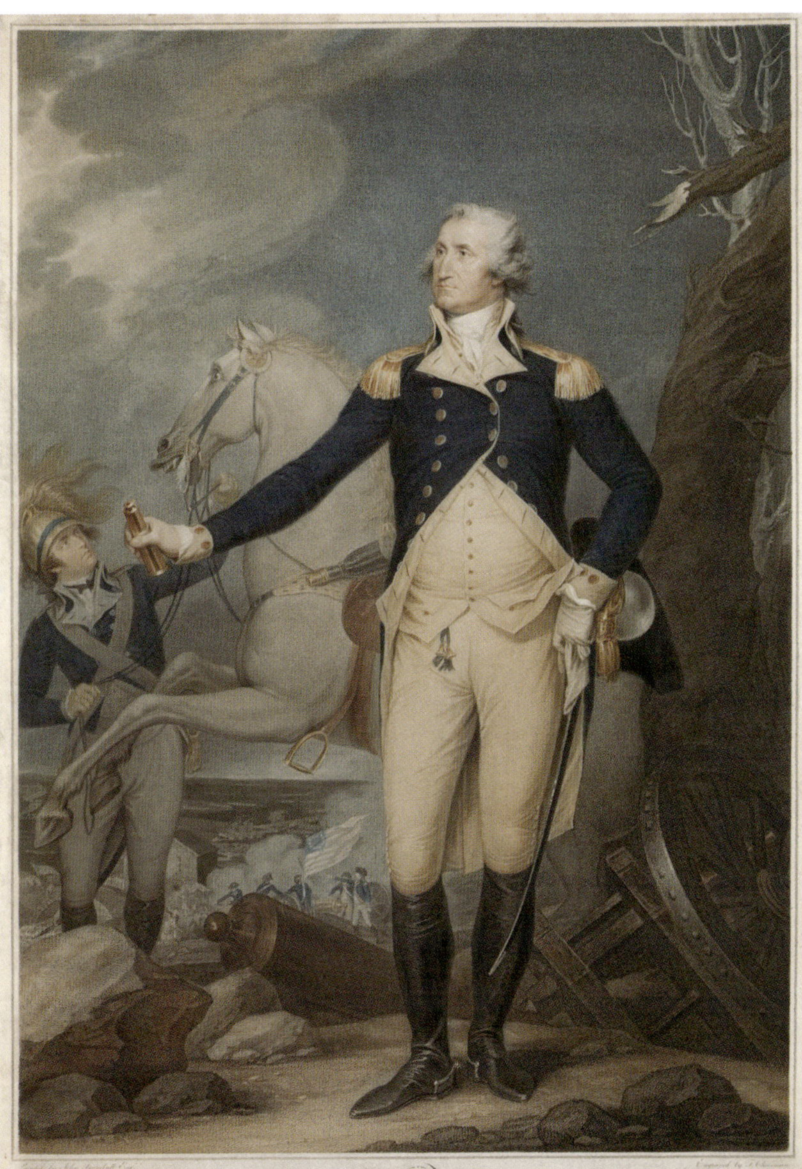

General Washington.

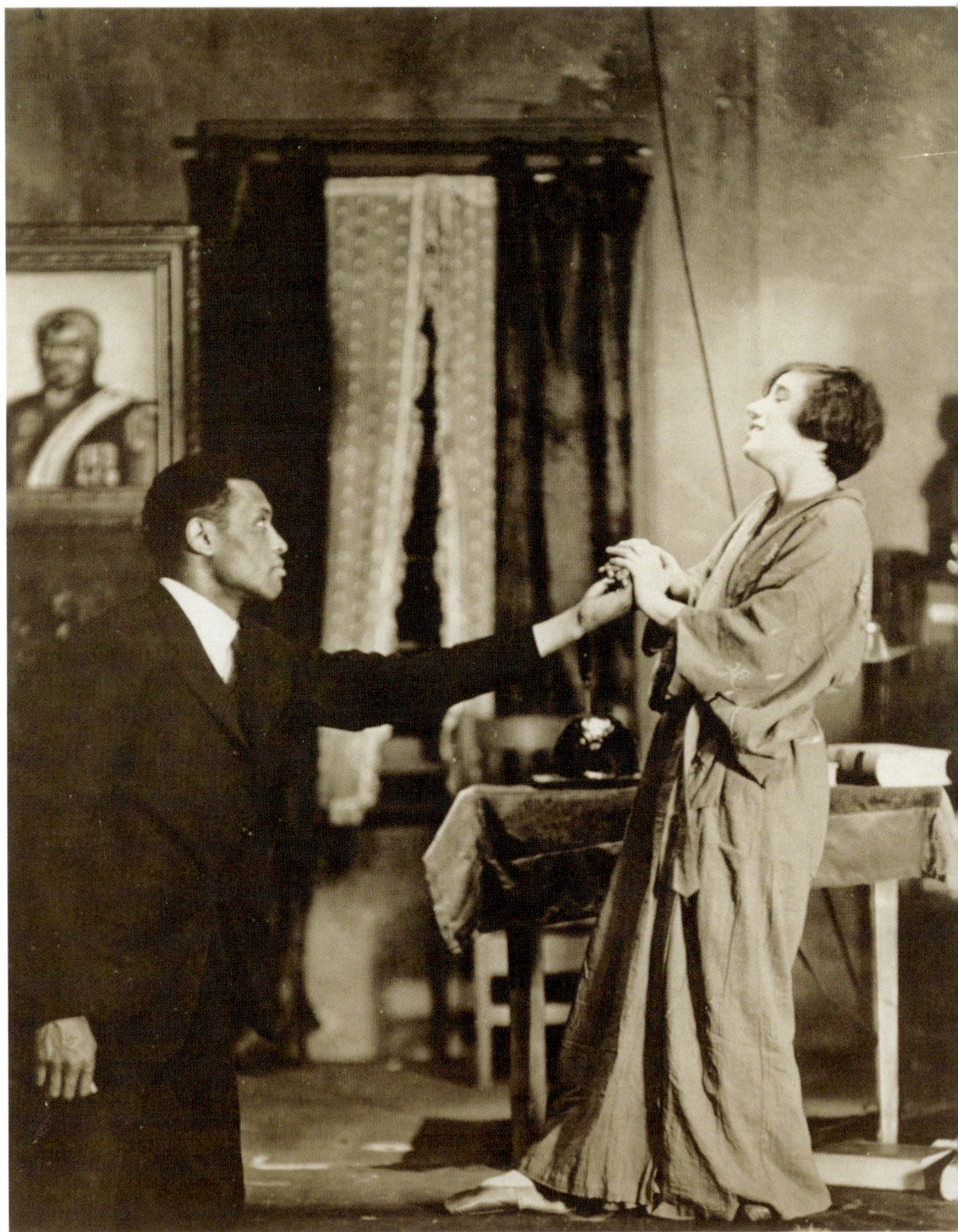

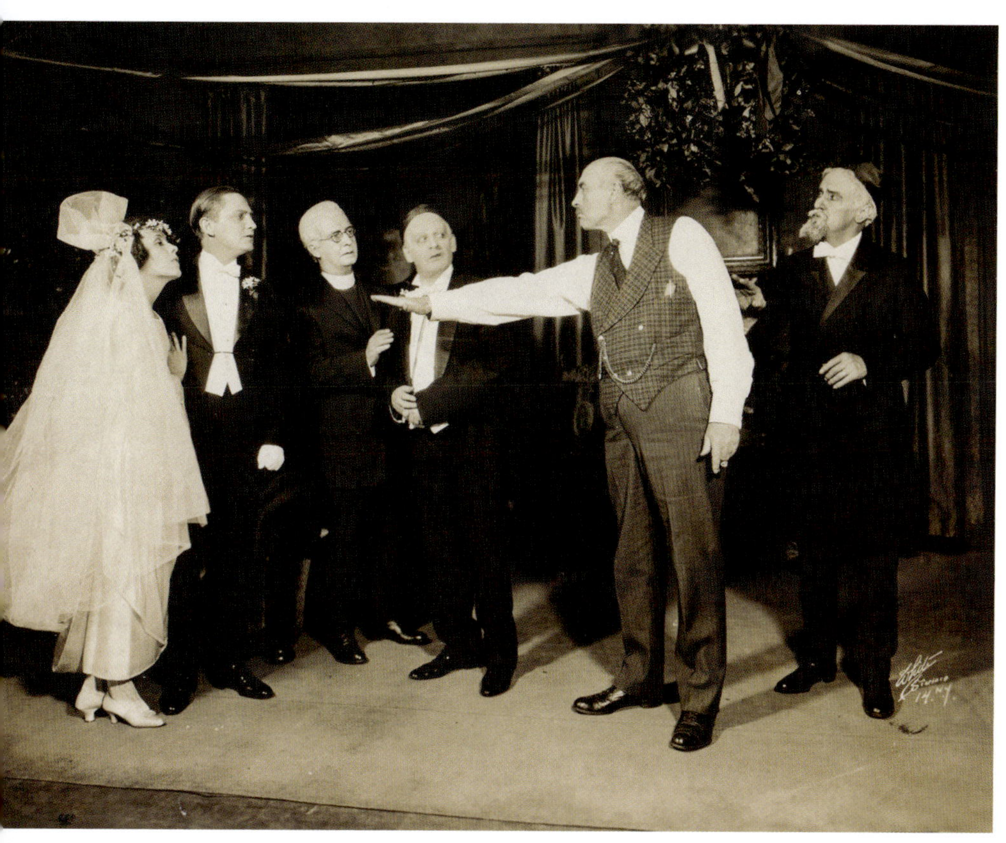

PLATE 5. White Studio, publicity still for *Abie's Irish Rose*, showing (*from left to right*) Marie Carroll, Robert Williams, Harry Bradley, Alfred White, John Cope, and Howard Lang playing the characters Rose Mary Murphy, Abie Levy, Father Whalen, Patrick Murphy, Solomon Levy, and Rabbi Jacob Samuels at the Fulton Theatre, New York City, 1922. Billy Rose Theatre Collection, The New York Public Library for the Performing Arts, © NYPL.

TE 4. Unidentified photographer, publicity still for
God's Chillun Got Wings, showing (*left to right*) Paul
eson and Mary Blair playing the characters Jim Harris
Ella Downey at the Provincetown Playhouse, New
k City, 1924. Billy Rose Theatre Collection, The New
k Public Library for the Performing Arts, © NYPL.

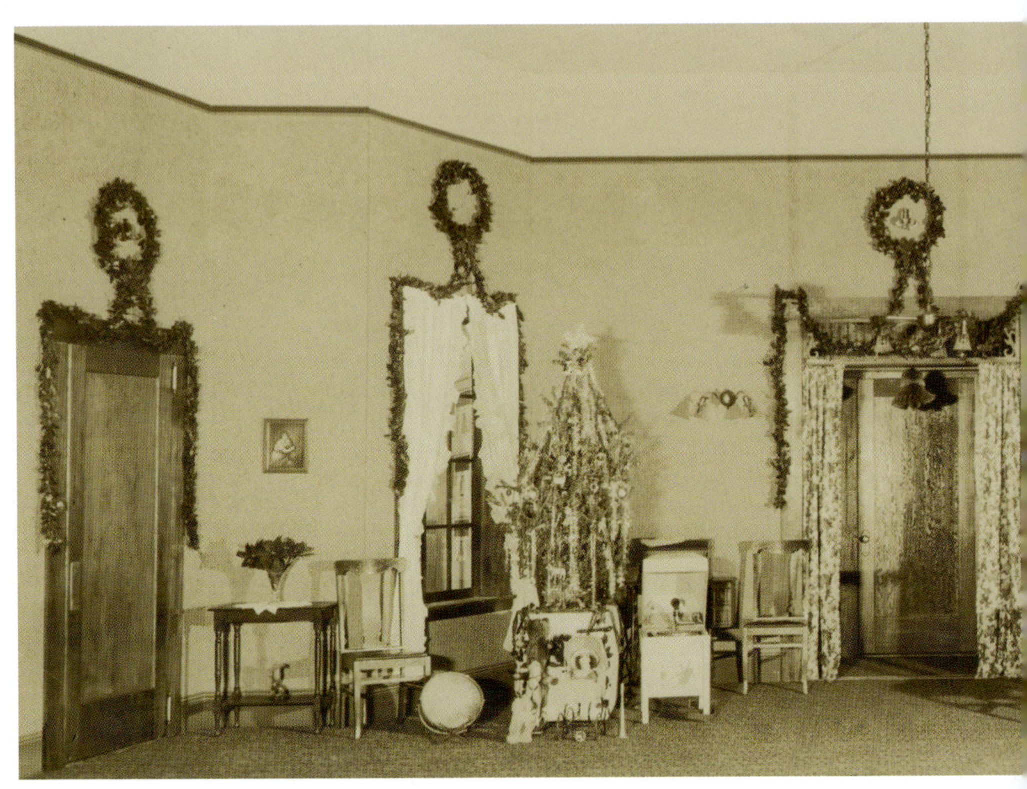

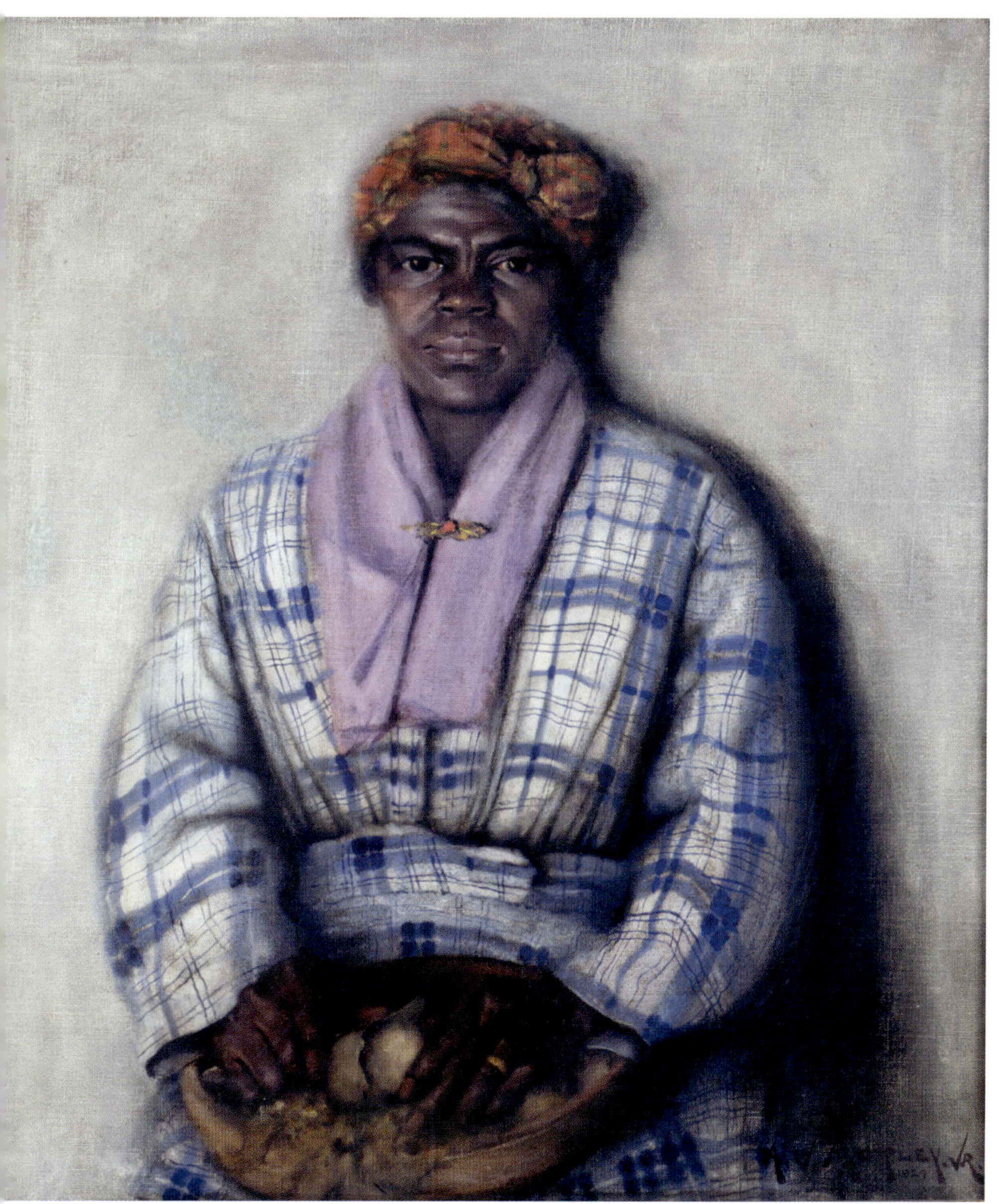

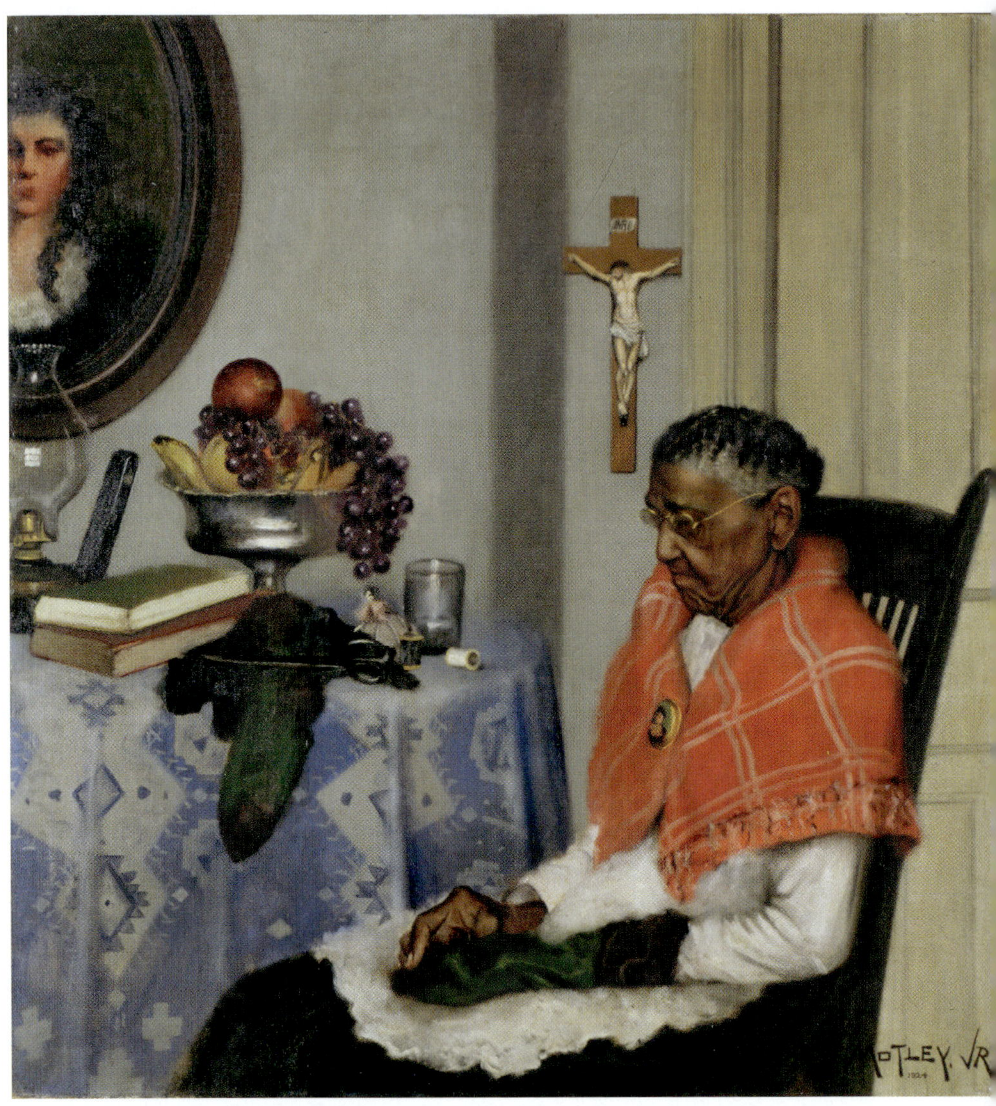

PLATE 8. Archibald J. Motley Jr., *Mending Socks*, 1924, oil on canvas, 43⅞ × 40 in. Ackland Art Museum, University of North Carolina at Chapel Hill, Burton Emmett Collection. © Estate of Archibald John Motley Jr. All reserved rights 2025.

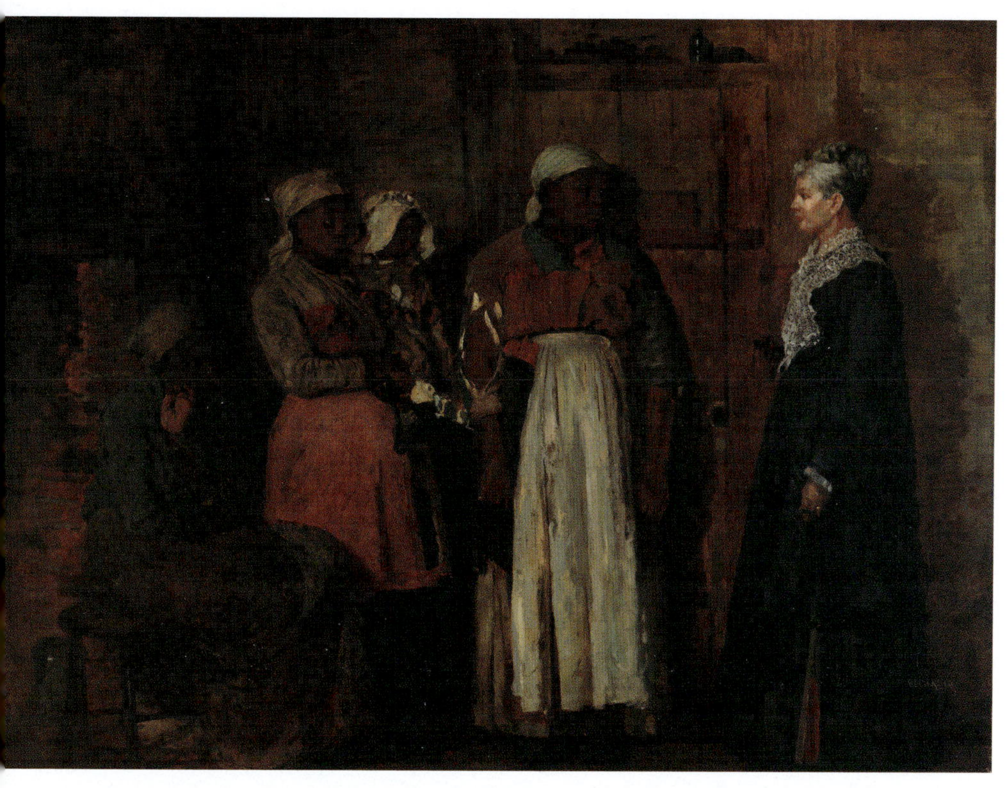

PLATE 9. Winslow Homer, *A Visit from the Old Mistress,* 1876, oil on canvas, 18 × 24 in. Smithsonian American Art Museum. Gift of William T. Evans. Courtesy of the Smithsonian American Art Museum.

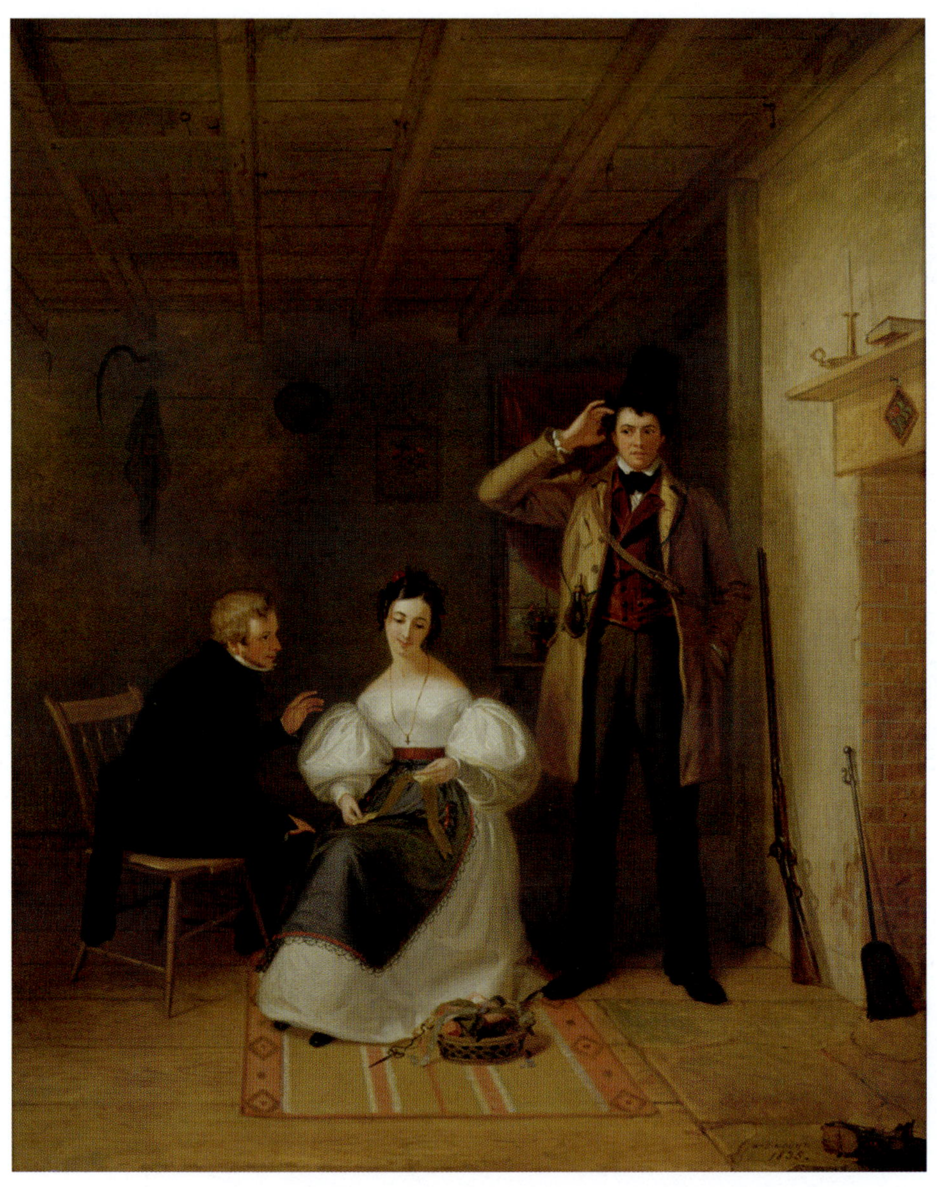

PLATE 10. William Sidney Mount, *The Sportsman's Last Visit*, 1835, oil on canvas, 21¼ × 17¼ in. Long Island Museum. Gift of Mr. and Mrs. Ward Melville, 1958.

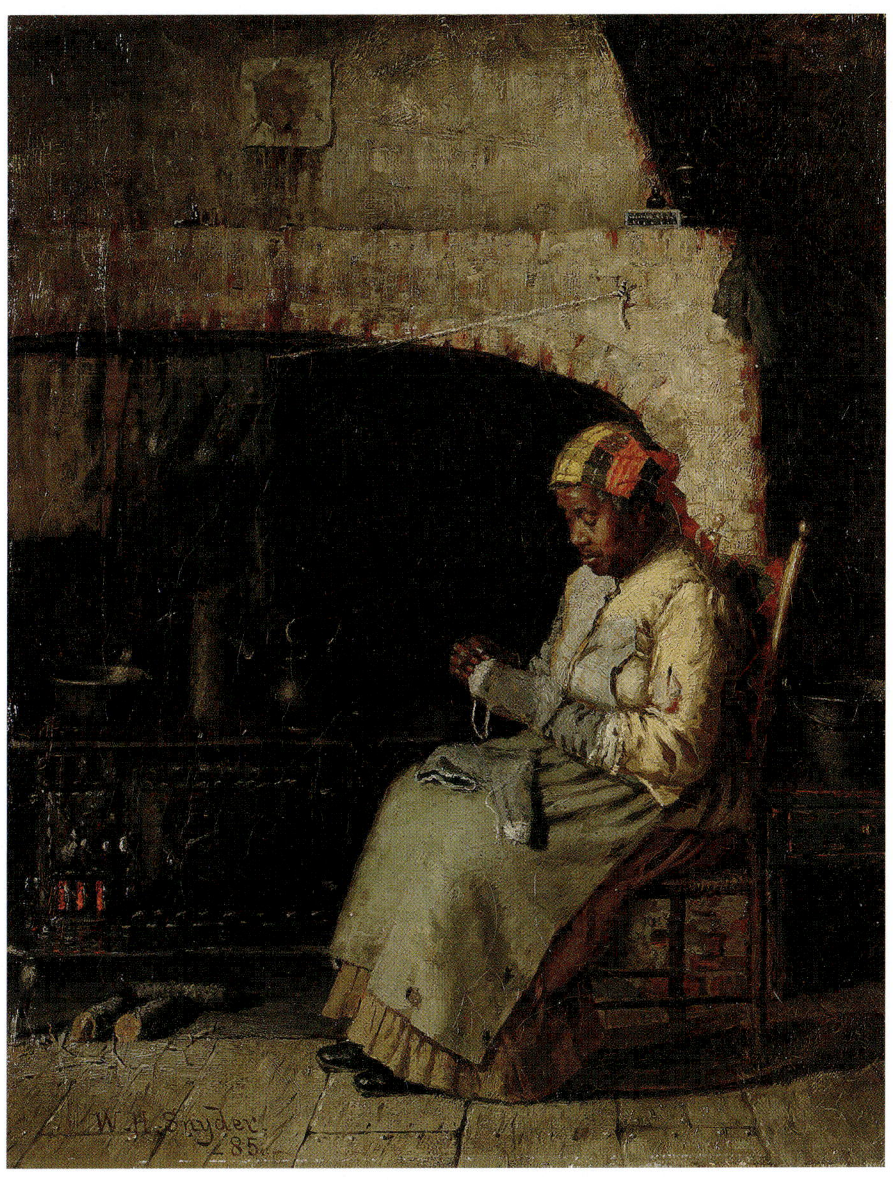

PLATE 11. William Henry Snyder, *Darning by the Hearth*, 1885, oil on canvas, 18 × 14 in. Private collection. Photo: Christie's Images/Bridgeman Images.

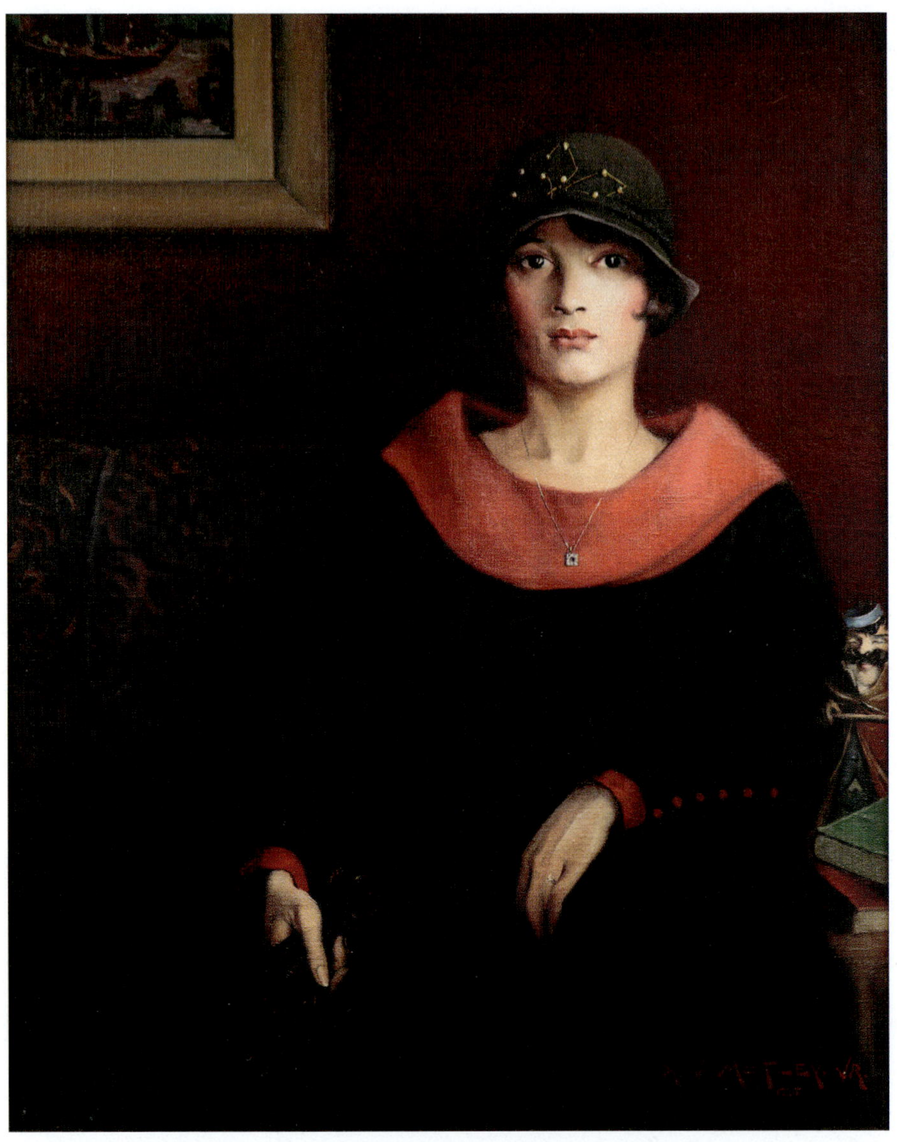

PLATE 12. Archibald J. Motley Jr., *The Octoroon Girl*, 1925, oil on canvas, 38 × 30¼ in. Courtesy of Michael Rosenfeld Gallery, LLC, New York, New York. © Chicago History Museum/© Estate of Archibald John Motley Jr. All reserved rights 2025/Bridgeman Images.

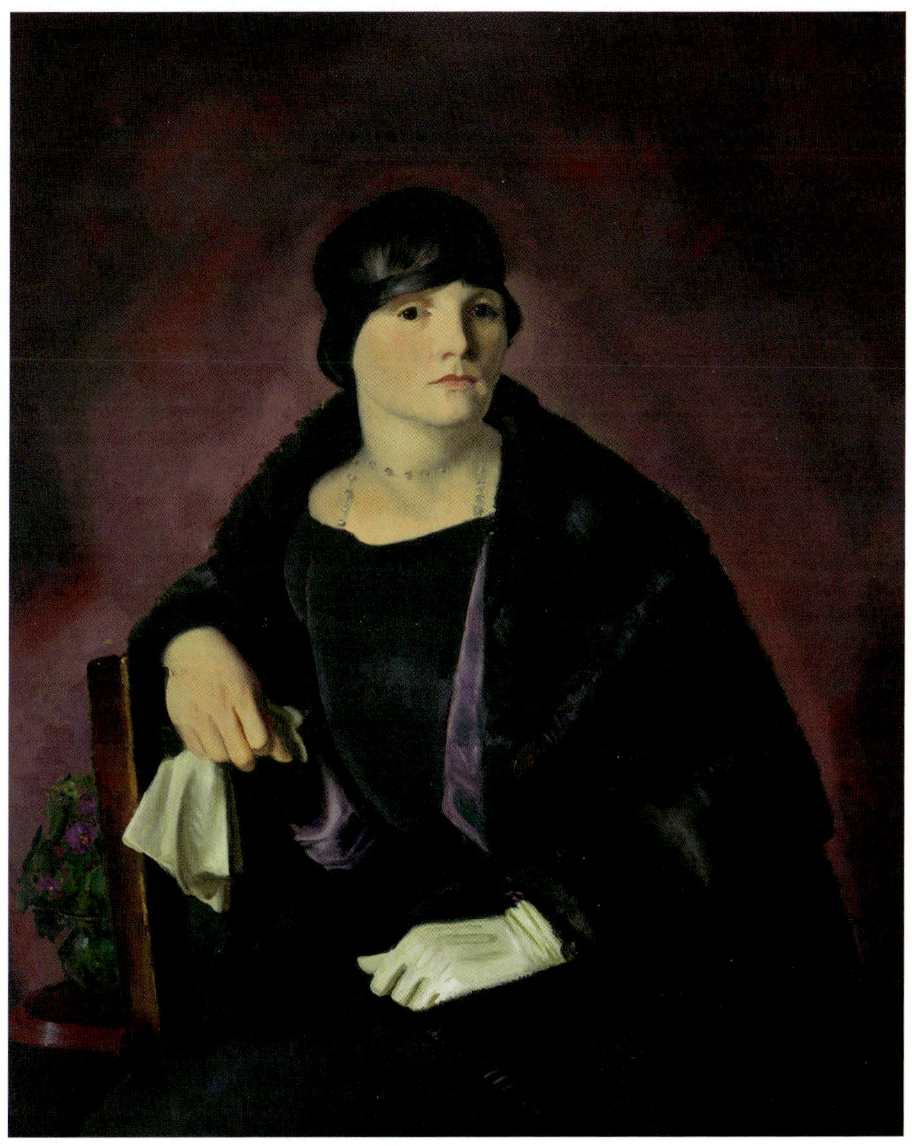

PLATE 13. George Bellows, *Mrs. Walter H. Richter*, 1922, oil on canvas, 40 × 32 in. Private collection. Photo: Christie's Images/Bridgeman Images.

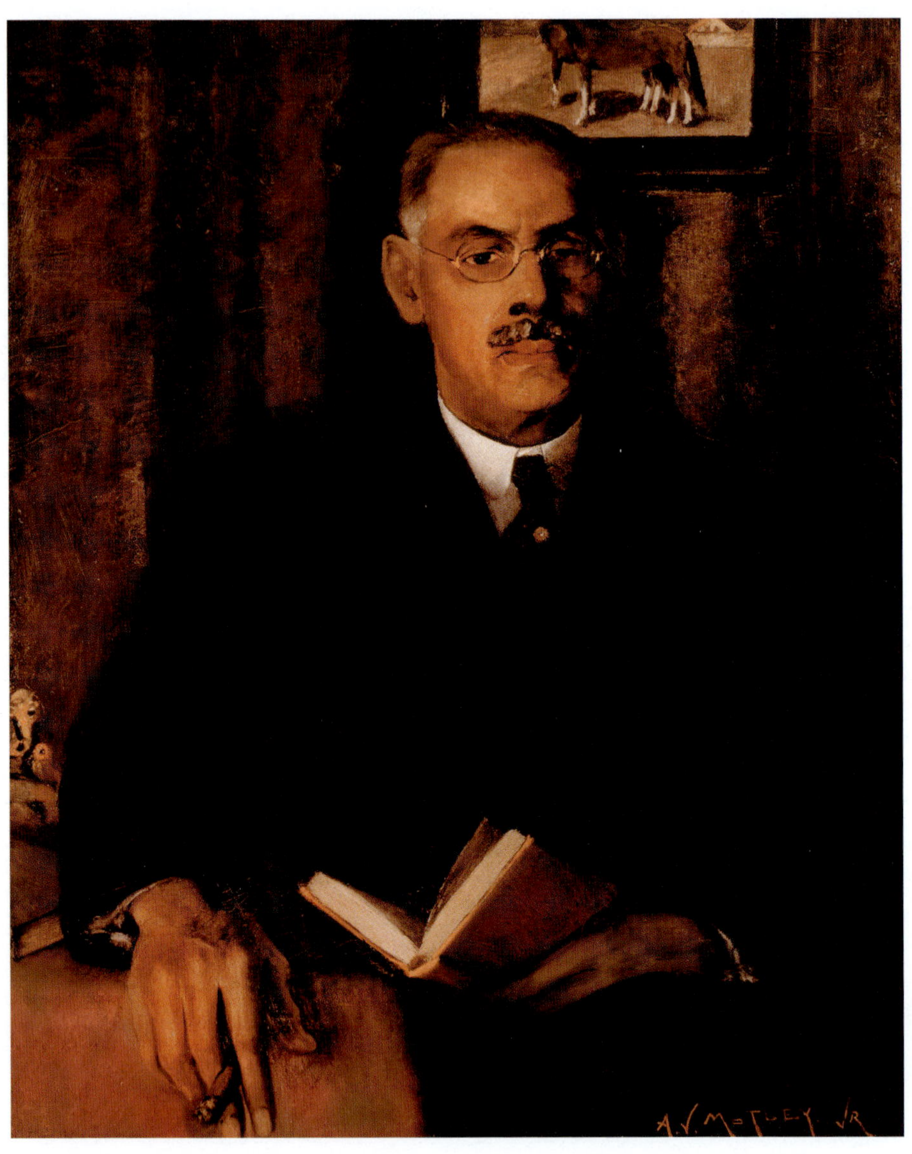

PLATE 14. Archibald J. Motley Jr., *Portrait of the Artist's Father*, ca. 1921, oil on canvas, 36 × 29 in. Private collection. © Chicago History Museum/© Estate of Archibald John Motley Jr. All reserved rights 2025/Bridgeman Images.

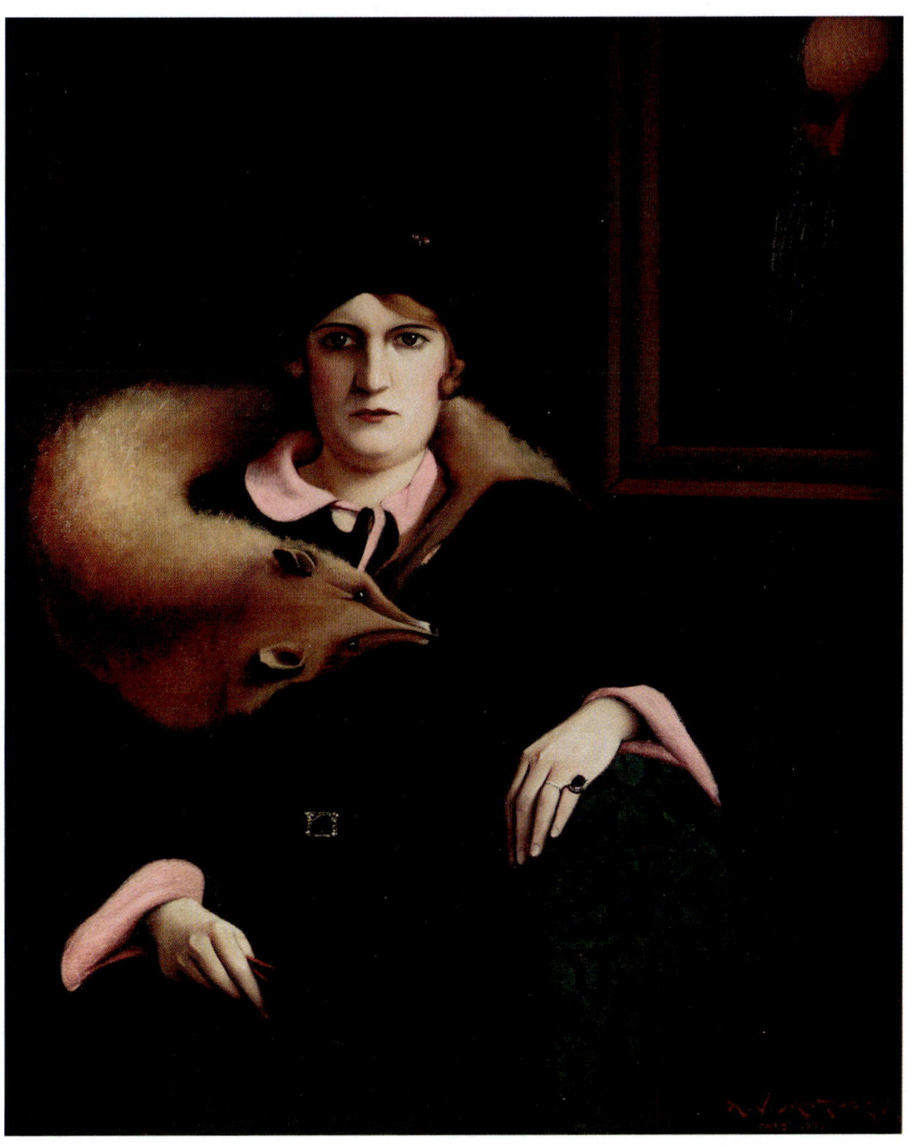

PLATE 15. Archibald J. Motley Jr., *Portrait of Mrs. A. J. Motley, Jr.*, 1930, oil on canvas, 39⅝ × 32 in. Private collection. © Chicago History Museum/© Estate of Archibald John Motley Jr. All reserved rights 2025/Bridgeman Images.

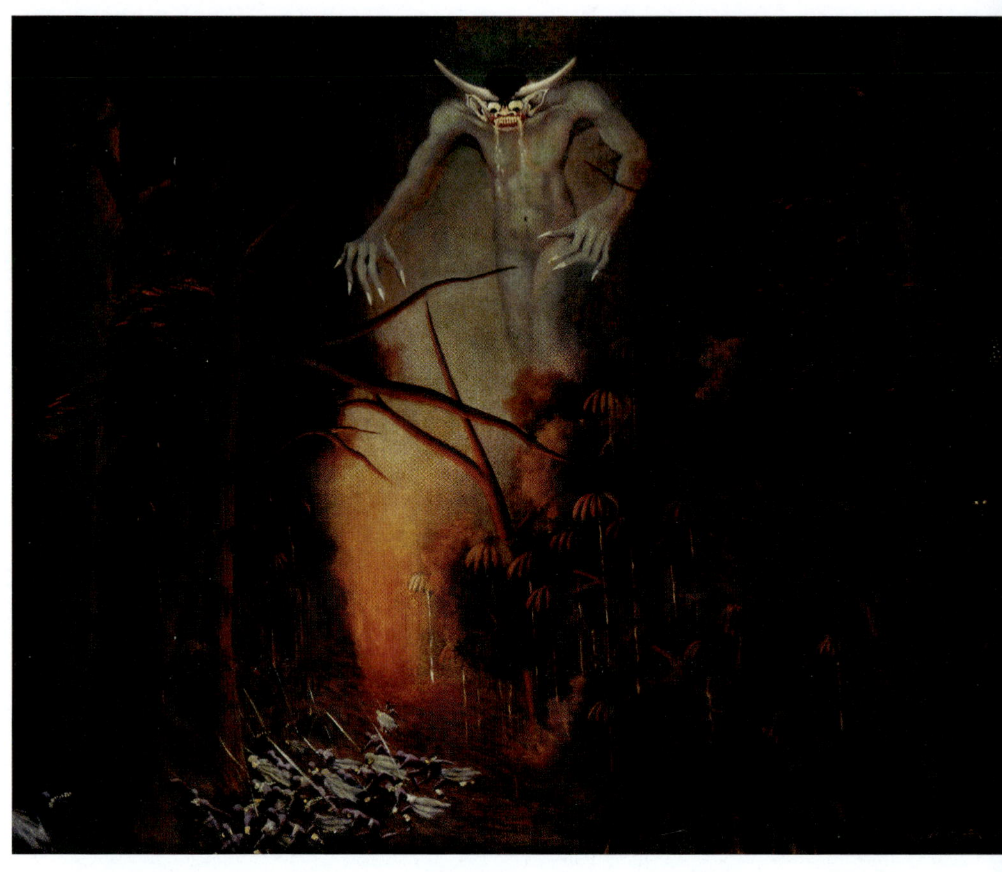

PLATE 16. Archibald J. Motley Jr., *Kikuyu God of Fire,* 1927, oil on canvas, 36 × 41⅛ in. Private collection. © Chicago History Museum/© Estate of Archibald John Motley Jr. All reserved rights 2025/Bridgeman Images.

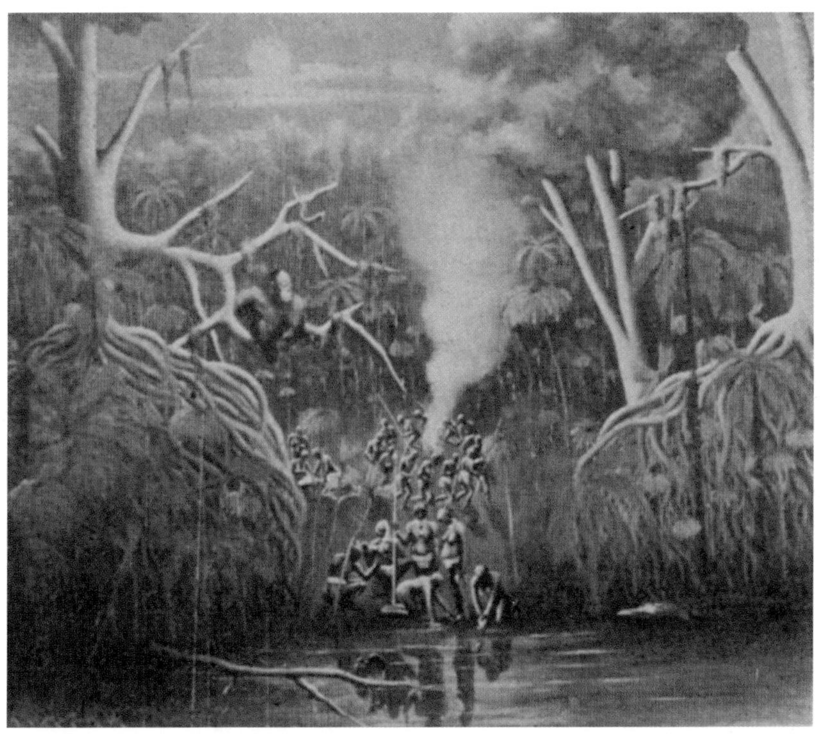

PLATE 17. Archibald J. Motley Jr., *Waganda Charm-Makers*, 1927, oil on canvas, 39½ × 45 in. Location unknown. Image from *Opportunity: A Journal of Negro Life*, April 4, 1928. Hanna Holborn Gray Special Collections Research Center, The University of Chicago Library. © Estate of Archibald John Motley Jr. All reserved rights 2025.

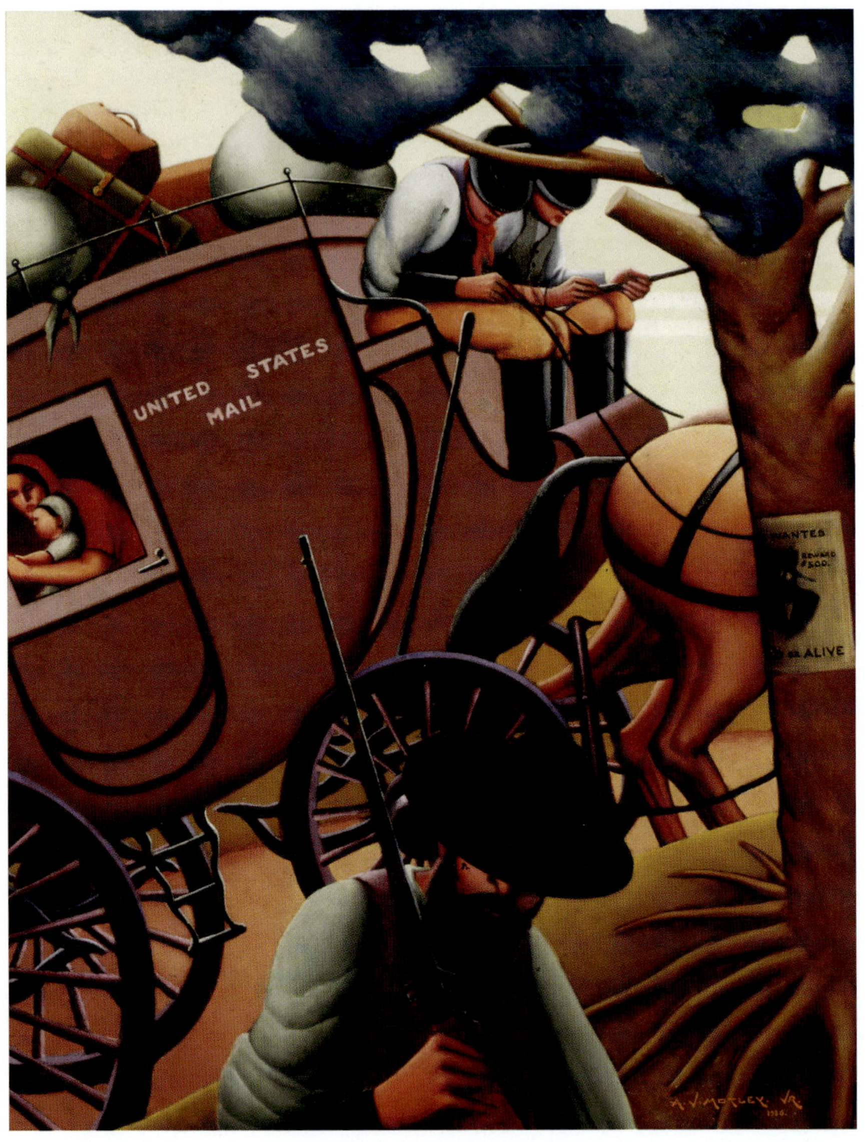

PLATE 18. Archibald J. Motley Jr., *United States Mail*, 1936, oil on canvas, 40 × 36 in. United States Postal Service, Wood River, Illinois. © Estate of Archibald John Motley Jr. All reserved rights 2025/Bridgeman Images.

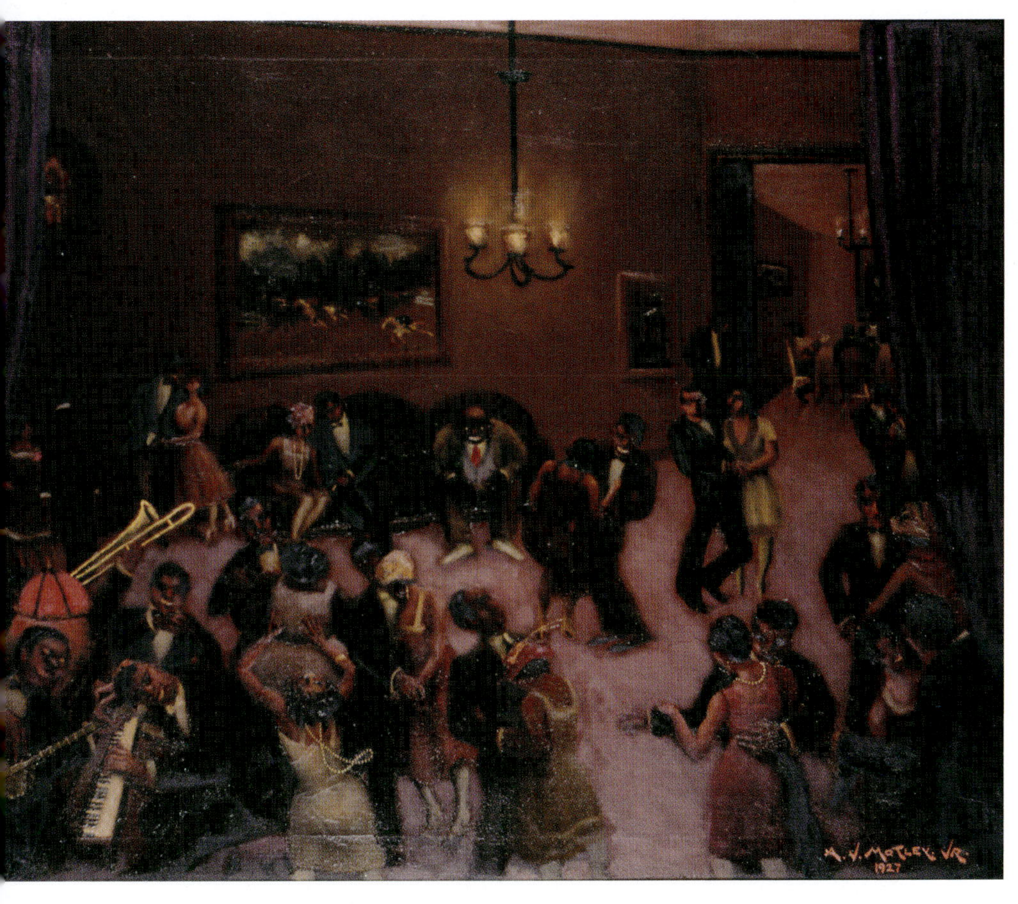

PLATE 19. Archibald J. Motley Jr., *Stomp*, 1927, oil on canvas, 30 × 36 in. Collection of Camille O. and William H. Cosby Jr. © Chicago History Museum/ © Estate of Archibald John Motley Jr. All reserved rights 2025/Bridgeman Images.

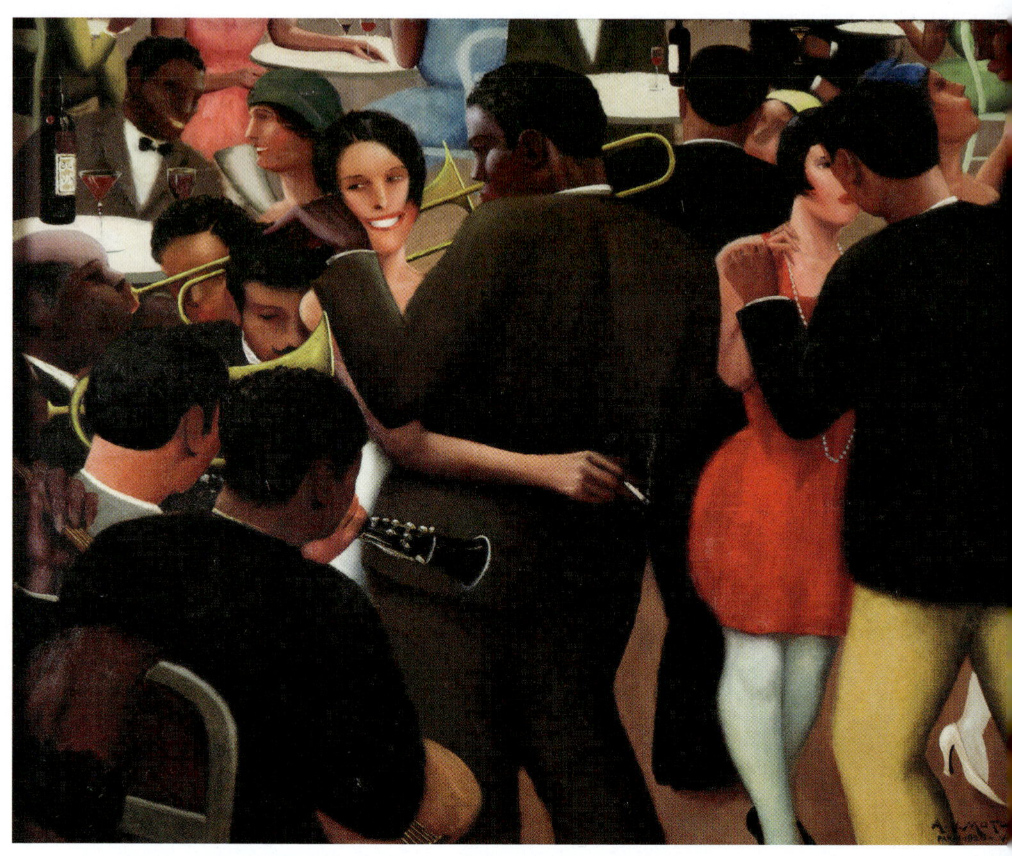

PLATE 20. Archibald J. Motley Jr., *Blues*, 1929, oil on canvas, 36 × 42 in. © Chicago History Museum/© Estate of Archibald John Motley Jr. All reserved rights 2025/Bridgeman Images.

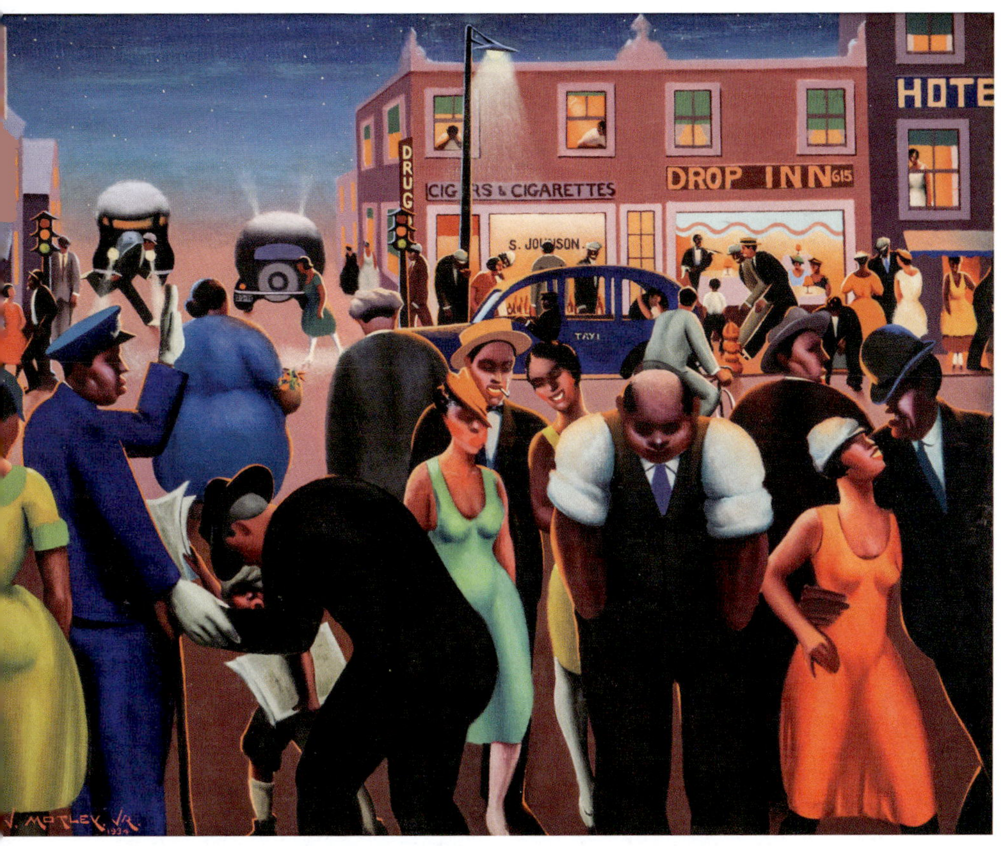

PLATE 21. Archibald J. Motley Jr., *Black Belt*, 1934, oil on canvas, 33 × 40½ in. Gift of the Harmon Foundation. Collection of the Hampton University Museum, Hampton, VA. © Chicago History Museum/© Estate of Archibald John Motley Jr. All reserved rights 2025/Bridgeman Images.

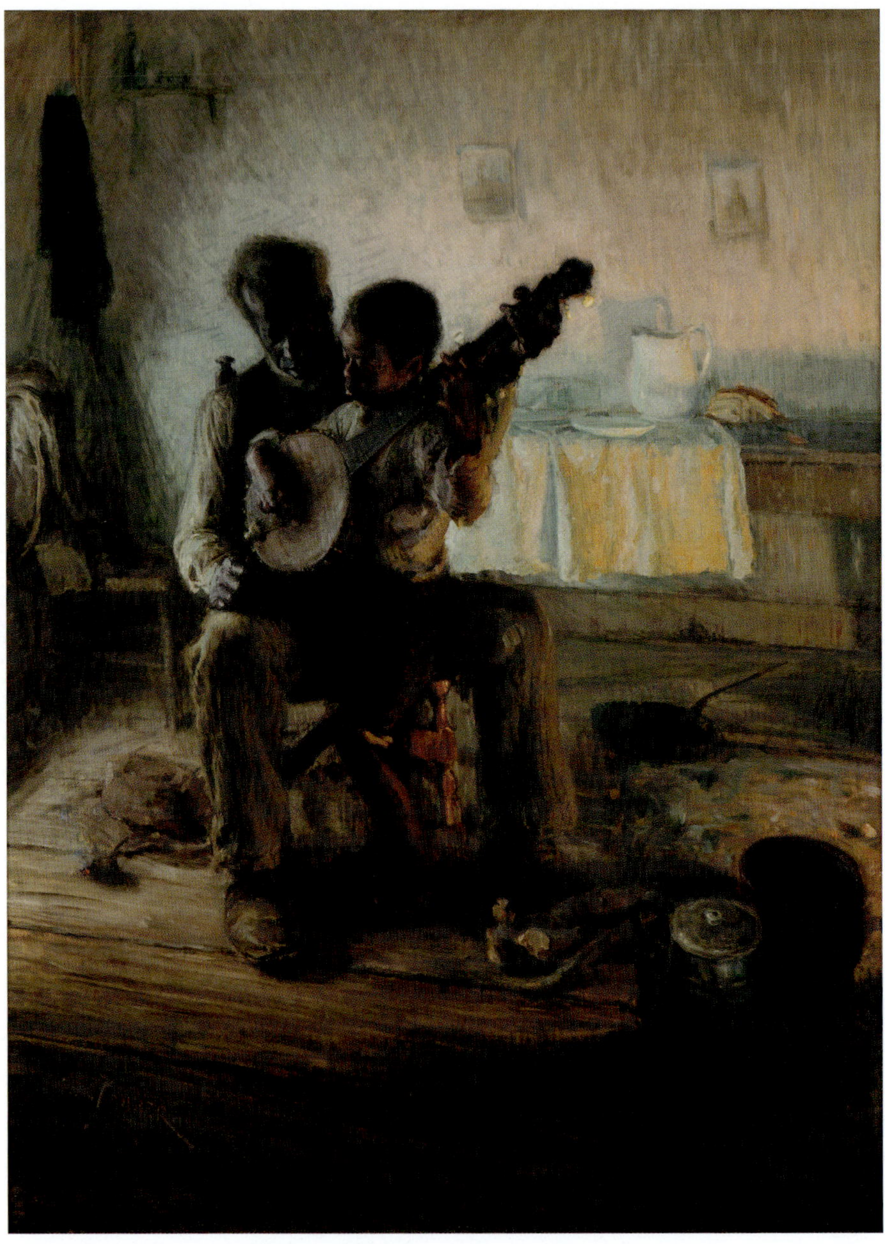

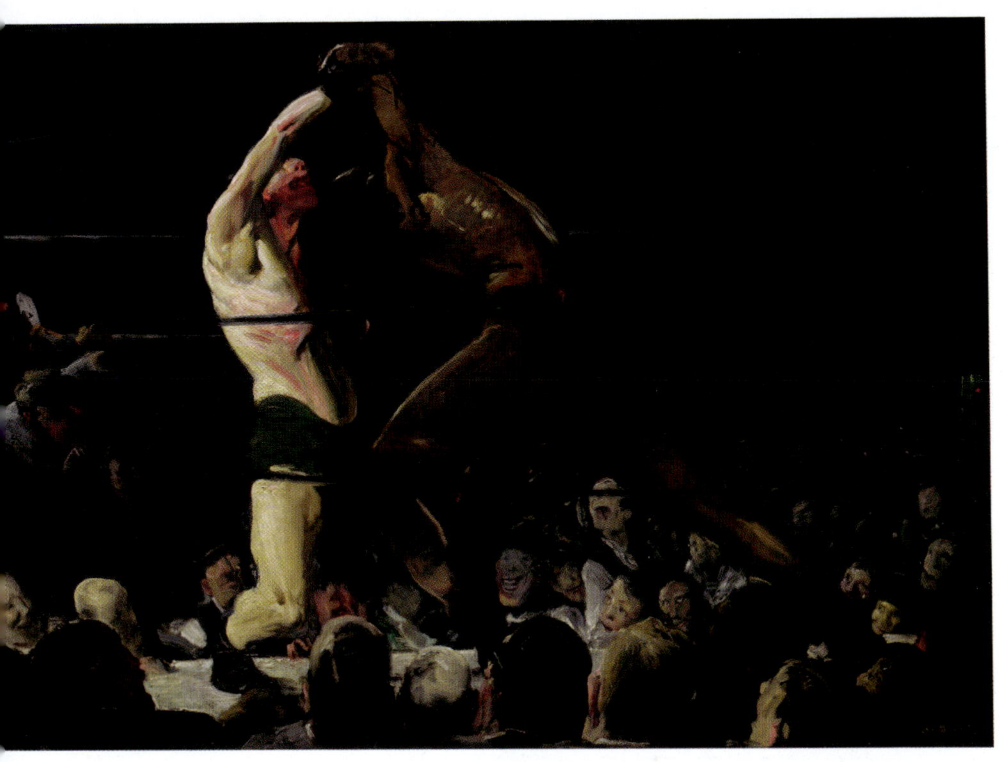

PLATE 23. George Bellows, *Both Members of This Club*, 1909, oil on canvas, 45¼ × 63³⁄₁₆ in. Chester Dale Collection, National Gallery of Art, Washington, DC. Courtesy National Gallery of Art.

TE 22. Henry O. Tanner, *The Banjo Lesson*, 1893, oil on vas, 49 × 35½ in. Gift of Robert C. Ogden. Collection of Hampton University Museum, Hampton, VA.

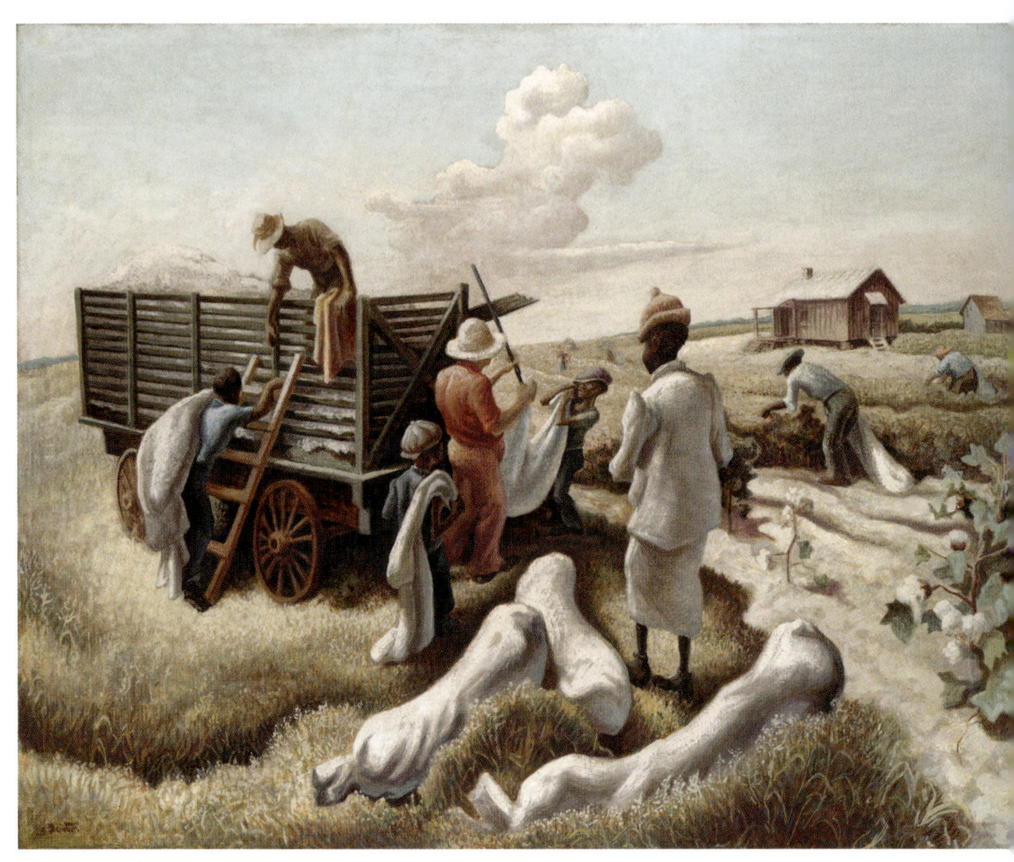

PLATE 24. Thomas Hart Benton, *Weighing Cotton*, 1939, oil and tempera on canvas, 32¹⁄₁₆ × 39½ in. Yale University Art Gallery. Purchased with the Stephen Carlton Clark, B.A. 1903, and John Hill Morgan, B.A. 1893, Funds; Collection of Mary C. and James W. Fosburgh, B.A. 1933, M.A. 1935, by exchange; and gifts from George Hopper Fitch, B.A. 1932, by exchange, William S. Kilroy, B.S. 1949, and Stanley Stone, B.S. 1916. © T. H. and R. P. Benton Trusts/Licensed by Artists Rights Society (ARS), New York.

that it "repeats the Thomas Nelson Page formula," before concluding: "These anecdotes of slavery, but a step above minstrel jokes, are all too happy for words, and too happy for truth." In a 1921 speech to an overflowing audience, the Black nationalist and activist Marcus Garvey slammed Du Bois as the "white man Negro" who had done nothing to support the Black working class. And, writing in 1936, Locke made the following sweeping statement about contemporary Black Americans: "Frankness compels the admission and constructive self-criticism dictates the wisdom of pointing out that the Negro's own conception of himself has been warped by prejudice and the common American stereotypes."[14] The absence of reference to stereotypes in Motley's art among interwar viewers should be seen as evidence that for Americans of the era, stereotypes were not present.

In surveying Motley's painting production during the interwar period, Locke divided the artist's output into three distinct themes: "realistic" portraits and studies of types; "fantastic compositions" of African religious and spiritual practices; and the "genre side of modern Negro life," showing contemporary residents of Chicago's South Side at leisure.[15] Making use of Locke's convenient divisions, this chapter analyzes representative works from each category. The analysis proceeds along one of two complementary lines: a Motley portrait, which appears nonstereotyped today, but which surfaced narratives strongly linked to stereotypes in the 1920s and 1930s, is scrutinized for how it managed to avoid the designation; and the artist's paintings of Africa and modern-day Chicago, a number of which began to look stereotyped in the late 1960s, are analyzed for why they read as naturalistic to Black and white audiences in the interwar period. The chapter contextualizes Motley's artwork, returning to "nonstereotyped" artworks their period complexity and to seemingly "stereotypical" artworks their naturalism.

Motley's best-known "realistic" portraits and studies of types include *Portrait of My Mother* (1919), *Mulatress with Figurine and Dutch Seascape* (ca. 1920), *Self-Portrait* (ca. 1920), *Portrait of the Artist's Father* (ca. 1921, plate 14), *Octoroon* (1922), *Portrait of My Grandmother* (1922), *Woman Peeling Apples* (*Mammy*) (*Nancy*) (1924, plate 7), *The Octoroon Girl* (1925, plate 12), *Aline, an Octoroon* (ca. 1927), *The Snuff Dipper* (1928),

Uncle Bob (1928), and, most famously, *Mending Socks* (1924, plate 8). *Mending Socks* depicts the artist's paternal grandmother, Emily Sims Motley, seated in a busy domestic interior as she darns a coarsely knit green sock; it was one of Motley's most widely exhibited and admired early paintings and his most reviewed painting from the interwar era. Museum visitors attending the Newark Museum of Art's 1927 exhibition of contemporary American painters voted it the "most popular" painting of the sixty-seven canvases in the show.[16]

In 1947, Motley produced a detailed explanation of his aims in creating *Mending Socks*:

> It is a painting of my grandmother on the paternal side, eighty-two years old when painted. I loved my grandmother very much. . . .
> I tried very hard to inject into the picture her kind understanding and also surrounded her with those things she loved best. Her old, faded brick-red shawl she wore continuously and always fastened it together with a hand-painted brooch of her only daughter. Every day all socks were gathered together for mending. She was very fond of fruit and read the bible daily. Above her head on the wall hangs her crucifix she loved so well and in the upper-left corner of the canvas hangs a portrait of a young lady, her mistress during the days of slavery, which is an oval shaped picture.[17]

In an interview conducted in 1978, Motley revealed more information on his grandmother's experience of slavery and on the genesis of *Mending Socks*. He began with Emily Sims Motley's recollections of her treatment by her former owners:

> She said they treated her just lovely, she got nice clothes, nice shoes, they made them take good care of themselves, they made them bathe. They had good food to eat; they had the same kind of food as the master and the family had. So she said it wasn't difficult at all. She said she liked it, she loved her master and mistress. And I think in that painting I did called *Mending Socks* you'll notice in the lefthand corner there's an oval painting of a woman. Well, the

woman in that painting was her young mistress. They gave her the picture when she was freed. And she took care of that, oh, like a very valuable diamond or something. She had it in the house there in a closet. So when I started that painting I told her, 'I'm going to put it in this painting.' She said, 'Oh, how beautiful that will be.' That's just what I did.[18]

Over his career, Motley accommodated foundations, patrons, art historians, and reporters interested in his work with interviews and written explanations of his art and working process, and there is strong evidence suggesting that he shared much of the background information quoted above with a range of contacts in the 1920s. The Harmon Foundation compiled information on the artists who loaned works to its 1929 traveling show, "Exhibit of Fine Arts by American Negro Artists." In Motley's file, they note: "His work covers a wide range of subjects and that in this Exhibit has been said to reveal several phases of Negro development. The *Octoroon Girl* is quite representative of the Northern metropolitan life; *Mending Socks* savours of slave days—the southern mammy with the suggestion of her status brought out by the picture of the mistress in the corner."[19]

Mending Socks received extensive discussion in the press, with reviews in both the white and Black press explaining the significance of the portrait hanging in the upper left of the composition. On February 3, 1925, the art critic for *The Chicago Daily News*, Marguerite B. Williams, wrote: "*Mending Socks* is a picture of his old grandmother, who is 86 years old, and bespeaks a sympathy and understanding of long standing between the ambitious young painter and the careworn old Negress. The faithful old mammy toils to the last as she sits in her rocking chair and darns the coarse family socks with her worn hands. Her crucifix hangs on the wall beside her and near by is the old kerosene lamp and the highly colored portrait of her young 'mistress,' relics of her early life in the south."[20]

Over the next two weeks, Black publications used Williams's copy to inform their readers about *Mending Socks* and Motley's success more generally. It was then common for Black publications to make use of wire services and, at times, to republish either credited or uncredited copy from large-circulation dailies. On February 11, *The New York Amsterdam News* printed a revised version of Williams's article under her byline, with the paragraph describing *Mending Socks* reproduced in full.[21] On February 14, *The Afro-American* published an edited and uncredited version of her article. The modified paragraph on the painting read: "*Mending Socks* is a picture of his old grandmother, who is 86 years old, and bespeaks a sympathy and understanding of long standing between the ambitious young painter and the careworn old lady. The faithful old lady toils to the last as she sits in her rocking chair and darns coarse family socks with her worn hands. Her crucifix hangs on the wall beside her and near by is the old kerosene lamp and the highly colored portrait of her young 'mistress,' relics of her early life in the south."[22]

The modifications made by the editors of *The Afro-American* are significant. In the description of *Mending Socks* in the files of the Harmon Foundation, and in the original review that appeared in the pages of *The Chicago Daily News*, there are hints of nostalgia for the antebellum South. The foundation claimed that "*Mending Socks* savours of slave days" through its depiction of a "southern mammy with the suggestion of her status," and the white newspaper wrote of the "toil" of "the faithful old mammy." The references to an "old Negress" and "faithful old mammy" are excised from the report in *The Afro-American*. The modified paragraph preserves the description of the relationship between the artist and his grandmother while toning down that between the grandmother and her former "mistress." Motley's descriptions of *Mending Socks* to interviewers, the Harmon Foundation's analysis of his artworks, and the exhibition reviews in the white and Black press all mention the relationship between former slave and former mistress. Depictions of "mammies" and of warm relations between selfless mistresses, their loyal slaves, and former slaves were charged tropes that featured prominently in late nineteenth- and early twentieth-century novels, short stories, plays, paintings, motion pictures, and advertisements created by whites.

Writing in 1937, the Harvard historian Paul Buck explained in his Pulitzer Prize–winning book, *The Road to Reunion, 1865–1900*, that the

Union victory in the US Civil War was the product of Northern military might combined with "a civil war in literature," the latter waged by writers in the North armed with novels and short stories that depicted the South's "'barbarism,' 'cruelty,' and 'injustice.'" Buck explained that Southern antebellum writers whose work touched on slavery were invariably seen as defenders of a system that threatened Northern interests. It was only with the destruction of slavery, and the South's acceptance of its place within the Union, that stories about plantation life could safely proliferate. The demise of slavery led Northern abolitionist writers to turn to other topics, with the literary vacuum filled by Southerners eager to reimagine the antebellum South for a national audience. Buck noted that the reconciliation of whites in the North and South was facilitated, in part, by literature populated with happy and nostalgic "'Uncles,' 'Mammies,' 'Colonels,' gracious ladies, fair maidens, and brave cadets." Northern whites enjoyed the revisionist stories of Southern life—which, while distorting the lives and motivations of both Black and white Southerners, posed no existential threat to the Union.[23]

Buck saw the Southern lawyer, diplomat, and author Thomas Nelson Page leading the literary charge to redefine the South. In essays, short stories, and novels produced from the late 1880s to the early 1920s, Page depicted slaves who were, according to Buck, "all of the faithful, devoted type and were used primarily as accessories to heighten the effect of pathos emanating from the departed grandeur of plantation days." And he added, referring to the era's novels and short stories on the South: "There was hardly a Negro in this fiction who could not have said with Virginia Frazer Boyle's darkey, 'dey was good ole days, dose times befoah de wah!'" Page's revisionist project extended to the depiction of slaveholders as well and included romanticized descriptions of the white mistress's selfless devotion to her slaves. In recounting her apocryphal ministrations to sick slaves, he wrote: "with her own hands administering medicines or food; ever by her cheeriness inspiring new hope, by her strength of courage, by her presence awaking faith; telling in her soft voice to dying ears the story of the suffering Saviour; with her hope soothing the troubled spirit, and lighting with her own faith the path into the valley of the dark shadow." The undergirding logic of postbellum plantation fiction, Buck explained, was that "the kindly and affectionate relations of the races under slavery were the true basis for a proper solution of the problems of races" in the post-Reconstruction era.[24]

During the same years that Buck described the cultural power of literature to shape perceptions of Black Americans, Locke discussed the analogous work performed by fine art painting. He catalogued the damage done by the tropes of adoring, comical, and contented slaves in the fine arts, writing: "The 'old faithful uncle,'—later Uncle Tom, Uncle Ned and Uncle Remus, the broad expansive 'mammy' from Aunt Chloe to Aunt Jemima . . . all became typical stereotypes, and scarcely any Nineteenth-Century art show was without its genre portrait study of one or more of these types . . . or some such glorification of the slave system." He noted that "the tradition was so strong [that] it has been and still is one of the mainstays of the literary and artistic defense of the 'lost cause' of the Confederacy. In fact, the cleverest argument for the slave system was this misrepresentation of the Negro as happy, content and 'naturally in place.'"[25] While the trend began with Southern white painters, it soon became popular with white artists in the North. The oil painting *A Visit from the Old Mistress* (1876, plate 9) by Winslow Homer (1836–1910) pictures a luxuriously dressed white woman facing three simply clad Black women and a child in a rough-hewn cabin illuminated by the fire in an open hearth. Homer's first biographer, William Howe Downes, described the Black women's depictions in 1911: "The three former slaves are observed and described most vividly and keenly. In their solemnity of demeanor, the humility of their expression, and the evident awe which the presence of the old mistress inspires, there is a blending of pathos and humor, which belongs to the situation. . . . The position and expression of the 'mammy' sitting on a stool near the fireplace are admirably caught."[26] Whether depicted on page or canvas, Black affection for their former owners was characterized by a docile subservience perfectly fitted to life under either slavery or Jim Crow.

Beyond their broad treatment of slaves' nostalgia for the antebellum South and loyalty to their owners, white writers and artists created particularized depictions of what they took as different slave types and their telltale attributes. In the post-Reconstruction period, no type received more attention than the "mammy," the slave responsible for nursing and raising white children, who in literature, fine arts, and advertising was stereotyped as elderly, asexual, heavyset, religious, and fiercely devoted to her charges. Page described the mammy as the mistress's loyal second, explaining that "her authority was . . . recognized through life, for her devotion was unquestionable. . . . She received, as she gave, an unqualified affection. If she was a slave, she at least was not a servant, but was an honored member of the family, universally beloved, universally cared for—'the Mammy.'"[27] In Page's formulation, it was preferable to be a slave than a servant, since the former nestled within the loving domestic family as an equal.

In *The Road to Reunion*, Buck acknowledged that the picture that emerged in postbellum Southern fiction "omitted much that was true and exaggerated the attractive features" of life under slavery, though he nonetheless concluded that the picture "rested upon a bedrock of fact, and distorted the actuality no more violently than had the abolitionist attack whose unfriendly picture it was now fortunately correcting." In Buck's estimation, the "omissions" and "exaggerations" of revisionist Southern literature provided a needed counterbalance to those promulgated in abolitionist sentimental fiction. Even as he worked as a historian to understand the role of literature in reconciling North and South, Buck bought into the romanticized picture of slavery that animated white descriptions of *Mending Socks*.[28]

Black academics largely agreed with Buck's assessment of how Southerners had won the peace, though they vigorously disputed his contention that the revisionist picture "rested upon a bedrock of fact." In a string of publications in the 1930s, Sterling A. Brown analyzed the formal qualities and political implications of the plantation fiction that glorified the antebellum South. He lamented that in such work "realism was subordinated to the purpose of showing the mutual affection between the races which the North had partly destroyed in a foolish war." And, he noted that "in the early twentieth century, under the influence of Thomas Nelson Page, a legion of writers wept over the vanished glory of the old plantation and presented Negroes of extreme devotedness to their masters."[29] Whereas Buck saw the literature's primary function as facilitating the reunion of whites in the North and South, Brown diagnosed a more malignant end. He contended that the generation of Southerners whose fathers fought the war "became elegists of a lost cause and cast a golden glow over the plantation past." The sons, "determined to resurrect slavery as far as they were able, needed as a cardinal principle the belief that Negroes were happy as slaves, and hopelessly unequipped for freedom." The ahistorical picture they promoted both explained the commitment of their fathers' generation to slavery and rationalized their present-day efforts to deny political rights and economic opportunities to Black citizens. As Brown summarized, "Designed originally to defend slavery, it is now a convenient argument for those wishing to 'keep the Negro in his place.'"[30]

From Reconstruction to the interwar period, a broad cross-section of Black Americans objected to the pernicious depictions that animated Southern literature and, increasingly, the cultural and commercial products of the North. Black activism on the issue came to a head with the national debate that culminated in 1923 over how "the mammy" of antebellum society would be remembered. In that year, the Senate passed, and the House debated, a bill that authorized the "erection, as a gift to the people of the United States, on public grounds of the United States in the city of Washington, D.C. . . . a monument in memory of the faithful colored mammies of the South."[31] The proposal originated with the Jefferson Davis Chapter of the United Daughters of the Confederacy, a hereditary association of white women whose ancestors fought for the Confederacy in the Civil War that was dedicated to advancing an idealized narrative of the war and the antebellum South. Through its benevolent, educational, and memorial-building campaigns, the United Daughters of the Confederacy perpetuated the "Lost Cause" mythology, which held that the Southern rebellion was a just cause made necessary by the Northern assault on their way of life. Lost Cause adherents categorically rejected slavery as being at the root of the conflict, but nonetheless defended slavery as a benevolent institution that exerted a civilizing influence on African Americans.[32] Citing the important work of the United Daughters of the Confederacy, the chief advocate of the bill in the US House of Representatives, Charles Stedman of North Carolina, explained: "The fidelity of these colored mammies has scarcely a parallel in history. The safety and comfort of 'their children,' as they called the boys and girls whom they nursed, gave them contentment and happiness. . . . They could not be seduced from their love and loyalty by either promise of reward or threats of violence." Stedman concluded: "No class of any race of people in bondage could be found anywhere who lived more free from care and distress. The very few who are left look back to those days as the happy and golden hours of their lives."[33]

The congressional debate on the monument ignited a passionate backlash from Black citizens across the country, led by the National Association of Colored Women and Black newspaper editors, who saw the memorial as both a rewriting of history and a means to impose upon them a docile ideal in the twentieth century. *The New York Amsterdam News* reprinted an editorial from the Black-owned *Philadelphia Tribune* in 1923 that argued that a monument to Black mammies was an affront "to every American citizen that descends from those saintly women who were sacrificed to the avaricious beastly natures of Southern gentlemen." Invoking the citizenship of Black Americans, the editorial pointedly disrupted the white stereotype of the mammy as a sexless slave devoted to the maintenance of the white household by highlighting her defenselessness in the face of white sexual predation. Then turning from the past to the present, the editorial went on to ask: "These men would erect a monument to commemorate what? A position of humility, subserviency, meniality, servility is the idea they desire branded and scorched into the brain and heart of every American who happens to be of African lineage."[34]

This context sheds light on why *The Afro-American* chose to edit Williams's description of *Mending Socks* to excise reference to a "faithful old mammy."[35] The editors surely sought to diminish the associations of love and subservience that whites wrote into—and read into—a range of literary and pictorial texts depicting Black characters. The editors of *The Afro-American* worked to reduce the likelihood of their readers seeing Motley's painting perpetuating a reviled stereotype that was firmly ingrained in white American culture. And yet we are confronted with two complicating facts: *The New York Amsterdam News* reproduced the paragraph without modification, to no recorded objection; and whether reviewers drew explicit attention to it or not, *Mending Socks* prominently featured a large, framed painting of a white woman—whose hairstyle and black oval frame date the portrait to the 1850s or 1860s—in the domestic space of an elderly Black woman for which there is no contemporaneous evidence of concern or complaint.[36]

In his 1933 essay "Negro Character as Seen by White Authors," Sterling A. Brown provided a way of unpacking why the painting did not elicit Black concerns of stereotyping. Brown opens his essay with the premise that "the Negro has met with as great injustice in American literature as he has in American life. The majority of books about Negroes merely stereotype Negro character." He goes on to list, and provide literary examples of, the dominant stereotypes of Black people that haunt American literature. After quoting from several texts that traffic in stereotypes of comic Black figures, Brown writes: "In pointing out the stereotype, one does not deny the rich comedy to be found in Negro life. One is insisting, however, that any picture concentrating upon this to the exclusion of all else is entirely inadequate." Toward the close of the essay he adds: "Few of the most apologistic of 'race' orators could deny the presence of contended slaves, of wretched freemen, in our past; nor of comic Negroes . . . , of self-pitying mulattoes, of brutes, of exotic primitives in our present. . . . What this essay has aimed to point out is the obvious unfairness of hardening racial character into fixed moulds. True in some particulars, each of these popular generalizations is dangerous when applied to the entire group." Brown argued that a described trait hardens into a stereotype only in the absence of other, complicating qualities apparent in an individual's makeup, or when the traits depicted in a single character are ascribed to everyone belonging to the character's race.[37] We saw this play out in debates over stereotypes in *All God's Chillun Got Wings,* with a number of progressive Black critics—including Brown, Du Bois, Robeson, and Locke—arguing that the play pushed beyond stereotypes because of the playwright's success in depicting individuals rather than racial types.

When it came to the depiction of love between compassionate mistresses and former slaves, the same point held true. Both Frederick Douglass and Harriet Jacobs wrote of kindhearted mistresses in autobiographies that chronicled their respective experiences of slavery, with Jacobs providing a particularly moving description of her love for her first mistress. Yet neither author was criticized for perpetuating this long-standing stereotype. In both cases, the depicted "kindness" was nestled within narratives that bristled with white brutality toward Black slaves and that illustrated how the decency of an individual could not compensate for the structural injustices of the slave system. The dominance of kindly mistresses and loving slaves within Page's writing stands in sharp contrast to fleeting examples of white kindness and Black love in the autobiographies of Douglass and Jacobs.[38] Much as Douglass's and Jacobs's writings communicated complex pictures of the authors' identities—and white-Black relations—so *Mending Socks* presented a sitter whose identity, and relationships, ultimately transcended her ties to an enslaver. Emily Sims Motley's connection to her former mistress was but one element of her identity as seen by period audiences.

Viewers in the 1920s were encouraged to see complexity in Grandmother Motley's identity because of the painting's ambiguous categorization; it was not obviously either a portrait or a genre painting, and this had significant implications for how audiences understood the sitter. *Mending Socks* had attributes of both types of painting. The arrangement of a single figure, prominently featured in a domestic interior space surrounded by personal effects, led a number of period reviewers to describe the painting as a portrait. In the late 1920s and early 1930s, newspaper reporters and art collectors referred to it as a "portrait of the old lady," "portrait of the artist's grandmother," and "fine character portrait." Motley supported this view when he wrote of *Mending Socks* to the Guggenheim Foundation in 1929: "I consider it the very best portrait I have painted."[39] But working against the categorization of the painting that Motley laid out in his correspondence was his decision to name the work *Mending Socks*. Portraits are typically titled with the sitter's name, familial affiliation, or profession, particularly when they depict little-known people. In declining to name his grandmother or define her relationship to him, and through his choice of a title that invoked a type of "women's work" common to genre paintings, the artist blurred the boundaries between these two painting types.

Genre painting was a lesser category of fine art that depicted ordinary and anonymous characters engaged in activities of "everyday life." Genre painting flourished in America during the nineteenth century, frequently drawing on stock characters borrowed from literary or theatrical sources, or from popular European prints and canvases. It commonly depicted working-class people engaged in sentimental and, at times, humorous activities that evoked viewer nostalgia for a bygone, preindustrial era. In William Sidney Mount's *The Sportsman's Last Visit* (1835), we glimpse the interior of an orderly but rough-hewn cabin in which a rugged would-be suitor is clearly losing out to his effete competitor for a young woman's affections (plate 10). Such scenes of rural life proved popular with urban audiences who enjoyed narratives about the supposed simplicity of country life.[40] *Mending Socks* fit with many period expectations for a genre scene, given its generic title, mundane subject matter, unnamed sitter, and nostalgic hints of the antebellum South. A number of contemporaneous reviewers reacted to the painting in ways that reveal their acceptance of the work as a genre painting. One reviewer described the painting's depiction of "a theme essayed by the great masters of the past, Rembrandt [and] Whistler," while another admired the canvas's depiction of a "native theme."[41] A review of Motley's one-person exhibition in New York City by the critic Marguerite B. Williams embodies the classificatory ambivalence posed by the painting. Williams labeled *Mending Socks* "a portrait study by Archibald Motley" and described the artist's aim to represent "Negro life and types." Writing specifically about *Mending Socks*, she declared: "Negro types in portraiture also have taken much of Archibald Motley's attention. Beginning with a portrait of his father, and one of his grandmother—whom he painted with sympathetic affection." The review is unusual for linking "portraiture," which focuses on unique individuals and their particularized traits, with "Negro types," which suggest broad categories of Black identity.[42]

The ambiguity of the canvas's categorization problematized a series of viewer expectations—related to style, subject matter, and the role of women—that, in turn, encouraged audiences to see the sitter's identity as multifaceted. As we saw in both *All God's Chillun Got Wings* and *Abie's Irish Rose*, the difference between a stereotyped and nonstereotyped rendering does not hinge on the objective accuracy of its character depiction, but rather on the ways in which it reinforces or subverts dominant representational norms. The breaking of conventions in the depiction of individuals who are subject to stereotypes tends to make those depictions read as naturalistic.

Art historians frequently describe genre paintings as backward-looking and nostalgic, befitting their conservative styles. Such conservatism is relative. Whether created in Europe or the US, genre painting tended to deploy styles that were a step or two back from those most current. Motley's painting was different. Reviewers made frequent reference to the painting's stylistic modernity. The *Negro History Bulletin* listed a series of Black painters that it deemed "traditional type or academic," before writing: "But Aaron Douglas, Archibald Motley, William H. Johnson, Hale Woodruff, Malvin Gray Johnson, and James Lesesne Wells, have been influenced by present tendencies in art." Reporting on an exhibition of Black art at the National Gallery of Art, an art critic favorably contrasted *Mending Socks* with a second Motley painting she characterized as "in the old tradition, academic" style.[43] Alain Locke deemed Motley a "Modernist" and described the "severe, realistic style" of his early portraits. The critic Marguerite B. Williams claimed: "Both 'The Mulattress' and 'Mending Socks' are painted in somewhat that same unpleasant and fearless realistic spirit that Bellows painted his Victorian types. Refusing to appropriate the conventional ideas of beauty of the older civilized races, he spares nothing to make his people real."[44] Both Locke and Williams commented on Motley's "realistic style," with Locke calling it "severe" and Williams deeming it "unpleasant." Williams describes the style in explicitly racial terms, seeing it rejecting the "conventional ideas of beauty of the older civilized races" in order to "make his people more real." Given that the painting style evident in *Mending Socks* was on the conservative side of progressive painting for the 1920s, Williams's perception of the artist's "refusal" to make use of "conventional ideas of beauty" surely says more about the inappropriateness of the style for the subject than about its departure from Western painting conventions.[45]

Not only was the style an unusual choice for a genre painting, but it was also unsuitable for a canvas that purported to offer a nostalgic picture of the grandmother's contended life under slavery. In Paul Buck's analysis of how postbellum Southern fiction reshaped white American perceptions of the South, the historian analyzed the stylistic conventions of writers of the New South. Buck explained that their "love and devotion . . . for the old" produced "a rich theme of nostalgia which gave [their writing] a piquant charm in a rapidly changing world." One result of their longing for a lost past, according to Buck, was that they cultivated a retrograde style of writing that "excluded from Southern literature of the [eighteen-]eighties all traces of grim realism." Addressing the novels and short stories depicting Black characters from the 1900s through the 1920s, Sterling A. Brown contrasted the "realism" characteristic of writing he admired with "unreal" plantation fiction, which he variously labeled "farce," "trite," "burlesque," and "melodrama."[46]

The painted equivalent of plantation fiction abounded in the galleries of the late nineteenth century. It is evident in the paintings of such artists as William Henry Snyder (1829–1910), who used an old-fashioned, soft-focused photographic style that hearkened back to genre scenes produced from the 1830s through the 1860s. In his *Darning by the Hearth* (1885, plate 11), we see the interior of a ramshackle and dimly lit domestic space in which a Black woman, in tattered dress and apron, sits in a rocking chair, with intent focus on her work. While the painting dates to the penultimate decade of the nineteenth century, viewers were hard-pressed to determine if the scene represented antebellum or postbellum society. An older style of painting was coupled with Black living conditions and a type of work that had changed little over time. Within the logic of the painting, the movement from slavery to freedom makes scant difference to Black Americans. While the female figures in both Snyder's and Motley's paintings strike similar poses in their rocking chairs as they engage in identical labor, the canvases are studies in difference: a backward-looking and nostalgic style versus a modern one; a decrepit versus a well-maintained interior; a darkened versus a brightly lit space; and, as we will explore in more detail, a poor versus a middle-class sitter; a type versus an individual; and an identity limited to darning versus one that had many facets.

Mending Socks also deviated from the stylistic norms of portraiture. A 1929 review juxtaposed Motley's *Octoroon Girl* to *Mending Socks*, noting that the former was a more traditional, "academic" painting. In the reviewer's estimation, *Mending Socks* was "more interesting but perhaps a little less well painted." A second reviewer reinforced the "academic" qualities of *The Octoroon Girl* (1925, plate 12), explaining that it was an "exceptional" and "sophisticated" portrait that "compare[ed] favorably with the best output of the Academy."[47] *The Octoroon Girl* shows a seated figure in three-quarter-length pose. She is elegantly attired, with gloves in hand, in a well-appointed interior that shows hints of books and a framed oil painting as symbols of material wealth and culture. A raking light highlights her hands and face as she gazes directly at the viewer. In *The Octoroon Girl*, the sitter's identity is communicated through her physical features, pose, solidly middle-class setting, and elegant outfit. The portrait displays conversancy with traditional European portraiture and with the stylistically progressive portraits produced by Motley's former teacher George Bellows (1882–1925) in such canvases as *Emma at the Window* (1920) and *Mrs. Walter H. Richter* (1922, plate 13). An anonymous art critic, whose review was published in both *The Afro-American* and *The Pittsburgh Courier*, praised Motley's "artistic ability, particularly as shown in *The Octoroon Girl*, an oil painting finely portraying a beautiful mulatto woman, seated with gloves in hand, dressed in dark red-trimmed clothing and wearing a hat."[48] In the review, "artistic ability" is never defined; it is simply coupled with the sitter's beauty and presentation as middle class. When Motley explained the creation of his series of "Octoroon" paintings, he pointedly named a half dozen stereotypes projected onto Black subjects that he wished to refute, before explaining his aim to illustrate Black sitters with "dignity, honesty, integrity, intelligence and understanding."[49] While it went unwritten, the "dignity, honesty, and integrity" of *The Octoroon Girl* stemmed largely from the application of a fashionable portraiture convention to a Black subject. An established, academic portrait formula took on a radical cast when applied to a Black female sitter.

Mending Socks looked "severe," even "unpleasant," because Motley lifted the brooding darkness of a Victorian parlor evident in *The Octoroon Girl*—and in many of his early portraits. He turned on the electric lights to sharply delineate the sitter and the plethora of objects around her.[50] The inclusion of so many disparate objects made for an unusual portrait of a female sitter. American portraits of women were historically spare. If they included additional objects, each one tended to serve a well-established symbolic role: a decorative bowl of fruit on an end table or a flower in the sitter's hand or lap were signs of female fecundity; implements for sewing, needlepoint, or knitting signaled industriousness; a Bible indicated piety; hints of stylish furniture and art, much as in *The Octoroon Girl*, signaled class standing or sophistication. Motley played with conventions. He added a second book to the presumed Bible, offering a visual suggestion of the sitter's wider interests. He also included an overflowing fruit bowl in the portrait of an octogenarian. The plethora of fruit and the age of the sitter nudged the display of fruit from symbolic to real. In addition, he cluttered the table with a small figurine pincushion, glass of water, and late nineteenth-century kerosene lamp—none of which were standard objects for a portrait. As nontraditional props, they could not have been readily decoded by audiences as symbols of the sitter's attributes. The objects in *Mending Socks* were sufficiently plentiful in number, and varied in their associations, that they broke from portraiture conventions and made the domestic space and the sitter appear more real.

At the heart of *Mending Socks* is the activity in which Grandmother Motley engages, sock darning. Her identity is most obviously signaled by this labor—communicated through the painting's title and the visual evidence of her focused concentration on the sock in her lap. During the 1920s, sock mending was associated with drudgery and, often, with working-class life. A guidebook to "modern marriage" from 1927 explained what it deemed as the fear held by many "fine-minded and imaginative young women" that marriage will lead inexorably to an old-fashioned and "unfair" arrangement in which "they will spend the morning . . . cleaning house, the afternoon washing dishes and cooking, and the evening sitting stupidly in the apartment, mending socks."[51] In Sinclair Lewis's *Main Street* (1920), Carol Kennicott sinks into despair after a tea with a local acquaintance, Mrs. Flickerbach, who complains bitterly about her missed opportunities in life. As someone with a "talent for tending to figures," Mrs. Flickerbach had hoped to become a "business woman," but instead finds herself with no career, trapped in a small Minnesota town she despises, "trying to forget washing and ironing and mending socks."[52] In Theodore Dreiser's 1918 short story "Married," we meet an artistic, socially progressive husband who marries a conventional and pragmatic Iowa farm girl. Dreiser pointedly contrasts the pleasure-seeking pursuits of the husband during his days as a bachelor with his wife's stolid, working-class values. The bride is confused by her husband's urbane, artistic world; as the narrator explains, "Out in Iowa, in the neighborhood of Avondale, there were no artists, no models, no budding actresses, no incipient playwrights. . . . There, people worked, and worked hard." The bride's mother, we are told, bent "daily over a cook-stove, preparing meals, washing dishes, sewing clothes, mending socks, doing the thousand and one chores which fall to the lot of every good housewife."[53]

In the culture of the 1920s, mending socks was old-fashioned, associated with the least appealing aspects of a women's married life, and strongly linked to rural life and economic necessity. In genre painting, the labor performed by women—whether mending, knitting, sewing, or spinning—stood as their defining characteristic. In Motley's painting, the sitter is not so limited. Grandmother Motley sits in a well-appointed, middle-class room. In addition to the framed oil painting in the background, her middle-class status is suggested by the neatly painted and intensely lit interior, her brooch and pristine white blouse, the brightly patterned tablecloth, and the large, silver ornamental fruit bowl on the table beside her. In explaining his grandmother's labor, Motley noted a daily ritual in his home: "Every day all socks were gathered together for mending."[54] Given the implausibility of a small household requiring daily sock darning, the statement makes clear that the daily task had more to do with the grandmother's industriousness and desire to be useful than with the family's need. Few viewers would have been aware of the Motley household's division of labor, but the depicted prosperity of the home was likely to have communicated a similar message. As with the portraits of wealthy white women engaged in needlework, the grandmother appears to toil by choice, not necessity.

Throughout Motley's childhood and early professional life, his family experienced financial insecurity. His father worked on the railroad for the Pullman Company as a dining car chef, a poorly paid job that was nonetheless deemed prestigious within the Black community, given the limited employment options available to Black men up through the interwar period. The elder Motley was forced to leave the job after an ailment left him paralyzed in one leg. He subsequently ran a four-chair shoeshine parlor in a rented space on Chicago's South Side, and the family often took in boarders. Motley Jr. served as a custodian at the Art Institute to cover his tuition while a student, and during the early years of his career—when *Mending Socks* was painted—he lived at home with his parents, worked a series of strenuous blue-collar jobs, and gave private art lessons to make ends meet. As Motley recalled years later, "I wasn't particular about the job, as long as I could make some money to live."[55] While finances were tight in the Motley household, there are few evident signs of financial precarity in the artist's paintings. His self-portraits and portraits of family members—particularly *Self-Portrait* (ca. 1920), *Portrait of the Artist's Father* (ca. 1921, plate 14), and *Portrait of Mrs. A. J. Motley, Jr.* (1930, plate 15)—use clothing, props, poses, and painting styles to depict upper-middle-class people, seemingly secure in their stations. The economic security depicted in *Mending Socks* is thus less a reflection of the conditions in the Motley household than a tactic for insulating the sitter from association with the era's ubiquitous pictures of impoverished, elderly Black women.[56]

In chapter 3, I quoted Sterling Brown asking why more Americans did not see in the struggle of the Black protagonist in Paul Green's *In Abraham's Bosom* (1927) "man's heroic struggle against great odds." Brown believed that Green had produced the type of complex, non-stereotyped Black characters that could stand as universal symbols of mankind, though he was aware of both the rarity of such depictions and the challenges white audiences faced in reading Black characters in this manner.[57] There is evidence that *Mending Socks* pushed Americans in that direction. Writing in *The Southern Workman*, a monthly published by the Hampton Institute, the art critic Rose Henderson wrote: "*Mending Socks*, a study of the artist's grandmother, reveals a rich apprehension of color values and a very human approach to character." And Carlyle Burrows, an art critic for the *New York Herald Tribune* and a contributor to *The Christian Science Monitor*, wrote that, in addition to Motley's *The Mulattress*, "there is another meritorious and utterly human document in the portrait of the artist's mother [*sic*], called 'Mending Socks.'"[58] That a Black art critic saw a "human approach" and that a white one perceived a "human document" in *Mending Socks* is testament to the ways in which the painting wove a complex set of associations (some of which flirted with stereotypes) into a rich character study of an individual. While the sentiments expressed by the critics did not attain Brown's ideal—of a Black woman standing as an unraced everywoman—they illustrated a notable advance in the reception of a seemingly prosaic canvas of an elderly Black woman mending socks. The sentiment starkly contrasts with the opinion of the *Washington Post* art critic whose 1992 exhibition review opened the chapter, with his claim of a "dehumanizing distance" between Motley and his subjects. Such distance was not produced by the artist but by audience perspectives on race that evolved over decades.

:::

Locke described the second major theme evident in Motley's oeuvre as "fantastic compositions of African tribal and voodoo ceremonials."[59] It is evident in *Devil-Devils* (ca. 1927), *Kikuyu God of Fire* (1927, plate 16), *Spell of the Voodoo* (ca. 1927), *Waganda Charm-Makers* (1927, plate 17), and *Waganda Women's Dream* (1927). These paintings reflected Motley's effort to picture the ceremonies and religious beliefs of peoples in east Africa, a region of the world that he had not visited. *Kikuyu God of Fire*, as described by a period art critic, depicts "weird fire-breathing monsters that the primitive African believed to inhabit the dank forests," while *Waganda Charm-Makers* illustrates, according to Motley, the application of charms "hung on the branch of some mighty forest tree supposed to be inhabited by a demon or deity; others are cast into a stream or lake to propitiate an offended river-deity."[60]

These five African-themed paintings were created by Motley in anticipation of his 1928 New Gallery exhibition at the suggestion of the gallery's president, George S. Hellman. The show was arranged through the efforts of Motley's most important mentor, Robert B. Harshe (1879–1938), the director of the Art Institute of Chicago. In May 1927, Motley wrote to Hellman to confirm details of the show. Hellman responded later that month with guidance: "My general suggestion to you would be that during the summer you paint some pictures showing various phases of negro life in its most dramatic aspects—scenes, perhaps, in which the voo-doo element as well as the cabaret element—but especially the latter—enter." In October 1927, Motley updated the gallery president on his progress, writing that he had "been quite successful in painting ten pictures which I think will meet with your approval. I used subjects concerning voodooism and the cabaret as you suggested in your last letter."[61]

The reception of Motley's African-themed paintings was more mixed than that of any other series that the artist produced during the interwar period. White critics were polarized in their assessments; they offered both the most laudatory and critical reviews. The leading white supporter was the *New York Times* art critic Edward Alden Jewell, who published a lengthy, illustrated exhibition review of Motley's New Gallery show in the *New York Times Magazine*. Jewell wrote that Motley's "unique" and "vivid pictures" "caught the spirit of life." He deemed the exhibition "significant both because of the quality of the paintings themselves and because it represented . . . the first one-man show by a Negro artist to be held in New York." Motley, Jewell summarized, "contributed eloquently to the artistic accomplishments of his race." While he was appreciative of Motley's portraits and scenes of contemporary Black life, it was the paintings of African religious practices that left the deepest impression on the critic and to which he devoted the bulk of his review.[62]

There are three key features to Jewell's racialized review: his breathless excitement over what he interpreted as the novel representation of primal scenes, his essentialization of Black identity, and his linkage of the artist's race to his capacity to create such imagery. In a typical passage, Jewell described his affective experience of the artworks: "Glistening dusky bodies, stamping or gliding, shouting or silent, are silhouetted against hot ritual fires. Myriad age-old racial memories drift up from Africa and glowing islands of the sea to color more recently ghostly memories of plantation days when black was black and slaves were slaves; these memories sift, finally, through negro life in Northern cities of the present, leaving everywhere their imprint and merging with a rich blur of tribal echoes." And he noted that Motley had chosen to depict "phases [of human life] of which he has knowledge and whose expression flows in his veins." Jewell ogles the "glistening dusky bodies" and imagines a Black racial memory that runs from tribal life in Africa, through antebellum plantation slavery, and up to Black Americans' experience of the modern, urban North. That Motley is able to capture all of this is testament to his knowledge and blood, social experience and racial heritage. That Jewell tacitly flattens history and essentializes Black identity is evident from his assertion that in Motley's paintings "the same fundamental rhythms are found, whether the setting be a jungle presided over by witchcraft or a cabaret rocking to the syncopation of jazz." Notwithstanding the passage of hundreds of years and dramatic changes to social, economic, and cultural conditions, Jewell imagines that a set of qualities intrinsic to Black people remains unchanged.[63]

In the reviews of Motley's New Gallery exhibition that followed, many white critics responded, as did Jewell, by linking the artist's racial identity to the style or subject matter of his work. After describing the different "racial strains" purportedly evident in Motley's portraits, an art critic posited: "Being himself a mixture of Caucasian, Indian and Negro, these types proved fascinating to him." Such references assured readers of the authenticity of Motley's depictions of nonwhites. Writing specifically of the artist's African-themed paintings, she explained: "Though research had to make up for actual first-hand knowledge of the African forest and of voodoo, there was something innate in this artist's makeup that made him sense and express the mystery that hovers over such themes."[64] Both Black and white artists are capable of researching their subjects with an eye toward creating more authentic representations, yet, in the estimation of the critic, only Black artists could draw on their "innate . . . makeup" to fully "sense and express" Black themes. A second critic surveyed the exhibition and claimed the artist was "going back for his material to the jungle and to the plantation, to the negro belts of modern cities, and weaving into all that rich racial fabric an emotion which no white man can experience." Seeing the same trajectory that Jewell detected in Motley's artwork—from Africa through to the South Side of Chicago—the critic described the resulting "racial fabric" as one that could be woven only by Black artists.[65] And, appraising an exhibition of Black art at the National Gallery of Art in 1929 that Motley participated in, a critic found the artists' "approach to their work unusual because it emanates from the temperament peculiar to the race." Critics were even able to see an artist's Blackness guiding the form of works of art that did not have an obviously racialized theme. In describing a painting of a nude that Motley created using a white model in Paris, a reporter for *The Chicago Daily News* claimed that "it has much of the exoticism Motley puts into his paintings of Negro models." And, in a complementary move, critics were equally capable of seeing a Black artist's disparate styles and subjects informed by his African origins. In another echo of Jewell's review, the art critic Marguerite B. Williams asserted that all of Motley's paintings of contemporary Black Chicago life "were swept by the primitive moods that seemed born of the tropical jungles."[66]

References to Motley's racial lineage were common in the writings of white art critics and reporters, whether or not the racial references were linked to the critics' specific arguments.[67] Knowledge of Motley's racial background was deemed relevant in its own right. After describing a mural commission that Motley had secured from the easel and mural divisions of the Works Progress Administration's Illinois Art Project, a painting illustrating "an 18th-century stage coach" with "passengers gazing out of the coach windows" (*United States Mail*, 1936, plate 18), a reporter offered this non sequitur: "Motley, in whose veins flow the blood of a French grandfather, a West Indian grandmother, and American Negro parents, has begun work on this mural."[68] When Jewell published his book *Modern Art: Americans* (1930), he noted the racial identities of just two of the fifty artists he featured in the volume—Motley and Julian Martinez, a San Ildefonso Pueblo painter, who were the only nonwhite artists included. Several white artists discussed in *Modern Art* depicted nonwhite characters in their paintings, suggesting that Motley's racial identification was not required for understanding his reproduced portrait of a Black sitter.[69] Motley's designation as Black was accorded such significance by white critics that it could overrule both other elements of the artist's biography and the visual evidence of his canvases. In a 1926 essay that attempted to parse the distinctions between the work of trained artists who rebelled against the stylistic restrictions of the academy and "naive" artists who painted without knowledge of high-art conventions, the critic Marguerite B. Williams wrote: "The problem of the young American-born artist reared in the more sophisticated atmosphere of schools is quite a different one from that of the young foreigner brought up close to the soil." As Williams made clear in her many articles devoted to Motley and his art, the artist was native-born, trained at one of the premier US schools of art, and frequently depicted urban subjects. And yet she went on to state: "The naivety of such artists as Marek Szwarc, Emil Armin and the Russian Petrusich, and one might also add the colored artist Archibald Motley, is all more natural and easy. To understand how much more complex is the world which confronts the habitue of the cities, the cosmopolitan, one has but to look at the work of Will Hollingsworth or A. S. Baylinson."[70]

A minority of white critics disparaged the paintings, branding them "unsuccessful" and "the cheapest, most blatant ten-twent-thirt illustrations," with "ten-twent-thirt" describing melodramatic entertainments with no artistic quality.[71] The art critic for *The New Yorker* opined: "We thought his best achievement was the canvas of the old lady mending socks. For the subjective things, Boys' imaginings of Voodooland, we do not care at all."[72] Such critics found the African-themed paintings incompatible with fine art, judging them instead to be cheap spectacles. *The New Yorker*'s critic went on to state: "Such things, to be real primitives, could hardly be executed by the young man who painted the sophisticated 'Octoroon' and 'Black and Tan Cabaret.'" A critic for the *New York Herald Tribune* affirmed this sentiment in his description of Motley's "Voodoo" paintings, which he deemed "imaginative, and strangely so, with fearful jungles and grotesque animals hovering around the lurid drama of the religious spectacle. But Mr. Motley is no ogre himself. As long as three years ago he drew attention by winning the Logan prize at the Chicago Art Institute exhibition with an academic and scholarly portrait of a girl, 'A Mulattress,' which appears with distinction in the present exhibition."[73] The critic for *The New Yorker* took it for granted that "primitive" artworks are necessarily created by naive artists and that a Black artist's ability to create authentic expressions of "primitive" life was compromised by his mastery of sophisticated Western styles of art. Along similar lines, the reporter for the *New York Herald Tribune* believed viewers would assume that the darkness of the "fearful jungles and grotesque animals" in the African paintings reflected on the character of the artist; he felt the need to reassure his readers that Motley was "no ogre," as evidenced by the painter's body of "academic and scholarly" artwork and institutional recognition. In *The New Yorker*, Western culture corrupted the "primitivism" of a nonwhite artist, and in the *New York Herald Tribune*, it was evidence of his humanity. In both cases, a Black artist's choice of subject and style posed challenges to audiences in discerning his true identity and nature.

White critics did not comment on stereotypes in Motley's paintings of Africa, even as their responses to the works surfaced long-standing Black stereotypes. In "Negro Character as Seen by White Authors," Sterling Brown explored seven dominant Black stereotypes with which white authors infused their fiction, including the "exotic primitive." As Brown explained, when white authors deploy the "exotic primitive" stereotype,

> the figure who emerges from their pages is a Negro synchronized
> to a savage rhythm, living a life of ecstasy, superinduced by jazz

(repetition of the tom-tom, awakening vestigial memories of Africa) and gin, that lifted him over antebellum slavery, and contemporary economic slavery. . . . A kinship exists between this stereotype and that of the contended slave; one is merely a "jazzed-up" version of the other, with cabarets supplanting cabins, and Harlemized "blues," instead of spirituals and slave reels.[74]

White responses to Motley's African paintings were filtered through this lens, seeing the continuity of primitive Blackness across time and geography. The paintings offered evidence that Black subjects remained tethered to qualities rooted in their "savage" pasts, imprinting what Jewell termed "tribal echoes" onto all of their behaviors and cultural productions. Motley, the critics believed, was able to tap into "racial memories" to re-create the ceremonies, look, and emotions of a world he had never experienced. The only thing that troubled the authenticity of the artist's African paintings was his obvious mastery of Western painting techniques. Several white critics expressed unease with his conversancy with the "sophisticated" artistic styles of the West. While it was broadly accepted that white artists could pick and choose their styles, nonwhite artists were granted less latitude. They could either fully embrace Western practices, as a sign of having been civilized, or they could employ their innate, primitive techniques. Moving between styles granted them an agency too reminiscent of the freedom accorded to whites and made "primitivism" too obviously a stylistic choice that was unconnected to their racial essence.[75]

Black critics were more unified in their praise of the paintings. In *Opportunity*, the canvases were deemed the "most interesting feature of the exhibition" at the New Gallery. Writing in *The Negro in Literature and Art in the United States* (1929), Professor Benjamin Brawley praised Motley's portraiture and scenes of contemporary life and added: "He also excels in the portrayal of African jungle life." The adjective that most frequently emerged from Black reviews was "imaginative."[76] Whereas white critics routinely offset references to the "imaginative" canvases with claims that the paintings' subjects and style were linked to the artist's "blood," Black audiences described the paintings as artistic interpretations of fantastical scenes. White critics tended to see the ideas and emotions of the African paintings as innate, while Black reviewers saw them as one creative strand among the artist's stylistically distinct themes. Black reviews made frequent note of the fact that Motley had never been to Africa. One critic stated: "His imaginative paintings of East Africa . . . caused the greatest amount of comment. To fully appreciate his African canvases, one should know that he has never been to the country of his scenes and that his work is purely imaginary, based, of course, upon research." A second complimented Motley for having "an imagination perhaps not shown to so great an extent save Tanner," before noting: "The interest is heightened when one learns that the artist has never set foot on the soil of the country whose institutions and customs he gives such vivid and startling interpretations."[77] And James Porter explained: "It is true, of course, that he had not been to Africa or even witnessed a demonstration of the activity represented in these paintings. . . . Yet the paintings have a verisimilitude."[78] Each of these critics deemed it noteworthy that Motley had not been to Africa or seen the ceremonies performed live, precisely because they did not perceive a link between his capacity to produce such scenes and his racial background. His cultural and physical distance from the depicted events made their "verisimilitude" all the more remarkable.

While many white and Black viewers saw in Motley's African paintings an example of "racial art" that nodded to the continent's primitive practices, white and Black audiences diverged on the question of whether or not such scenes revealed anything about the developmental state of contemporary Black Americans. Black intellectuals in the 1920s—including Brawley, Du Bois, and Locke—referred to the peoples of Africa and their arts as "primitive" and, at times, "savage," but in contrast to whites' perspective, they tended not to see such references reflecting on the qualities or social advancement of modern members of their race.[79] In his essay "The Legacy of the Ancestral Arts," Locke acknowledged the validity of a series of characteristics commonly ascribed by whites to Black Americans and agreed that Black people and their arts were indeed "free, exuberant, emotional, sentimental and human." But he went on to confound reader expectations by claiming that Africans and their arts were historically "rigid, controlled, disciplined, [and] abstract." Locke argued that slavery stripped Africans of their characteristic qualities and arts, and that in response to the new conditions they encountered in the Americas, "African spirit blended itself in with entirely different culture elements and blossomed in strange new forms," which resulted in "a curious reversal of emotional temper and attitude." While accepting that characteristic traits could be identified in Black Americans, Locke diminished their significance by arguing that they were the product of local, social conditions, and not "race psychology." In his most radical move, he attributed to Africans many of the characteristics that Europeans and European Americans had historically lauded as signs of their civilized state, which highlighted his belief that they were also social products and not innate to the Anglo-Saxon race.[80]

Black Americans in the 1920s not only undermined the idea of fixed qualities that linked Black people across time and geography, but in imagining their links to Africa and Africans, they selectively fashioned a usable past. As the historian Clare Corbould has explored, for most of the nineteenth century, the majority of Black Americans subscribed to the white narrative of Africa as an uncivilized continent that was valued primarily for its natural resources. Any symbolic links between Black Americans and Africa were then fostered by religious leaders who invoked the Israelites' exodus from Egypt and the book of Psalms's reference to the future "redemption" of Ethiopia, which congregants were told were signs of Black Americans' freedom and deliverance to come. In the aftermath of the Great War, a confluence of events secularized and altered Black Americans' symbolic relationship to Africa. Corbould notes that Black interest in Africa during the 1920s was promoted by Marcus Garvey's Universal Negro Improvement Association (UNIA), which advanced Black pride, economic self-sufficiency, and a Black American nation-building effort in Africa; by the National Association for the Advancement of Colored People (NAACP), as it sought to link global diasporic communities in pushing for the decolonization of Africa; by American and European fascination for "the primitive" and an accompanying explosion of interest in African music, dance, and visual arts; and, finally, by the 1923 opening of Tutankhamen's tomb. The dark skin color of ancient Egyptians, as revealed in tomb paintings, sculpture busts, and sarcophagi, was validating to the Black public in providing visual evidence that the world's first great civilization was Black. For a people long accused of having made no meaningful contributions to culture or civilization, the artifacts revealed by the excavation offered a powerful counterargument.[81]

Corbould traces two dominant strains in how Black Americans of the 1920s thought about their relationship to Africa: neocolonialists like Garvey invested in a cyclical model of history and believed that Africans required the aid of Black Americans to reclaim the lost power and culture emblematized by ancient Egypt, while a majority of the Black public accepted a model of history that saw human progress as a continual forward march. This second group largely ignored present-day Africans to focus on the links between ancient Africans and modern-day African Americans, who, as survivors of slavery and builders of the modern US, were seen as the spiritual inheritors of Africa's ancient accomplishments. Neither strain of thought showed much respect for modern Africans, who were either dismissed as a backward people in need of Western aid, or deemed irrelevant players who stood between the past greatness of the Egyptians and the admirable achievements of modern-day Black Americans.[82] In a commencement address at the Hampton Institute in June 1923, James Weldon Johnson sought to inspire graduates by both linking them to an ancient Black civilization and explaining away the present-day backwardness of Africa. He declared: "Popular opinion has it that the Negro in Africa has been from time immemorial a savage. This is far from the truth. . . . The truth is that the torch of civilization was lighted on the banks of the Nile; and we can trace the course of that torch . . . up through Egypt, around the borders of the Mediterranean, through Greece and Italy and Spain, on into Northern Europe." And he concluded: "The fact that dark ages fell upon Africa and her people is no more of a discredit than the fact that dark ages fell upon the buried empires of Asia Minor or Asia or ancient Greece."[83] Black viewers of all political persuasions were unlikely to then perceive meaningful connections between themselves and the figures in Motley's paintings of tribal religious life. The canvases' representations of indigenous ceremonies and myths possessed voyeuristic appeal, without illustrating any ties to the pinnacle of African civilization. In contrast to white audiences of the 1920s, Black viewers would have read the canvases as further evidence of both cultural discontinuity and the seismic changes catalyzed by social context.[84]

In *The Negro Genius* (1937), Benjamin Brawley provided an analysis of the paintings of Motley and Aaron Douglas and the sculpture of Richmond Barthé, noting the tendency of critics to ascribe African influences to the men's work. Deeming such influence "overemphasized" and "indirect," Brawley cautioned that "the influence may be said to be not so much African as what is regarded as modern. To assert then, as is sometimes asserted, that American Negro painting and sculpture of to-day find their real roots in Africa, is perhaps to claim just a little too much." Brawley did not believe that the African influences evident in the art of Black Americans derived from racial memory or even primary research, but that they resulted from the secondhand influence of European modernists. According to Brawley, the Black "memory" of Africa came to them largely through whites. The role of white artists in introducing African themes to Black Americans further complicates efforts to see in the themes evidence of racial continuity. Perhaps because of this, there were a number of prominent Black voices during the period that—while deeply invested in the unique contributions that Black artists had to make in advancing Black arts—explicitly argued for the role whites could play in the development and promotion of "Negro art."[85]

The sociologist Charles S. Johnson penned an editorial in *Opportunity* in January 1925 that effusively praised the African-themed artwork of the German-born Winold Reiss that illustrated that issue of the journal. Johnson extolled the artwork for recording Negro life "with faithfulness to reality" and concluded his tribute by noting: "In art as in literature and music we are beginning to realize that Negroes have a distinct and inimitable contribution to make to the culture of America, and we may salute with gestures of appreciation those trailblazers who both sense and assist the coming of this more complete recognition."[86]

Locke was similarly laudatory in his praise of Reiss's illustrations for *The New Negro* (1925), which he characterized as "deliberately conceived and executed as a path-breaking guide and encouragement to this new foray of the younger Negro artists" in creating a "racial school of art." In the same year, the Black dramatist and activist Montgomery Gregory looked back and hailed Harriet Beecher Stowe's novel *Uncle Tom's Cabin* (1852) and Dion Boucicault's play *The Octoroon* (1859). Gregory explained that these white-produced artworks represented "the first instance where an attempt [was] made to present to the American public in a realistic manner the authentic life of the Negro." He deemed novel and play "a distinct gain for Negro drama."[87] Writing in *Modern Negro Art* (1943), James A. Porter listed the non-Black artists who had advanced "the pictorial and plastic interpretation of Negro life." Porter praised "Miguel Covarrubias' *Negro Drawings*, and Winold Reiss' appealing charcoal and crayon studies of Black Americans, and the presentation of Black characters in such plays as Eugene O'Neill's *Emperor Jones* and DuBose Heyward's *Porgy*" for creating artworks in which "the unself-conscious life of the Negro can be observed truthfully."[88] For Johnson, Locke, Gregory, and Porter, sensitive depictions by white artists could validate and promote "Negro art" through the circulation of more complex depictions of Black subjects.

There are even examples of Black intellectuals of the interwar period going further and praising whites for contributing to the creation of "Negro art." Reviewing an anthology of Southern plays in 1925, Montgomery Gregory singled out for praise *The Last of the Lowries* by the white playwright Paul Green. After noting the failure of the volume's editor to list Green's work as "a Negro play," Gregory stated: "It should be so classified."[89] In *Plays of Negro Life* (1927), Locke wrote optimistically of the development of a "national Negro Theatre," but cautioned: "Vital as the Negro actor and dramatist are to this development, theirs is and can be no monopoly of the field." He added: "White actors have been very successful in some Negro parts. . . . And a play like *Judge Lynch* [by the white playwright John W. Rogers Jr.] . . . with entirely white characters, may yet be so much a play of the peculiar situations of race, as to be indisputably a drama of Negro theme and motive."[90]

Montgomery Gregory wrote in 1927: "With the possible exception of Eugene O'Neill," Paul Green has given us "the finest contribution of Negro plays yet written." And Sterling A. Brown opened his review essay "Concerning Negro Drama" by lauding a 1930 play written by a white author as a "Negro dramatic success." In his essay "Negro Character as Seen by White Authors," Brown presented the "manifest truth" that "the sincere, sensitive artist, willing to go beneath the clichés of popular belief to get at an underlying reality, will be wary of confining a race's entire character to a half-dozen narrow grooves. He will hardly have the temerity to say that his necessarily limited observations of a few Negroes in a restricted environment can be taken as the last word about some mythical *the* Negro. He will hesitate to do this, even though he had a Negro mammy, or spent a night in Harlem, or has been a Negro all his life."[91] And, finally, the argument was put most directly by Locke in 1936, when he boldly stated: "Beyond a certain point the race of the painter or sculptor is not the significant thing. In the last analysis it is the adequacy of the interpretation that counts."[92] Each of these critics sought to promote Black writers and actors; none thought that literature or fine arts created by whites could ever completely capture the Black experience. But believing that race was more a social product than not, they each maintained that white artists could—with the right knowledge and sympathy—contribute to the promotion and creation of Black culture.

These responses are striking, but they are also rare. Their novelty highlights the degree to which period audiences continued to see biology as the ultimate backstop for racial identity. It is no surprise that white and Black conservatives would have held to a racial litmus test for the production of "white" and "Black" art. The reviewers troubled by Motley's mixing of subjects and styles that were academic (i.e., "white") and primitive (i.e., "Black"), or those convinced that his African paintings were informed by his blood, are more expected than those claiming that white artists could contribute to Black culture. Rather than categorizing as "Black" those paintings, plays, films, and novels that sensitively depicted the complexity of Black identities, experience, and culture—regardless of the racial identification of their creators—the vast majority of progressives effectively used the "one-drop rule" as a gatekeeper for determining who was eligible to create Black art. While racial identity was no guarantee of one's capacity to produce art that captured the Black experience, it remained, for most, the minimum requirement for creating art deemed "Black."

: : :

Locke described Motley's third theme as the "genre side of modern Negro life" and listed the following paintings as examples: *Stomp* (1927, plate 19), *Blues* (1929, plate 20), *The Plotters* (1933), *The Barbecue* (ca. 1934), *The Liar* (1936), and *Chicken Shack* (1936). A selection of additional canvases that may be included are *Black Belt* (1934, plate 21), *Picnic* (1934), *Saturday Night* (1935), and *Street Scene* (1936).[93] The paintings show Black Americans at leisure in the dance halls, bars, parks, and streets of a largely segregated Chicago. The depicted characters dance, eat, drink, stroll, watch, and, above all, socialize in bustling interior spaces and streetscapes that are typically rendered with a flat painting style, skewed perspective, and vibrant colors. The paintings were widely praised by both white and Black critics. White viewers claimed: "Motley seems to be entitled to first place in art as representative of his people"; noted that his modern genre scenes have "originality, strength, and vigor"; and commended him for "remarkable interpretations of his race."[94] Black critics were equally effusive, though they placed more emphasis on his racial contributions. Locke credited Motley with helping to build a new "racial school of art," Porter lauded works infused with "racial expression," and Brawley celebrated his "racial subjects" and deemed his art "outstanding among the modernists."[95]

The division that Locke described between Motley's scenes of African religious life and his canvases of contemporary Black leisure was less visible to white observers. White racial preconceptions effaced the distinctions between Motley's individual artworks and the thematic strands Black viewers identified in his oeuvre. Recall the previously cited quotation from Jewell, claiming that "the same fundamental rhythms are found, whether the setting be a jungle presided over by witchcraft or a cabaret rocking to the syncopation of jazz," and from Williams, stating that all of Motley's paintings of Black Chicago life "were swept by the primitive moods that seemed born of the tropical jungles." In his review of Motley's New Gallery exhibition, the art critic for *Time* magazine continued the theme of Black primitivism while reversing the direction of influence that Jewell and Williams described. According to *Time*'s reviewer, in creating his African paintings, "painter Motley has seen the crowd of anxious dark faces at a fortune teller's door, waiting to be told what numbers to bet on in a gambling game. He paints the same crowd, their black skins grey in the light of a jungle moon, capering through the mad tendrils of a mango grove."[96] Instead of seeing "primitive" Africans setting the parameters for contemporary Black behavior, he imagines modern Black urbanites modeling ancient tribal life. Through critics' focus on the "fundamental rhythms," "primitive moods," or present-day superstitions shared by Africans and African Americans, the specificity of the canvases was sacrificed to confirm the essential continuity of Black life across time, culture, and geography.

Just as the white reception of Motley's African paintings was guided by the critics' internalized stereotypes of Blackness, so was their understanding of his genre scenes. One critic claimed that "the gayety and childlike quality characteristic of the negro is evidenced in the figure compositions which are taken from contemporary life—street scenes, picnics and dance halls," while a second observed that the paintings captured "the child-like abandon of his people" in scenes "imbued with the negro's natural love of bright colors."[97] And a collection of critics described that Black peoples' "eloquent feeling for rhythm," "fine sense of rhythm," "free expression of . . . rhythm," or "rhythmic presentation of Negro life" found ready expression in Motley's modern genre scenes.[98] Wedded as they were to long-standing stereotypes of Black people belonging to a childlike race, drawn to bright colors, and naturally instilled with rhythm, gaiety, and a lack of inhibition, the responses to the paintings obviously preceded looking.

It is worth quoting Locke's description of Motley's third theme at length, as his detailed description of the painter's scenes of contemporary Black life aids in illuminating the more complex reactions of Black audiences. Locke described the modern genre paintings as created in

> a broad, higher-keyed and somewhat lurid color scheme, with an emphasis on the grotesque and genre side of modern Negro life. [Since 1930, Motley] seems more and more fascinated by the grotesqueries and oddities of Negro life, which he sometimes satirically, sometimes sympathetically, depicts. His style, once curiously restrained [in his early portraits], is now highly imaginative, free in rhythm, riotous in color, a combination of Dutch realism with American humor and tempo. . . . Very little of the humor and swashbuckler of Negro life has found its way into Negro art work . . . so Motley's Rabelaisian turn is a promising departure.[99]

After referencing both humor and satire, Locke linked Motley to the French Renaissance writer François Rabelais, an author famous for his biting, satirical novels that critiqued the morality of his day. Both Black and white reviewers remarked on the humor of Motley's genre paintings, though the references are more numerous among white writers. Whites saw "telling pictures of crowded cabarets and social clubs dedicated to hilarious moments," praised Motley for being an artist who "tells a good story and is not afraid of humor," and noted that "sometimes his pictures struck a hilarious note."[100] Locke's quoted passage is typical of period references to humor in Motley's paintings in its vague declaration that the artworks exhibit "American humor," without an accompanying explanation of the source. Absent specificity in the references to humor, it remains possible to talk broadly about differences between how Black and white audiences were amused by the paintings.

Given that Black critics, including many progressive intellectuals and academics, consistently praised Motley's genre scenes, did not comment on their stereotyping, saw them presenting naturalistic pictures of Black life, and described the depictions as "modern" scenes that broke from convention, the humor they perceived was surely unrelated to the stereotypical tropes through which Black characters in American art and literature traditionally generated laughter.[101] Black progressives such as Locke would not have found the paintings funny if the humor simply replicated those familiar stereotypes that they reviled. And considering the abundant evidence that white reviewers filtered the paintings through then-dominant stereotypes ascribed to Black people, it is more likely than not that they laughed at internalized stereotypes that they brought with them to the paintings. Up through the early decades of the twentieth century, images of Black characters in fine arts were sufficiently rare, and the white expectation of Black figures in fine arts and popular culture being comical was sufficiently strong, that the mere sight of a Black figure in a painting cued white audiences to smile expectantly. Recall the critics who saw humor in Brown's *A Card Trick* and Homer's *A Visit from the Old Mistress* and consider that the associations of Black characters with comedy were so pervasive that a white critic, evaluating Motley's dignified *Portrait of the Artist's Father* (plate 14), claimed: "Its finer qualities are the sincerity and sympathy of the characterization, and its sensitive humor."[102]

Locke's reference to the grotesque in Motley's art was unique to him and was the closest that an interwar critic came to labeling the paintings stereotyped. During this era, a number of Black intellectuals explicitly linked comical and grotesque depictions to Black stereotypes. In Montgomery Gregory's essay "The Drama of Negro Life," which Locke published in *The New Negro*, the author traced what he saw as the pernicious influence of Harriet Beecher Stowe's comic character Topsy from *Uncle Tom's Cabin*. Gregory argued that while the novel faded from consciousness, "'Topsy' survived" and provided us with "fearful progeny." He stated: "The earliest expression of Topsy's baneful influence is to be found in the minstrels made famous by the Callenders, Lew Dockstader, and Primrose and West. These comedians, made up into grotesque caricatures of the Negro race, fixed in the public taste a dramatic stereotype of the race that has been almost fatal to a sincere and authentic Negro drama."[103] Elise Johnson McDougald's "The Task of Negro Womanhood," which was also published in *The New Negro*, explored the limiting picture of Black womanhood constructed by the fine arts in American culture. Black women, McDougald explained, understood "that the ideals of beauty, built up in the fine arts, have excluded her almost entirely. Instead, the grotesque Aunt Jemimas of the street-car advertisements, proclaim only an ability to serve, without grace of loveliness." In *The Negro in American Fiction*, Sterling A. Brown applied "grotesque" to Black characters who had been distorted beyond recognition by white writers. In reference to Erskine Caldwell's short story "Blue Boy," which appeared in *Kneel to the Rising Sun* (1935), he wrote: "'Blue Boy' is the ugly anecdote of a Negro idiot whose grotesque tricks entertain a group of satiated 'high class ladies and gentlemen.'"[104]

Elsewhere in *Negro Art: Past and Present* Locke unambiguously deploys "grotesque" in the sense advanced by Gregory, McDougald, and Brown. When discussing representations of Black figures in American visual culture, he claimed that colonial representations hewed to naturalism and that depictions of Black characters became "grotesque" only with the "Negro's lapse into chattel slavery and plantation bondage." According to Locke, naturalistic depictions became rare by the nineteenth century, largely replaced by images that illustrated Black figures "in the background corner as a clownish, grotesque object setting off the glory of his master or as the comic subject of his amused condescension. The 'old faithful uncle,'—later Uncle Tom, Uncle Ned and Uncle Remus, the broad expansive 'mammy' from Aunt Chloe to Aunt Jemima, the jigging plantation hands in tattered jeans and the sprawling pickaninnies all became typical stereotypes." But this use of grotesque is balanced in Locke's writing by its attachment to positive attributes and valued representations.[105]

In *Negro Art: Past and Present*, Locke wrote approvingly of the African portraits created by the German artists Julius Hüther, Walter von Ruckteschell, and Georg Kolbe, each of whom, he believed, captured the "race soul" of Africans. "Whatever else may be said of the German colonial record," Locke argued, "it must in all fairness be admitted that their literary and artistic approach to the African has been thorough, sympathetic and understanding." Locke saw in the artists' work a "revealing interpretation of the deepest human values; it is there in the mellow, sleepy but mystic eyes, the sensuous but genial lips, the grotesque mask-like simplicity of countenance, the velvety tones and textures of the African skin, the strength, vitality and structural beauty of body, so common to African types, despite their otherwise great diversity." He also deployed the positive associations of "grotesque" when he used the word to describe African art he admired. In his analysis of the sculpture of Guinea, for example, he explained that the works are valued for their ability to "say much with little" and as a "primitive anticipation of Cubism." And he concluded: "Grotesque and generally to larger scale than most African sculpture, it is striking in its bold simplicity and crudity,—a crudity, however, associated with technical skill. . . . No art ever reduced art expression to barer or more basic essentials."[106] In both of these examples, Locke uses "grotesque" to refer to forms that are made strange and unexpected through their radical simplification. According to *Webster's International Dictionary of the English Language* (1907), *grotesque* did not have either exclusively positive or negative associations. It was then defined as "'wildly or strangely formed'; whimsical; extravagant; or irregular forms and proportions; fantastic; ludicrous; antic."[107] Given Locke's use of *grotesque* as a descriptor for art that he both disparaged and admired, and his determination that Motley's genre paintings of modern Black life offered "a promising departure," it seems evident that he used the word to highlight the break of Motley's paintings from period conventions for depicting Black life. What he took as the fantastical qualities of the paintings separated them—for the better—from the standard representations of Black characters.

Writing in the *Negro History Bulletin* in 1939, a reviewer highlighted an aspect of Motley's genre paintings that went unnoticed by white periodicals. He observed: "All of Motley's paintings did not deal with the people highest up in life. He understood the lowly and tried to portray them in such paintings as 'Stomp,' 'Black and Tan Cabaret,' 'Barbecue in a Garden,' 'Carnival,' and 'Parade.'"[108] Whereas white critics saw in Motley's paintings generic depictions of "Black life," the *Negro History Bulletin* made finer distinctions, understanding that they often featured working-class people. As late as 1936, Locke expressed disappointment that despite their expression of "reformist and proletarian" sympathies, most Black artists remained hesitant to create artwork that grappled with "the street level of the masses and the contemporary social scene."[109] Not only had Motley taken up this subject, but he rendered it in a manner that was unique in American art. White racial expectations in the 1920s and 1930s constricted the range of professions and behaviors deemed acceptable for Black men and women, as well as the nature of their representations in art. In normative depictions, Black characters were entertainers or athletes, living in poverty or suffering oppression and, most commonly, engaged in manual labor. Motley's genre paintings illustrated segregated spaces where Black Americans were not on display for white audiences, but were simply enjoying life; and in contrast to virtually all of the depictions of working-class Black characters created by whites in early twentieth-century America—including in fine art, literature, and advertising—Motley's paintings gave the men and women of his canvases a life beyond labor, beyond poverty, and beyond oppression. The lively scenes were pointed departures from Henry O. Tanner's *The Banjo Lesson* (1893, plate 22), with its evident signs of poverty and portrayal of Black figures as entertainers; George Bellows's *Both Members of This Club* (1909, plate 23), with its anonymous Black boxer defined by the spectacle of his physical struggle against a white combatant for the entertainment of whites; and Thomas Hart Benton's *Weighing Cotton* (1939, plate 24), in which faceless Black laborers toil in endless fields and assume the shape and size of the commodity-filled sacks they stuff and lug.[110] Motley's art was "grotesque" in the sense that it was wildly out of sync with conventional portrayals. Locke argued that "art has to pioneer in the discovery of new interests and new beauty." For many Black observers of the era, that is precisely what Motley's scenes of everyday life accomplished.

During the interwar period, Motley enjoyed a rare position for a Black artist, as both his professional accomplishments and art appealed to a diverse range of viewers. White critics, museum visitors, and art patrons valued his paintings of tribal life and urban Black leisure, which lent themselves to confirming a host of traits deemed innate to Black people. Many whites saw in the paintings the comforting signs of Black primitivism, rhythm, gaiety, and a lack of inhibition that had featured in the art and literature of the nineteenth century and continued up through the interwar period. At the same time, Motley's portraits—which ranged stylistically from academic to slightly advanced—were experienced as progressive depictions that gently pushed whites to view Black sitters as more complex individuals. Conservative Black viewers celebrated the artist's obvious mastery of academic painting techniques, as well as the awards bestowed on him by the Art Institute of Chicago, Harmon Foundation, and Guggenheim Foundation, and his sales to prominent white collectors. They joined with progressive Black audiences in their appreciation for Black subjects that they understood as breaking from common stereotypes. Nowhere in Motley's modern genre scenes were poor, laboring, or oppressed people. During the 1920s, more progressive Black critics found appeal in Motley's almost exclusive focus on Black life and supposed African aesthetic, which combined to constitute a "racial art." With the rise of socialism and communism among Black progressives in the 1930s, the same paintings were even more prized for their respectful attention to working-class subjects.[111]

In the later decades of Motley's life, he was occasionally confronted by Black critics and artists troubled by what they interpreted as stereotypes in his art. To an interviewer in 1972, Motley recalled: "I know that there are many of the Negro artists [who] have criticized me. It's come to me through various channels. . . . They say that I have made fun of the Negro, and all that. I think it's stupid." In the same interview, Motley recounted that the journalist Harry Henderson "was the first man that I ever talked to who ever told me right to my face that I was criticized." Henderson spoke with the artist in the 1960s while researching the coauthored book he eventually published with Romare Bearden, *A History of African-American Artists, from 1792 to the Present* (1992). With regard to his Black critics, Motley recalled telling Henderson that he "had no idea what they're talking about." In 1980, the art historian and artist David Driskell made his final visit to Motley's studio, just four months before the artist's death in January 1981. He met with him in his capacity as curator of the Camille O. and William H. Cosby Jr. Collection, with an eye toward acquiring additional paintings for the collection. Driskell reported that "he found Motley reluctant to engage in a conversation about race or the so-called 'exaggeration of black physiognomy' so often attributed to him in some of the earlier paintings." Driskell interpreted Motley's disinclination to engage as a sign that the painter "did not wish to be reminded of the failure so often associated with being black in America."[112]

Such exchanges invariably proved frustrating and confusing to a painter who had dedicated his life's work to representing Black subjects "honestly and sincerely." What neither Motley nor his critics appreciated were the ways in which changes in America's racial context transformed some of his nonstereotyped portrayals from the first half of the century into stereotyped ones in the century's second half. Taking Motley to task for painting stereotypes during the interwar period is akin to criticizing him for referring to people of his race as "Negro" in 1920, rather than as "African-American," "African American," "black," or "Black." In other words, it is to judge him by a standard that did not then exist. In the decades during which he created his most famous paintings, they were honest and sincere depictions because period audiences consistently took them as such; it was not the artist, but an altered racial context, that produced stereotypes.

ENGAGING WITH OUR PAST

Inventing Stereotype has multiple aims: excavating the intellectual genealogy of the concept of stereotype; explaining the distance between the concept and its subsequent deployment by scholars and members of the general public; recuperating the racial complexity of a selection of plays and paintings from the 1920s and 1930s; demonstrating the transitory nature of stereotypes, which emerge and dissolve with changing social contexts and distinct audiences; exposing how stereotypes exist relative to representational norms and without regard for their capacity to capture the authentic attributes of an individual or group; and, finally, illuminating what debates over stereotypes can and cannot reveal about America's art and racial values.

Inventing Stereotype argues that racial stereotypes become visible *as* stereotypes when a viewer's racial picture conflicts with the one apparent to them in representations. Neither the values of the individual viewer nor those embedded within works of art or literature are static.

Individual viewers undergo changes in perspective over time, and the values apparent in representations shift because their meanings are derived from their locations within the broader visual and literary fields. As representational norms shift, and the canon of art and literature shifts, so too does the racial meaning of individual works. Even at a moment in time, there exists no singular "meaning" for a work, because its audience is composed of people divided into innumerable ideological camps, each with distinct perspectives. All of this explains why works of art and literature can be both stereotyped and nonstereotyped at the same moment in time, and why they can move from stereotyped to nonstereotyped (and vice versa) over time.

Unseen stereotypes are also a function of a work's relation to other works of literature and art and to viewers' racial values. Stereotypes may go unseen because a given play or painting appears less wedded to stereotypical depictions than the majority of period representations; the work may, for instance, illustrate a diverse array of complicated characters who respond to psychological and social forces in ways that appear less formulaic than in dominant representations. They may also go unseen because the work is credited with performing other, important racial work that inoculates it against stereotypes. Or it may be because the work gives welcome attention to disempowered groups or shows them treated equitably by members of the dominant group. While it is also possible that stereotypes are unseen because viewers have internalized them—and, hence, naturalized them as real—one should question how a stereotype may be said to exist within a society when there is no contemporaneous evidence of it having been apprehended. Given that there is no representational art without stereotypes, what separates "stereotyped" from "nonstereotyped" artworks is a viewer's detection of stereotypes at particular moments in time.

Scholars of literature and the fine arts often link specific artistic styles to "progressive" or "reactionary" ideological positions. Most commonly, they associate radical styles with progressive politics and conservative styles with reactionary views. The impulse is evident in these pages in my discussion of Mount's and Snyder's genre paintings—specifically, my reference to their retrograde styles being associated with canvases that sought to validate and preserve the status quo. The complexity of viewer reactions to the plays and paintings discussed in *Inventing Stereotype* consistently refutes the idea of style (or subject) having any consistent or obvious link to particular ideologies. Both O'Neill and Motley were celebrated for their distinctive approaches to realism, but that did not prevent viewers from seeing in their plays and paintings support for a breathtaking range of political positions. For differing reasons, Motley's modern genre scenes looked naturalistic to both white and Black audiences during the interwar years. For white conservatives the paintings' naturalism was rooted in their confirmation of a host of stereotypes that viewers held about Black Americans, while for Black conservatives and progressives their naturalism was based on the artworks' refutation of those same stereotypes. This observation dovetails with another insight that emerges in this book—that the perception of stereotypes is not evidence of a viewer's progressive politics, just as failure to see stereotypes is not evidence of a conservative position. Recall that *All God's Chillun Got Wings* contained stereotypes for conservatives but was nonstereotyped for progressives, and that *Abie's Irish Rose* looked stereotyped to progressives but nonstereotyped to conservatives. One's detection of stereotypes says nothing on its face about one's politics or about the ideologies embedded within the artwork under consideration.

Inventing Stereotype's resolute focus on the art and audiences of the interwar period contains important lessons for twenty-first-century readers. The disparate and, often, surprising responses of viewers to artworks in the 1920s and 1930s suggest the perils of critics and historians making pronouncements on the presence or absence of stereotypes in older artworks without a careful study of artworks' period reception. It is one thing to claim that a play or a painting from the 1920s looks stereotyped to audiences today—given our current racial context—and another to overwrite the perspectives of its first audiences by declaring that it contains stereotypes that its initial viewers failed to perceive. When audiences today assert that an artwork originally seen as nonstereotyped is tainted with stereotypical physiognomies, speech, or actions, the past is distorted. Because racial identities, viewer expectations and values, the representational field, and stereotypes themselves alter over time, our modern perspective is of limited utility in recuperating the past.

Artworks judged stereotyped by their original audiences are the least likely artworks to be read, published, performed, or displayed today. Modern corporations, institutions, and individuals are generally wary of perpetuating stereotypes, and wary as well of the controversy that would ensue from championing the value of continuing engagement with such works. There is a similar hesitancy today to circulate artworks that were once seen as free of stereotypes but that modern viewers now judge as stereotyped. The result is that the vast majority of artworks in circulation today are those that offer palatable racial messages but, since the artworks' modern racial meaning is produced by current sensibilities, there is not necessarily a connection between its palatability today and its original significance.

The unspoken norms that restrict which works of art and literature we circulate today play a significant role in distorting our understanding of the past. When we do not engage with works that were judged as stereotyped by their original audiences, we constrict the range of evidence available to analyze the past; when we do not display or stage works that originally appeared nonstereotyped but look stereotyped today, we substitute our ways of seeing for those of the works' original audiences; and in ensuring that the majority of works circulating today do not obviously conflict with current racial politics, we tamp down the ideological distinctions between past and present. Each of these processes flattens the past and ahistorically heightens its similarities to the present. And the damage goes beyond impairing our understanding of race. In light of the importance that progressive twenty-first-century Americans place on getting their racial politics correct, and because cultural products do not confine themselves to expressions of a single theme, the exclusion of works of literature and art from the canon for any single criterion negatively impacts our understanding of a host of related and unrelated issues. To speak only of identity, our approach to race hinders our ability to fully analyze class, gender, religion, sexual orientation, and so on, since facets of each are left behind when we limit the cultural artifacts that are permitted to speak of the past. While the impetus to censor stems from the laudable aim of not perpetuating racist ideologies in the present, it is difficult to imagine how we can come to terms with our past when we ignore those works of literature and art that complicate our present.

Acknowledgments

I thought about racial stereotypes long before I learned the term. German stereotypes of Jews haunted my childhood, and, later, US stereotypes of Black Americans catalyzed my scholarly work. While my thinking and teaching have circled around the issue for years, it was only a decade ago that I began to sketch out the contours of *Inventing Stereotype*—a project that aimed to address stereotypes head-on. I am gratified to complete this book and to acknowledge the people and institutions who aided me along the way.

At the University of California, Santa Cruz, which was my academic home for nearly fourteen years, I benefited from the consistent financial support of the Arts Research Institute and Arts Dean's Fund. Former Dean David Yager invigorated the Arts Division at Santa Cruz and was a steadfast supporter of my work. Smart, dedicated, and warmhearted graduate and undergraduate research assistance provided crucial support during preliminary stages of my research. I thank Lorraine Affourtit, Jordan Reznick, and Lauren Tomicich for their diligent work and comradery.

In 2015–16, I had the good fortune to devote significant time to the project as the Archie K. Davis Fellow at the National Humanities Center. The center boasts enviable facilities, dedicated staff, and phenomenal library support. My thanks to center staff Brooke Andrade, Karen Carroll, Sarah Harris, Cassie Mansfield, Robert Newman, and Sam Schuth. The academic colleagues in my cohort of fellows formed a wonderful cadre of engaged and supportive interlocutors. I enjoyed daily lunches and spirited conversations with all of the fellows, but am particularly grateful to have met Mick O'Malley, Jan Radway, and Jack Sasson.

An early draft of chapter 1 benefited from feedback from the Art History Intermezzo Group at Duke University and the Social Science Research Seminar at Wake Forest University. Conversations about my project with Chris Castiglia, Susan Fellows, Chris Reed, and Daniel Sherman sharpened my arguments. The press's two anonymous readers approached the manuscript from distinct epistemological perspectives. They each offered generously detailed and thoughtful critiques of my project. I hope that both see the published book improved for their feedback. David Barquist identified and dated decorative arts, and Amy Mooney responded to many questions on Archibald Motley Jr. I am grateful to both for their responsiveness.

At the University of Chicago Press, I value the support and encouragement of Executive Editor Karen Levine, who showed enthusiasm for this project from the start. Karen is a thoughtful, warm, and detail-oriented editor whom I cannot thank enough. At the press, I also benefited from the efficient work of senior editorial associate Victoria Barry, who expertly shepherded the book into production, and from the aid of my production editor, Lindsy Rice, and promotions manager, Adrienne Meyers. My copyeditor, Marian Rogers, skillfully edited the manuscript, catching discomfiting typos and sharpening my prose. Josephine Yanasak-Leszczynski secured images and reproduction rights; I am thankful to her for her skillful work.

At the School of the Art Institute of Chicago, a semester-long sabbatical in fall 2023 allowed me to bring the book to completion. My thanks to President Emerita Elissa Tenny for encouraging me to take the time away. My executive assistant, Emilie Yardley-Hodges, provided all manner of high-energy morale and logistical support. I am thankful to our Dean of the Library and Special Collections, Melanie Emerson, for aiding me in sourcing images and connecting me to her colleagues at the University of Illinois at Chicago libraries. Dean of Libraries and University Librarian, Rhea Ballard-Thrower, at the University of Illinois at Chicago graciously provided me with an office in the Richard J. Daley Library during my sabbatical, and Associate University Librarian for Administrative Services, Linda Naru, helped acclimate me to the campus and its scholarly resources. The available office, collections, and databases were invaluable.

I am grateful for the staff aid, collections, and electronic resources I accessed at the following additional libraries, archives, and special collections: Ryerson Library at the Art Institute of Chicago; Flaxman Library at the School of the Art Institute of Chicago; Abakanowicz Research Center at the Chicago Historical Society; Manuscript Reading Room and Newspaper and Current Periodical Reading Room at the Library of Congress; Special Collections at the Northern Illinois University Founders Memorial Library; McCormick Library of Special Collections and University Archives at Northwestern University; Main Library of the San Francisco Public Library; and Sterling Memorial Library Manuscripts and Archives and Beinecke Rare Book & Manuscript Library at Yale University. In addition, I benefited from the rich collections of the New York Public Library, primarily the Schomburg Center for Research in Black Culture; Performing Arts Research Collections— Billy Rose Theatre Division; and Archives and Manuscripts Division.

Finally, I thank Vicky Gwiasda. While she is not an academic administrator, she lived the pandemic, racial reckoning, and war in Gaza with me. Absent her steadfast support, I could not have managed those years.

Notes

INTRODUCTION

1. Guy C. McElroy, *Facing History: The Black Image in American Art, 1710–1940* (San Francisco: Bedford Arts Publishers, 1990), 95; H. Barbara Weinberg and Carrie Rebora, eds., *American Stories: Paintings of Everyday Life, 1765–1915* (New Haven: Yale University Press, 2009), 144. While the dating of *A Card Trick* is uncertain, with the year estimated by art historians ranging from 1880 to 1892, the leading scholar of Brown's art dates the work to ca. 1891–92. See Martha Hoppin, *The World of J. G. Brown* (Chesterfield, MA: Chameleon Books, 2010), 198.

2. *Art and Artists of All Nations: Over Four Hundred Photographic Reproductions of Great Paintings* (New York: Arkell Weekly Company, 1894), 12; *Famous Paintings of the World: A Collection of Photographic Reproductions of Great Modern Masterpieces* (New Haven: Butler & Alger, 1897), 24.

3. "Japheth" was a son of Noah whom many nineteenth-century Christians believed to be the father of the white race. For discussions of this narrative in the US context, see Thomas Virgil Peterson, *Ham and Japheth: The Mythic World of Whites in the Antebellum South* (Metuchen, NJ: Scarecrow Press, 1978); Stephen

R. Haynes, *Noah's Curse: The Biblical Justification of American Slavery* (New York: Oxford University Press, 2002), 89, 99–103.

4. For a comprehensive biography of Locke, see Jeffrey C. Stewart, *The New Negro: The Life of Alain Locke* (New York: Oxford University Press, 2018). For the philosopher's contributions to racial theory, see Alain Locke, *Race Contacts and Interracial Relations: Lectures on the Theory and Practice of Race*, ed. Jeffrey C. Stewart (Washington, DC: Howard University Press, 1992). For his complex relationship to the visual arts, see Kobena Mercer, *Alain Locke and the Visual Arts* (New Haven: Yale University Press, 2022).

5. Alain Locke, *Negro Art: Past and Present* (Washington, DC: Associates in Negro Folk Education, 1936), 45–48; Locke, *The Negro in Art: A Pictorial Record of the Negro Artist and of the Negro Theme in Art* (Washington, DC: Associates in Negro Folk Education, 1940), 140.

6. Rebecca Zurier, Robert W. Snyder, and Virginia McCord Mecklenburg, *Metropolitan Lives: The Ashcan Artists and Their New York* (New York: W. W. Norton, 1995), 125, 129; Marianne Doezema, *George Bellows and Urban America* (New Haven: Yale University Press, 1992), 154. See also Dora Apel, *Imagery of Lynching: Black Men, White Women, and the Mob* (New Brunswick: Rutgers University Press, 2004), 86–88.

CHAPTER 1

1. For the five-part series, see Walter Lippmann, "Barriers to Information: Toward a Critique of Public Opinion," *Century Magazine* 103, no. 1 (1921): 121–31; Lippmann, "The Habits of Our Eyes: Toward a Critique of Public Opinion," *Century Magazine* 103, no. 2 (1921): 243–52; Lippmann, "The Making of a Common Will: Toward a Critique of Public Opinion," *Century Magazine* 103, no. 3 (1922): 441–50; Lippmann, "The Nature of News: Toward a Critique of Public Opinion," *Century Magazine* 103, no. 4 (1922): 603–12; Lippmann, "Intelligence: Toward a Critique of Public Opinion," *Century Magazine* 103, no. 5 (1922): 739–47. His first reference to "stereotype" appeared in "The Habits of Our Eyes" in December 1921. The professor of psychology Leonard S. Newman argues that Lippmann did not invent the modern concept of stereotype but simply broadened it. Newman notes that the original use of *stereotype*, to describe a printing technique, had evolved by 1850 to stand for "anything constantly repeated without change." As I will discuss in some detail, this differs in significant ways from Lippmann's formulation. In addition, whether or not Lippmann may be said to have invented the concept, there is no doubt that it was Lippmann's writings that sparked an explosion of interest in stereotype and that his texts set the parameters for the discussions in academic and popular

circles. Leonard S. Newman, "Was Walter Lippmann Interested in Stereotyping? *Public Opinion* and Cognitive Social Psychology," *History of Psychology* 12, no. 1 (2009): 7–18.

2. *Webster's Revised Unabridged Dictionary* (Springfield, MA: G. & C. Merriam, 1913), 1412.

3. Lippmann, *Public Opinion*, 13. The contemporary psychologist Leonard Newman has pointed out that "what Lippmann called a stereotype was what a contemporary psychologist would recognize as the broader concept of a 'schema.'" Newman, "Was Walter Lippmann Interested in Stereotyping?," 12. Newman explains that psychologists today define stereotype as an example of a schema that applies specifically to social, ethnic, racial, and national groups. In other words, while Lippmann imagined a broad definition for his stereotype concept, its focus today is on the narrower classification of human groups. The Swiss child psychologist Jean Piaget was the first to describe a schema in this modern sense in 1923; it was subsequently developed by the British psychologist Frederic Bartlett in 1932. Given that both publications fall after *Public Opinion*, I am not concerned to parse the stereotype/schema distinctions and will continue to use Lippmann's formulation. My attention is not to the actual operation of the mental processes but to Lippmann's influential formulation of it, and with the ways in which subsequent audiences in the 1920s and 1930s interpreted and applied his concept. See Jean Piaget, *Le language et la pensée chez l'enfant* (Paris: Delachaux & Niestlé, 1923); Frederic Charles Bartlett, *Remembering: A Study in Experimental and Social Psychology* (Cambridge: Cambridge University Press, 1932).

4. Lippmann, *Public Opinion*, 104.

5. *Webster's Revised Unabridged Dictionary*, 218, 1558.

6. Ibid., 1558.

7. Lippmann, *Public Opinion*, 89.

8. Lippmann, *Public Opinion*, 162; Ronald Steel, *Walter Lippmann and the American Century* (Boston: Little, Brown, 1980), 27–28.

9. The idea of the modern stereotype was first alluded to in print in Graham Wallas, *Our Social Heritage* (New Haven: Yale University Press, 1921), 78–80, though Wallas's ideas first took form in 1899 notes for his "A Prolegomenon to Politics." See Martin J. Wiener, *Between Two Worlds: The Political Thought of Graham Wallas* (Oxford: Clarendon Press, 1971), 76; H. G. Wells, *Experiment in Autobiography: Discoveries and Conclusions of a Very Ordinary Brain (Since 1886)* (New York: Macmillan, 1934), 511.

10. Wallas, *Our Social Heritage*, 78. Lippmann's epigraph for *Public Opinion* excerpts a passage from *The Republic of Plato*, trans. Benjamin Jowett (Oxford: Clarendon Press, 1888), 214, which describes the chained prisoners trapped in a cave. Lippmann, *Public Opinion*, vii.

11. Ibid., 78–80. While Wallas is credited extensively in *Public Opinion* for his insights, Lippmann makes no mention of his description of a proto-stereotype concept. It seems of note that in a passage by Freud referenced in Lippmann's text, the psychoanalyst links dreams to painting. See Lippmann, *Public Opinion*, 156; Sigmund Freud, *The Interpretation of Dreams*, trans. Dr. A. A. Brill (New York: The Modern Library, 1994), 291–92.

12. Sinclair Lewis, *Main Street: The Story of Carol Kennicott* (New York: Harcourt, Brace and Howe, 1920).

13. Lippmann, *Public Opinion*, 13–14; Lippmann's linkage of stereotypes to pictures and art was widely embraced, though it did have detractors. For a prominent critic, see Francis G. Wilson, "Concepts of Public Opinion," *American Political Science Review* 27, no. 3 (1933): 378.

14. For the description of Clemenceau's mental picture, see Lippmann, *Public Opinion*, 82; for Lippmann's distrust of eyewitness reporting, see 79–80, 82–83.

15. Lippmann, *Public Opinion*, 84, 160.

16. Bernard Berenson, *Three Essays in Method* (Oxford: Oxford University Press, 1927), vii.

17. Lippmann, *Public Opinion*, 83.

18. For Berenson's foundational books on the Renaissance, see Bernard Berenson, *The Venetian Painters of the Renaissance* (New York: G.P. Putnam's Sons, 1894); Berenson, *Venetian Painting* (Privately printed, 1895); Berenson, *The Florentine Painters of the Renaissance* (New York: G.P. Putnam's Sons, 1896); Berenson, *The Central Italian Painters of the Renaissance* (New York: G.P. Putnam's Sons, 1897).

19. John Dewey, "Public Opinion," *New Republic*, May 3, 1922.

20. Steel, *Walter Lippmann and the American Century*, 180.

21. For Lippmann's prior publications, which include four original books and two volumes of previously published essays, see Walter Lippmann, *A Preface to Politics* (New York: Mitchell Kennerley, 1914); Lippmann, *Drift and Mastery* (New York: Mitchell Kennerley, 1914); Lippmann, *Stakes of Diplomacy* (New York: Henry Holt, 1915); Lippmann, *The Political Scene: An Essay on the Victory of 1918* (New York: Henry Holt, 1919); Lippmann, *Liberty and the News* (New York: Harcourt, Brace and Howe, 1920).

22. Gilman explicitly links Lippmann and Berenson, noting how the men's "rejections of a 'Jewish' identity" enhanced the perceived "objectivity" of their work. Sander L. Gilman, *Jewish Self-Hatred: Anti-Semitism and the Hidden Language of the Jews* (Baltimore: Johns Hopkins University Press, 1986), 317–19. Berenson and Lippmann shared several biographical similarities in addition to their efforts to distance themselves from their Jewish heritage. They both

attended Harvard, became disillusioned with Allied uses of propaganda and the crushing terms forced on Germany in the Treaty of Versailles, and sought to develop more systematic methods for the study of their chosen fields. In his youth, Lippmann even imagined that he would become an art historian. Rachel Cohen, *Bernard Berenson: A Life in the Picture Trade*, Jewish Lives (New Haven: Yale University Press, 2013), 196; Meryle Secrest, *Being Bernard Berenson: A Biography* (New York: Holt, Rinehart and Winston, 1979), 300; Eisig Silberschlag, "Berenson as a Critic of Hebrew Literature," *Hebrew Studies* 23 (1982): 145–53. Steel, *Walter Lippmann and the American Century*, 156, 178–79, 186–96, 372–74.

23. Lippmann, *Public Opinion*, 84.

24. Ibid., 80, 81. The phrase "great, blooming, buzzing confusion" as a metaphor for how babies see the world, comes from William James. See William James, *Principles of Psychology* (New York: Henry Holt, 1890), 1:488. Embedded in James's reference to the mental chaos experienced by the child is a racial undercurrent, for James saw the experience of babies and "primitive savages" in identical terms. See James, *Principles of Psychology* (New York: Henry Holt, 1890), 2:299.

25. Lippmann, *Public Opinion*, 84–85. Note that the ellipsis is present in Lippmann's text.

26. Berenson, *The Central Italian Painters of the Renaissance*, 62–66.

27. Ibid., 66–67.

28. Ibid., 9.

29. Lippmann, *Public Opinion*, 104, 95–96.

30. Berenson, *The Central Italian Painters of the Renaissance*, 66–67.

31. Lippmann, *Public Opinion*, 408.

32. Ibid., 84.

33. Ibid., 29.

34. Ibid., 319–20.

35. Susan T. Fiske and Shelley E. Taylor, *Social Cognition*, 2nd ed. (New York: McGraw-Hill, 1991); David L. Hamilton and Jeffrey W. Sherman, "Stereotypes," in *Handbook of Social Cognition*, ed. Robert S. Wyer Jr. and Thomas K. Srull, 2nd ed. (Hillsdale, NJ: Lawrence Erlbaum Associates, 1994), 2:1–68; Susan T. Fiske, "Stereotypes, Prejudice, and Discrimination," in *The Handbook of Social Psychology*, ed. Susan T. Fiske, Daniel T. Gilbert, and Gardner Lindzey, 4th ed. (New York: McGraw-Hill, 1998), 2:357–411; Sander L. Gilman, *Difference and Pathology: Stereotypes of Sexuality, Race, and Madness* (Ithaca, NY: Cornell University Press, 1985).

36. Daniel J. Kevles, *In the Name of Eugenics: Genetics and the Uses of Human Heredity* (New York: Alfred A. Knopf, 1985), 63; Herbert Spencer Jennings, *The Biological Basis of Human Nature* (New York: W.W. Norton, 1930), 228.

37. For more on social Darwinism, see Richard Hofstadter, *Social Darwinism in American Thought* (Boston: Beacon Press, 1992); Robert C. Bannister, *Social Darwinism: Science and Myth in Anglo-American Social Thought* (Philadelphia: Temple University Press, 1979).

38. For a counterexample that illustrates positive eugenics advocated by conservatives, see Kevles, *In the Name of Eugenics*, 85.

39. For an outline of the goals and beliefs of mainstream US eugenics, see Harry H. Laughlin, *Eugenics Record Office Report Number 1* (Cold Spring Harbor, NY: Eugenics Record Office, 1913), 2.

40. For the progressive strain in eugenic thinking during the interwar period, see Michael Freeden, "Eugenics and Progressive Thought: A Study in Ideological Affinity," *Historical Journal* 22, no. 3 (1979): 651; Frank Dikötter, "Race Culture: Recent Perspectives on the History of Eugenics," *American Historical Review* 103, no. 2 (1998): 467; Diane Paul, "Eugenics and the Left," *Journal of the History of Ideas* 45, no. 4 (1984): 567; Kevles, *In the Name of Eugenics*, 21, 87–88.

41. Kevles, *In the Name of Eugenics*, 57–60, 85, 63–64.

42. Joel Williamson, *New People: Miscegenation and Mulattoes in the United States* (New York: The Free Press, 1980), 106, 188–89.

43. Ibid., 92–93.

44. Matthew Frye Jacobson, *Whiteness of a Different Color: European Immigrants and the Alchemy of Race* (Cambridge, MA: Harvard University Press, 1998), 93–96; Glenda Elizabeth Gilmore, *Gender & Jim Crow: Women and the Politics of White Supremacy in North Carolina, 1896–1920*, 2nd ed. (Chapel Hill: University of North Carolina Press, 2019), 71–72. For how class was exploited to divide white from Black Americans in the early twentieth century, see Bryant Simon, *A Fabric of Defeat: The Politics of South Carolina Millhands, 1910–1948* (Chapel Hill: University of North Carolina Press, 1998), 188–218.

45. Williamson, *New People*, 98–108.

46. Ethel Wolfskill Hedlin, "Earnest Cox and Colonization: A White Racist's Response to Black Repatriation, 1923–1966" (PhD diss., Duke University, 1974), 1–13.

47. For more on Cox, see William H. Tucker, *The Funding of Scientific Racism: Wickliffe Draper and the Pioneer Fund* (Urbana: University of Illinois Press, 2002), 11–43; Jonathan Peter Spiro, *Defending the Master Race: Conservation, Eugenics, and the Legacy of Madison Grant* (Burlington: University of Vermont Press, 2008), 245–48, 252–55, 260–65; Hedlin, "Earnest Cox and Colonization," 1–13.

48. Earnest Sevier Cox, *White America* (Richmond, VA: White America Society, 1923), 61, 309.

49. Ibid., 9, 27, 61–62.

50. Ibid., 246.

51. Thomas Jackson Woofter Jr., *The Basis of Racial Adjustment* (Boston: Ginn, 1925), 42; Alexander Harvey Shannon, *The Negro in Washington: A Study in Race Amalgamation* (New York: Walter Neale, 1930), 12.

52. Earnest Sevier Cox, *The South's Part in Mongrelizing the Nation* (Richmond, VA: White America Society, 1926), 16.

53. Edward Byron Reuter, *The Mulatto in the United States* (Boston: The Gorham Press, 1918), 103–4.

54. Lothorp Stoddard, *The Rising Tide of Color: Against White World-Supremacy* (New York: Charles Scribner's Sons, 1922), 301–2.

55. For the distinctive anxieties that white-looking Black Americans spurred in nineteenth-century whites, see Jessie Morgan-Owens, *Girl in Black and White: The Story of Mary Mildred Williams and the Abolition Movement* (New York: W. W. Norton, 2019).

56. Shannon, *The Negro in Washington*, 41, 108, 137–38; Robert Wilson Shufeldt, *America's Greatest Problem: The Negro* (Philadelphia: F.A. Davis, 1915), 139; Louis Fremont Baldwin, *From Negro to Caucasian, or How the Ethiopian Is Changing His Skin* (San Francisco: Pilot, 1929), 25–29, 36; Albert Stowe Leecraft, *The Devil's Inkwell: A Story of Humanity* (Houston: Albert Stowe Leecraft, 1923), 35.

57. Madison Grant, *The Passing of the Great Race* (New York: Charles Scribner's Sons, 1918), 77, 46–47, 73–74, 245; Spiro, *Defending the Master Race*, 245.

58. Charles B. Davenport and Morris Steggerda, *Race Crossing in Jamaica* (Washington, DC: Carnegie Institution of Washington, 1929), 470.

59. Quoted in Spiro, *Defending the Master Race*, 246–47.

60. Cox, *White America*, 320; Shufeldt returned the favor with a positive review of Cox's book. He described it as a book with "a keen appreciation of the meaning and results of race mixing" and noted its debt to his own pioneering work published "many years before." See Robert Wilson Shufeldt, "White America—A Timely Book," *Medico-Legal Journal* 41 (June 1924): 85–87.

61. Robert Wilson Shufeldt, "Hybridization of Our Race with the Negroes in the United States," *Religio-Philosophical Journal* 1, no. 34 (1891): 533.

62. Robert Wilson Shufeldt, *The Negro: A Menace to American Civilization* (Boston: The Gorham Press, 1907), 90–91, 14. For an almost identical argument, see Shufeldt, *America's Greatest Problem*, 111–12; for a brief biography of Shufeldt, see Kalman Lambrecht, "In Memorium: Robert Wilson Shufeldt, 1850–1934," *The Auk: A Quarterly Journal of Ornithology* 52, no. 4 (1935): 359–61; for another argument on how "Black" attributes endured even after miscegenation removed outward, physical signs of Blackness, see William Hannibal Thomas, *The American Negro: What He Was, What He Is, and What He May Become* (New York: Macmillan, 1901), 105–6.

63. Michael Yudell, *Race Unmasked: Biology and Race in the Twentieth Century* (New York: Columbia University Press, 2014), 25. For the distinctions between mainline, reform, and new eugenicists, see Kevles, *In the Name of Eugenics*, 88–89, 164–75, 267–68.

64. Jennings, *The Biological Basis of Human Nature*, 205. For an anthropologist's take on the difficulty scientists have in keeping their prejudices in check, see Melville J. Herskovits, "The Racial Hysteria," *Opportunity* 2, no. 18 (1924): 166.

65. Kevles, *In the Name of Eugenics*, 173–74.

66. Franz Boas, *The Mind of Primitive Man* (New York: Macmillan, 1921), 20–29. The book was first published in 1911 and reprinted in 1921, just prior to the publication of *Public Opinion*.

67. Franz Boas, "The Problem of the American Negro," *Yale Quarterly Review* 10 (January 1921): 384, 392.

68. Boas's address, "Human Faculty as Determined by Race," is quoted in George W. Stocking Jr., ed., *A Franz Boas Reader: The Shaping of American Anthropology, 1883–1911* (Chicago: University of Chicago Press, 1982), 227, 228.

69. George W. Stocking Jr., *Race, Culture, and Evolution: Essays in the History of Anthropology* (New York: The Free Press, 1968), 196.

70. Ibid., 300, 306–7. For the array of factors leading to the dominance of a sociohistorical model of race, see Howard Winant, "Race and Race Theory," *Annual Review of Sociology* 26 (2000): 176–77.

71. Boas, *The Mind of Primitive Man*, 115.

72. Bardin is quoted in Shufeldt, *America's Greatest Problem*, 202. See also James Bardin, "The Psychology Factor in Southern Race Problems," *Popular Science Monthly* 83 (October 1913): 368–74.

73. Spiro, *Defending the Master Race*, 246–47; Madison Grant, *The Passing of the Great Race*, 4th rev. ed. (New York: Charles Scribner's Sons, 1921), 281, 282, 418; as the reference on p. 282 makes clear, Boas is not exclusively used as a foil.

74. Shufeldt, *America's Greatest Problem*, 184.

75. W. E. B. Du Bois, *The Conservation of the Races* (Washington, DC: The American Negro Academy, 1897), 6, 8; Howard Brotz, ed., *African-American Social and Political Thought, 1850–1920* (New Brunswick, NJ: Transaction, 1992), 483–86.

76. David Levering Lewis, *W. E. B. Du Bois: Biography of a Race, 1868–1919* (New York: Henry Holt, 1993), 190.

77. W. E. B. Du Bois, *The Health and Physique of the Negro American: A Social Study Made Under the Direction of Atlanta University by the Eleventh Atlanta Conference* (Atlanta: Atlanta University Press, 1906), 11:110.

78. Herbert Aptheker, ed., *Writings by W. E. B. Du Bois in Periodicals Edited by Others* (Millwood, NY: Kraus-Thomson Organization Limited, 1982), 2:49–50.

79. W. E. B. Du Bois, *Dusk of Dawn: An Essay Toward an Autobiography of a Race Concept* (New York: Harcourt, Brace, 1940), 117. For modern debates on Du Bois's conceptualization of race, see Chike Jeffers, "Du Bois, Appiah, and Outlaw on Racial Identity," in *The Oxford Handbook of Philosophy and Race,* ed. Naomi Zack (New York: Oxford University Press, 2017), 204–13. Alain Locke may be seen as the early twentieth-century theorist who most fully articulated the separation of biology from race, but he did so in a series of lectures in 1915 and 1916 that were not widely known until their eventual publication in 1992. For the lectures, see Alain Locke, *Race Contacts and Interracial Relations: Lectures on the Theory and Practice of Race,* ed. Jeffrey C. Stewart (Washington, DC: Howard University Press, 1992). The philosopher Jacoby Adeshei Carter has explored how Locke's approach to race anticipated many twenty-first-century perspectives. Jacoby Adeshei Carter, "Between Reconstruction and Elimination: Alain Locke's Philosophy of Race," in Zack, *The Oxford Handbook of Philosophy and Race,* 198.

80. Kwame Anthony Appiah, *Lines of Descent: W. E. B. Du Bois and the Emergence of Identity* (Cambridge, MA: Harvard University Press, 2014), 158–60; see also 143–65.

81. Herbert Aptheker, ed., *The Correspondence of W. E. B. Du Bois: Selections, 1877–1934* (Amherst: University of Massachusetts Press, 1973), 1:302; Aptheker, *Writings by W. E. B. Du Bois in Periodicals Edited by Others,* 2:320–21, 163.

82. Aptheker, *The Correspondence of W. E. B. Du Bois,* 1:301.

83. For Du Bois's class-based biases against poor Black Americans, see Lewis, *W. E. B. Du Bois,* 96, 149, 243–44.

84. Herbert Spencer Jennings, "Heredity and Environment," *Scientific Monthly* 19, no. 3 (1924): 236–37.

85. Herbert Spencer Jennings, "Undesirable Aliens: A Biologist's Examination of the Evidence Before Congress," *The Survey,* December 15, 1923, 310.

86. Jennings, "Heredity and Environment," 238.

87. Jennings, *The Biological Basis of Human Nature,* 284, 285, 287.

88. Francis Glaton, *Hereditary Genius: An Inquiry into Its Laws and Consequences* (New York: D. Appleton, 1871), 339–40; H. G. Wells, *The Outline of History: Being a Plain History of Life and Mankind* (New York: Macmillan, 1921), 111; Cox, *White America,* 314. For evidence that even opponents of the 1924 Johnson-Reed Act tended to accept the existence of a racial hierarchy and that their argument was over which ethnic and racial groups should be excluded, see Jacobson, *Whiteness of a Different Color,* 86.

89. Lippmann nonetheless held the typical period prejudices of men of his race and class. He ascribed traits to various racial and ethnic groups that corresponded to dominant stereotypes. He wrote of the "slave morality of the Negro" and chastised Jews for sparking antisemitism with their "bad economic habits" and resistance to discarding those "differences" that made them "other." Lippmann, *Public Opinion*, 148; Steel, *Walter Lippmann and the American Century*, 189.

90. Walter Lippmann, "A Future for the Tests," *New Republic*, November 29, 1922, 10; Lippmann, "The Great Confusion: A Reply to Mr. Terman," *New Republic*, January 3, 1923, 145–46. For more on Lippmann's critique, see Steel, *Walter Lippmann and the American Century*, 207–8.

91. Lippmann, *Public Opinion*, 24, 93.

92. Ibid., 24–25.

93. Walter Lippmann, *An Inquiry into the Principles of the Good Society* (Boston: Little, Brown, 1937), 212, 213, 226, 232, 58–59.

94. Lippmann, *Public Opinion*, 93. Lippmann's interest in how social constructs might impact human biology may also have been supported by Berenson's idiosyncratic interpretation of the power of Renaissance art. When Berenson concluded his discussion of the Renaissance male bodily ideal, he claimed: "After five centuries of constant imitation of a type first presented by Donatello and Masaccio, we [Europeans] have, as a race, come to be more like that type than we ever were before. For there is no more curious truth than the trite statement that nature imitates art." Influenced, no doubt, by the selective application of Darwinian evolutionary theory and turn-of-the-century eugenicists, Berenson imagined that pictorial ideals could exert an influence on human biology. Berenson, *The Central Italian Painters of the Renaissance*, 67.

95. For Wallas's investment in eugenics, see Graham Wallas, *The Great Society: A Psychological Analysis* (New York: Macmillan, 1920), 55–56; Wiener, *Between Two Worlds*, 131, 171.

96. Wallas, *Our Social Heritage*, 14, 17.

97. Ibid., 17–18. For another example of an author cited in *Public Opinion* who believed in the capacity of the social realm to influence biology over time, see Lippmann's reference on p. 107 to John Bagnell Bury, *The Idea of Progress: An Inquiry into Its Origin and Growth* (London: Macmillan, 1924), 167–68.

98. Wallas, *Our Social Heritage*, 16–17.

99. Ibid., 17.

100. Wallas, *The Great Society*, 5.

101. Ibid., 7.

102. Ibid., 62–63.

103. Ibid., 68. For my understanding of Wallas's philosophy, I am indebted to Wiener, *Between Two Worlds*, 98–126.

104. For authors cited in Lippmann's text, beyond Wallas, who advanced a biological understanding of race, see Howard C. Warren, *Human Psychology* (Boston: Houghton Mifflin, 1919), 421; Wells, *The Outline of History*, 66–67, 113. There is suggestive evidence that some readers may have picked up on Lippmann's idea of groups coming to resemble their stereotypes. In *Man and Civilization: An Inquiry into the Bases of Contemporary Life*, 3rd rev. ed. (London: Constable, 1929), 268, after listing a series of groups (racial, religious, and political) that are commonly stereotyped in US society, John Storck claimed: "The resultant general frenzy much often happens which tends to make these groups what they are supposed to be."

CHAPTER 2

1. "Boston Professors Learn What Their Students Don't Know," *Chicago Daily Tribune*, February 4, 1932, 15.

2. Edward L. Bernays, *Crystalizing Public Opinion* (New York: Boni and Liverlight, 1923); Abbott Lawrence Lowell, *Public Opinion in War and Peace* (Cambridge, MA: Harvard University Press, 1923); Mary Parker Follett, *Creative Experience* (New York: Longmans, Green, 1924); Alain Locke, "The New Negro," in *The New Negro: An Interpretation*, ed. Alain Locke (New York: Albert and Charles Boni, 1925), 4; Locke, "The Legacy of the Ancestral Arts," in Locke, *The New Negro*, 267; William Stanley Braithwaite, "The Negro in American Literature," in Locke, *The New Negro*, 29; Montgomery Gregory, "The Drama of Negro Life," in Locke, *The New Negro*, 155; Walter White, "The Paradox of Color," in Locke, *The New Negro*, 363.

3. For a sample of such headlines, see "Feels Shakespeare Revival Will Be Epoch in Theatre: Billie Burke Predicts New Type of Play if Production of Classics Departs from Stereotype," *The [Baltimore] Sun*, November 27, 1922, 4; "Says Actors Fail in Use of 'Make-Up': Princess Matchabelli Declares They Achieve Only Stage Stereotypes," *New York Times*, January 18, 1926, 21; Alexander Will, "Popular Stereotype of Negro Is Wrong Never Did Exist," *Philadelphia Tribune*, March 6, 1926, 15.

4. Harry Dexter Kitson, *Journal of Applied Psychology* 6, no. 3 (1922): 306; Clyde L. King, *Annals of the American Academy of Political and Social Science* 103 (September 1922): 154; "The Springs of Public Opinion," *The Nation and Athenaeum* 31, no. 23 (1922): 734; Robert Park, *Journal of Sociology* 28, no. 2 (1922): 234.

5. "Beverley Nichols, Likable Visitor," *New York Times*, March 17, 1929, BR22; Grace Kingsley, "Director Braves Hazards of Mountain Wilds Making Film with Native Actors," *Los Angeles Times*, December 12, 1926, C27–28; "Laemmle May Picture Life of Bavarian Ruler," *Los Angeles Times*, May 26, 1929, 19.

6. "The Springs of Public Opinion," 734; "Women's Club Notes," *Beatrice [Nebraska] Daily Sun*, December 11, 1927; "Twenty-Three Fantastic and Eerie Stories," *New York Times*, November 23, 1924, 16; Grace Kingsley, "Flashes: It Is a Wham 'Young Blood' Is a Joyous, Tingling Tonic," *Los Angeles Times*, May 4, 1926, A11; "Pet Theories Punctured," *Los Angeles Times*, February 19, 1925, A4.

7. Alexander Will, "Popular Stereotype of Negro Is Wrong Never Did Exist," *Philadelphia Tribune*, March 6, 1926, 15; Florence Guy Seabury, "Stereotypes," in *Our Changing Morality: A Symposium*, ed. Freda Kirchwey (New York: Albert & Charles Boni, 1924), 231; Sterling A. Brown, "A Literary Parallel," *Opportunity* 10, no. 5 (1932): 152–53; George W. Jacobs [George S. Schuyler], "Negro Authors Must Eat," *The Nation*, June 12, 1929, 711.

8. Harry Elmer Barnes, *The Twilight of Christianity* (New York: Vanguard Press, 1929), 375.

9. Lowell, *Public Opinion in War and Peace*, 7, 92. For another period example of an author assuming that stereotypes capture reality, see Anne O'Hare McCormick, "The Mass Offensive of Women," *New York Times*, April 14, 1929, 80.

10. Walter Lippmann, *Public Opinion* (New York: Harcourt, Brace, 1922), 95, 118.

11. Ibid., 132, 361, 358–59, 123.

12. Ibid., 358, 341; for Lippmann's view of Upton Sinclair, see 335–37.

13. Lippmann, *Public Opinion*, 361.

14. For more on Wood, see A. L. Jackson, "The Onlooker: Climbing Up," *Chicago Defender*, November 3, 1923, 24; "The Opportunity Dinner," *Opportunity* 3, no. 30 (1925): 176–77.

15. "Fighting for Utopian Dreams," *New York Times*, October 22, 1922. For an additional newspaper report that notes Wood's expertise in analyzing "the American Negro," see "Noted Lecturer Here for Tonight," *Daily Telegraph*, November 2, 1923, 16.

16. A. L. Jackson, "The Bookshelf: Author Gives Inside Facts on His Novel," *Chicago Defender*, January 13, 1923; see also Clement Wood, "The Problem of James Crow," *Chicago Defender*, January 6, 1923; Wood, "Alabama: A Study in Ultra-Violet," *The Nation*, January 10, 1923, 33–35.

17. "Howard U. Students Hear Novelist Cite Cultural Progress," *Washington Post*, March 16, 1924, ES17. For the extensive Black press coverage of the talk, see Roscoe Simmons, "The Week," *Chicago Defender*, March 22, 1924, A1; "Students Hear Author Tell of 'Race Problem,'" *Chicago Defender*, March 22, 1924, 8;

"Distinguished Author Addresses Howard Students," *Philadelphia Tribune*, March 22, 1924, 9; "Howard U. Students Hear Novelist Cite Cultural Progress," *Pittsburgh Courier*, March 22, 1924, 13; "Noted Author Talks at 135th St. Library," *New York Amsterdam News*, February 21, 1923, 12; "Howard U. College in Midst of Exams," *Evening Star*, March 16, 1924, sec. 1, 26; "Clement Wood at Howard," *The Hill Top*, March 29, 1924, 5, 8.

18. "Noted Author Talks at 135th St. Library," 12.

19. Simmons, "The Week," A1.

20. "Howard U. Students Hear Novelist Cite Cultural Progress," 13; "Students Hear Author Tell of 'Race Problem,'" 8.

21. For a white review critical of the novel's "stereotyped" treatment of Black characters, see John V. A. Weaver, "Assorted Novels," *Bookman* 56, no. 4 (1922): 492; for a Black review that is largely positive, see A. L. Jackson, "The Bookshelf," *Chicago Defender*, November 18, 1922, 14.

22. Charles S. Johnson, "Nigger—A Novel by Clement Wood," *Opportunity* 1, no. 1 (1923): 30; Mary White Ovington, "'Nigger' Book Chat," *Afro-American*, November 24, 1922, 9.

23. Clement Wood, "The Characters of 'Nigger,'" *Opportunity* 1, no. 2 (1923); Jackson, "The Bookshelf: Author Gives Inside Facts on His Novel."

24. "Noted Author Talks at 135th St. Library," 12.

25. Wood, "Alabama," 35.

26. Franz Boas, "The Problem of the American Negro," *Yale Quarterly Review* 10 (January 1921): 394–95. For other white authors who articulated the benefits of interracial contact, see Chicago Commission on Race Relations, *The Negro in Chicago: A Study of Race Relations and a Race Riot* (Chicago: University of Chicago Press, 1922), 645–46; John Louis Hill, *When Black Meets White* (Chicago: The Argyle Publishers, 1922), 143–49. For a scientific examination of stereotypes from the 1920s that sees their diminishment possible through "face-to-face inter-[racial] stimulation," see Stuart A. Rice, "'Stereotypes': A Source of Error in Judging Human Character," *Journal of Personnel Research* 5 (May 1926): 267–76.

27. Vachel Lindsay, "The Negro in Art: How Shall He Be Portrayed?," *The Crisis* 32, no. 1 (1926): 35.

28. Clement Wood, *The Messenger* 5, no. 4 (1923): 674. See also William Pickens, "Arkansas: A Study in Suppression," *Messenger* 5, no. 1 (1923): 565–68.

29. DuBose Heyward, "The Negro in Art: How Shall He Be Portrayed?," *The Crisis* 31, no. 5 (1926): 220; William Lyon Phelps, "The Negro in Art: How Shall He Be Portrayed?," *The Crisis* 31, no. 6 (1926): 280.

30. Clement Wood, "The Problem of James Crow," *Chicago Defender*, January 6, 1923, 13. For more on Wood's views on Black identity, see Clement Wood, *The Glory Road: An Autobiography* (New York: Poets' Press, 1936); for Wood's

penchant to mimic Black dialect on stage, see "Lecture Was a Pleasing One," *Bluefield Daily Telegraph*, November 3, 1923, 10; for another period example of whites seeing stereotypical qualities rooted in the traits of living Black people, see Alexander A. Goldenweiser, "Racial Theory and the Negro," *Opportunity* 1, no. 8 (1923): 231.

31. Sterling A. Brown, *The Negro in American Fiction* (Port Washington, NY: Kennikat Press, 1937), 3; James Weldon Johnson, "Race Prejudice and the Negro Artist," *Harper's Monthly Magazine* 14 (June 1, 1928): 775; Charles S. Johnson, "Public Opinion and the Negro," *Opportunity* 1, no. 7 (1923): 201–2.

32. Johnson, "Race Prejudice and the Negro Artist," 775; Alain Locke, *A Decade of Negro Self-Expression*, John F. Slater Fund 26 (Charlottesville: The Michie Company, 1928), 5; Jacob Milton Sampson, "Race Consciousness and Race Relations," *Opportunity* 1, no. 5 (1923): 15, 17; Graham Romeyn Taylor, "Race Relations and Public Opinion," *Opportunity* 1, no. 7 (1923): 197. There were Black observers who argued that they needed to "sell" whites on their abilities and promise, but they still tended to see the problem as one of white perception. See "Selling Ourselves," *Philadelphia Tribune*, October 23, 1926, 16; "High Points of N.A.A.C.P. Speeches," *Pittsburgh Courier*, July 5, 1930, A9; George S. Schuyler, "Views and Reviews," *Pittsburgh Courier*, July 12, 1930, 10.

33. "Why Jim Crow Schools," *Philadelphia Tribune*, May 10, 1928; Alain Locke, ed., *The New Negro: An Interpretation* (New York: Albert and Charles Boni, 1925), 8. For a rare instance of a Black academic advocating interracial contact as a means to combat stereotypes, see "Morgan Dean Speaks at Belair High," *Afro-American*, November 1, 1930, 11.

34. Locke, *The New Negro*, 4.

35. James Weldon Johnson, "Dilemma of the Negro Author," *American Mercury* 15 (December 1928): 480; Claude McKay, "A Negro Writer to His Critics," *New York Herald Tribune: Books*, March 6, 1932, 1, 6; W. E. B. Du Bois, "Criteria of Negro Art," *The Crisis* 32, no. 6 (1926): 297; Langston Hughes, "The Negro Artist and the Racial Mountain," *The Nation*, June 23, 1926, 693.

36. Johnson, "Race Prejudice and the Negro Artist," 769–70; Johnson, *Black Manhattan* (New York: Alfred A. Knopf, 1930), 306; Alain Locke, "Goat Alley," *Opportunity* 1, no. 2 (1923): 30; Jacobs [Schuyler], "Negro Authors Must Eat," 710; Brown, "A Literary Parallel," 153; Joel Elias Spingarn, "The Negro in Art: How Shall He Be Portrayed?," *The Crisis* 31, no. 6 (1926): 279; Lippmann, *Public Opinion*, 170.

37. W. E. B. Du Bois, "The Contribution of the Negro to American Life and Culture," *Pacific Review*, June 1921, 127–32; James Weldon Johnson, *The Second Book of Negro Spirituals* (New York: Viking Press, 1926), 18–19.

38. Montgomery Gregory, "The Spirit of Phyllis Wheatley," *Opportunity* 2, no. 18 (1924): 181. Despite the appeal to arts and humanities scholars of the fine arts and literature serving as vehicles for racial justice, Henry Louis Gates Jr. soberly reminds us: "No people, in all of human history, has ever been liberated by the creation of art. None." In Henry Louis Gates Jr., *Stony the Road: Reconstruction, White Supremacy, and the Rise of Jim Crow* (New York: Penguin Press, 2019), 228. The optimism expressed by Gregory and others in the 1920s for the power of representation would quickly fade.

39. Frederick Douglass, "Pictures and Progress," manuscript fragment, 1865, pp. 15, 13, Frederick Douglass Papers, Library of Congress. In Lippmann's era, Franz Boas accentuated the links between the human "will" to make art and our shared humanity. Franz Boas, *Primitive Art* (Oslo: H. Aschehoug, 1927), 11.

40. Frederick Douglass, "A Tribute for the Negro," *The North Star*, April 7, 1849, 2; Frederick Douglass, "The Negro as a Man," ca. 1850s, p. 23, Frederick Douglass Papers, Library of Congress; Douglass, "Pictures and Progress," 18; John W. Blassigame, ed., *The Frederick Douglass Papers: Speeches, Debates, and Interviews*, vol. 3, series 1 (New Haven: Yale University Press, 1985), 462. Laura Wexler's insights on Douglass were integral to my thinking on this topic. See Laura Wexler, "'A More Perfect Likeness': Frederick Douglass and the Image of the Nation," in *Pictures and Progress: Early Photography and the Making of African American Identity*, ed. Maurice O. Wallace and Shawn Michelle Smith (Durham: Duke University Press, 2012), 18–40. The "Pictures and Progress" speech is often interpreted to promote the unique potential of photography. While Douglass's speech doubtlessly advances an argument on photography's promise, it takes a more expansive view of "pictures," giving clear attention to paintings and literature as well. That said, the potential of photography was unique. When whites compared engravings and photographs, or paintings and photographs, they were not comparing two representations with equal cultural authority; they compared an image produced through a subjective, artistic process with one created by a mechanical-chemical means generally taken by nineteenth-century Americans to be more objective. Douglass's hope was that a sufficient number of photographs of Black subjects would shift the balance of power, and compel whites to glimpse the gulf between the false depictions in other media and the more truthful renderings in photographs. Because photographs could draw attention to the gap between an individual's real appearance and society's stereotypical picture of his or her group, photography, Douglass argued, held a unique potential for catalyzing meaningful racial reform.

41. Du Bois, "Criteria of Negro Art," 297.

42. Alain Locke, "The American Negro as Artist," *American Magazine of Art* 23, no. 3 (1931): 178; Du Bois, "Criteria of Negro Art," 297, 290, 292; Madeline G. Allison, "Stories in Sculpture," *Opportunity* 2, no. 15 (1924): 81.

43. George S. Schuyler, "The Negro-Art Hokum," *The Nation*, June 16, 1926, 662–63; Hughes, "The Negro Artist and the Racial Mountain"; the two essays were subsequently reproduced together in the Black press. See George S. Schuyler and Langston Hughes, "Two 'New Negroes' Discuss Negro Art in the 'Nation,'" *New York Amsterdam News*, June 23, 1926. For reactions to the exchange, see "American Negro Art," *Opportunity* 4, no. 44 (1926): 238–39; "Negro Art 'Made in America' Is Hokum," *Sioux City Journal*, July 11, 1926, 24.

44. Schuyler, "The Negro-Art Hokum," 662.

45. Ibid., 662–63. Bert Williams (1874–1922) was a vaudeville entertainer and comedian; Aunt Jemima (1889–2021) was a fictional character and, later, brand name for a pancake mix; Uncle Tom (1852) is the title character of Harriet Beecher Stowe's novel *Uncle Tom's Cabin; or, Life Among the Lowly*; Jack Johnson (1878–1946) was the first Black world heavyweight boxing champion (1908–15), who was hounded by law enforcement for his relationships with white women; Florian Slappey was a fictional detective in the short stories and novels of Octavus Roy Cohen (1891–1959). Schuyler's understanding of stereotypes being rooted in the qualities of real people was one shared by many period whites. When Wood described for his audience at Howard University what white people picture when mention is made of Black Americans, the novelist stated: "The stereotype would be Jack Johnson instead of Jim [James Weldon] Johnson." "Clement Wood at Howard," 8. Contrasting the controversial boxer with the writer and civil rights activist, Wood distinguished bad from good stereotypes, both of which he deemed real.

46. Hughes, "The Negro Artist and the Racial Mountain," 692–94; Schuyler, "The Negro-Art Hokum," 663. For an argument on how the "American" label did not then apply to Black people, see W. E. B. Du Bois, "Postscript," *The Crisis* 35, no. 3 (1928): 96.

47. Hughes, "The Negro Artist and the Racial Mountain," 692–94.

48. White, "The Paradox of Color," 363–64. For additional examples of this sentiment, see "Selling Ourselves," *Philadelphia Tribune*, October 23, 1926, 16; "Why Jim Crow Schools," *Philadelphia Tribune*, May 10, 1928.

49. It is worth remarking that studies conducted by twenty-first-century cognitive and social psychologists have shown "that essentialism often follows from acts of categorization and explanation . . . and that it contributes to system justification processes." The act of stereotyping helps reinforce essentialist notions of identity. See John T. Jost and David L. Hamilton, "Stereotypes in Our

Culture," in *On the Nature of Prejudice Fifty Years After Allport*, ed. John F. Dovidio, Peter Glick, and Laurie A. Rudman (Malden, MA: Blackwell, 2005), 219.

CHAPTER 3

1. Ronald Steel, *Walter Lippmann and the American Century* (New Brunswick, NJ: Transaction, 1999), 116–54.

2. Lippmann, *Public Opinion*, 90–91, 95, 114.

3. For the psychological processes by which we endow artificial groups, such as races, with essences, see M. Rothbart and Marjorie Taylor, "Category Labels and Social Reality: Do We View Social Categories as Natural Kinds?," in *Language, Interaction and Social Cognition*, ed. G. R. Semin and Klaus Fiedler (Thousand Oaks, CA: Sage, 1992), 11–36. For evidence that people act as if racial and ethnic differences are innate, see Michael Omi and Howard Winant, *Racial Formation in the United States* (New York: Routledge Press, 2015). For how we make sweeping generalizations about individuals designated as members of a racial group, see Nick Haslam, Louis Rothschild, and Donald Ernst, "Are Essentialist Beliefs Associated with Prejudice?," *British Journal of Social Psychology* 41 (2002): 87–100; Vincent Yzerbyt, Steve Rocher, and Georges Schadron, "Stereotypes as Explanations: A Subjective Essentialistic View of Group Perception," in *The Social Psychology of Stereotyping and Group Life*, ed. Russell Spears and Penelope J. Oakes (Oxford: Wiley-Blackwell, 1997), 20–50. For how stereotypes justify actions against out-groups, see Henri Tajfel, *Human Groups and Social Categories: Studies in Social Psychology* (Cambridge: Cambridge University Press, 1981); John T. Jost, Mahzarin R. Banaji, and Brian A. Nosek, "A Decade of System Justification Theory: Accumulated Evidence of Consensus and Unconscious Bolstering of the Status Quo," *Political Psychology* 25, no. 6 (2004): 881–919. For "categorization" and "explanation" leading to the essentialization of people seen as belonging to racial groups, see Gregory L. Murphy and Douglas L. Medin, "The Role of Theories in Conceptual Coherence," *Psychological Review* 92 (1985): 289–316; Rothbart and Taylor, "Category Labels and Social Reality," 11–36.

4. Lippmann, *Public Opinion*, 365; see also 369–416 (Part VIII).

5. Ernst H. Gombrich, *Art and Illusion: A Study in the Psychology of Pictorial Representation* (Princeton: Princeton University Press, 1969), 65, 90. *Art and Illusion* was based on a series of lectures that Gombrich delivered in 1956. For scholarship that has expanded on Gombrich's insights, see Michael Baxandall, *Painting and Experience in Fifteenth-Century Italy* (Oxford: Oxford University Press, 1972), Svetlana Alpers, *The Art of Describing: Dutch Art in the Seventeenth*

Century (Chicago: University of Chicago Press, 1983), and Michael Baxandall, *Patterns of Intention: On the Historical Explanation of Pictures* (New Haven: Yale University Press, 1985). For the psychological studies important to Gombrich's deployment of "schema," see Jean Piaget, *Le language et la pensée chez l'enfant* (Paris: Delachaux & Niestlé, 1923); Frederic Charles Bartlett, *Remembering: A Study in Experimental and Social Psychology* (Cambridge: Cambridge University Press, 1932).

6. Eugene O'Neill, "All God's Chillun Got Wings," *American Mercury* 1, no. 2 (1924): 129–48.

7. John Corbin, "Among the New Plays: Mixed Marriages," article clipping with no publication, date, or page number preserved, Center Scrapbooks, SC Micro R-707, reel 17, "Theater" section, Schomburg Center for Research in Black Culture, New York Public Library.

8. For a comprehensive overview of the controversy, see Robert M. Dowling, *Eugene O'Neill: A Life in Four Acts* (New Haven: Yale University Press), 281–82. For an excellent period summary of the debate, see George Jean Nathan, "The Theatre," *American Mercury* 2, no. 5 (1924): 113–19.

9. Edmund Wilson, "*All God's Chillun* and Others," *New Republic*, May 28, 1924, 22.

10. "Mixed Race Play Arouses Revolt," *Morning Telegraph*, February 22, 1924, 7; Karl Decker, "O'Neill Bows Low to Publicity Bunk," *Morning Telegraph*, February 23, 1924, 1–2. For additional coverage in the paper, see James P. Sinnott, "God's Chillun Got Wings—Weak Ones," *Morning Telegraph*, March 8, 1924, 1, 7; "'Chillun' Angels' Wings Are Singed," *Morning Telegraph*, March 1, 1924, 1, 7; Karl Decker, "Jim Crow Theatre City's Next Novelty," *Morning Telegraph*, March 5, 1924, 1. For a selection of the paper's references to the Klan in the year that the play premiered, see "The Town in Review," *Morning Telegraph*, February 13, 1924, 1; "The Town in Review," *Morning Telegraph*, February 17, 1924, 1; "The Town in Review," *Morning Telegraph*, February 27, 1924, 1.

11. "Role Opposite Negro Spurned," *New York American*, February 22, 1924, 6; James Weldon Johnson, *Black Manhattan* (New York: Alfred A. Knopf, 1930), 213. For additional coverage in the *New York American*, see "Negro-White Play Has New Mystery," *New York American*, February 23, 1924, 3; "O'Neill's Play Hits New Snag," *New York American*, March 2, 1924, 3.

12. "All God's Chillun," *Time*, March 17, 1924, 16; "Art Above Nature," *Florence [SC] Morning News*, March 14, 1924, 4. For additional white reviews that were highly critical of the play from across the country, see "Play on Race Problem Is Flat Failure," *Amarillo Globe*, May 28, 1924, 1; "The Play That Was Too Well Advertised," *Anaconda Standard*, April 6, 1924, 33; "The Play That Was Too

Well Advertised," *Ogden Standard Examiner*, April 11, 1924, 11; Alice Bohe, "On the New York Stage," *Berkeley Daily Gazette*, June 3, 1924, 10; Maurice Henle, "However, Comma—," *The Bee*, March 29, 1924, 8; Malcolm Ellis, "Romance Will Oust Realism from Theater," *Davenport Democrat and Leader*, July 27, 1924, 19; "Inviting Suppression," *Kingston Daily Freeman*, March 3, 1924, 4; Arthur Brisbane, "Today," *Nevada State Journal*, March 5, 1924, 1; Arthur Brisbane, "Today," *The Capital*, March 24, 1924, 1; Arthur Brisbane, "This Week," *Ukiah Republican Press*, March 19, 1924, 2; Percy Hammond, "Percy Hammond's Letter," *Ogden Standard-Examiner*, March 19, 1924, 16; Hammond, "Percy Hammond's Letter," *Ogden Standard-Examiner*, March 25, 1924, 6.

13. Paul Robeson, "Reflections on O'Neill's Plays," *Opportunity* 2, no. 24 (1924): 369.

14. Will Anthony Madden, "Why Did Eugene O'Neill Write *All God's Chillun Got Wings*?," *Pittsburgh Courier*, April 12, 1924, 13; "Negroes Protest New O'Neill Play: Boston Will Ban *All God's Chillun Got Wings* as Insulting Colored Race," *Morning Telegraph*, February 24, 1924; "Negro Clergy Bitter at Play," *New York American*, March 15, 1924, 24; Brown and Powell quoted in Dowling, *Eugene O'Neill*, 284. For additional Black reviews critical of the play, see George Schuyler, "Views and Reviews," *Pittsburgh Courier*, October 4, 1930, 10; William Stanley Braithwaite, "The Negro in Literature," *The Crisis* 28, no. 5 (1924): 204–10; "The Negro on the Screen," *Pittsburgh Courier*, September 21, 1929, 12.

15. Tony Langston, "White Actress to Star with Paul Robeson in Eugene O'Neill's Drama," *Chicago Defender*, March 1, 1924, 1, 5; "'All God's Chillun Got Wings' Creates But Little Interest in New York Opening," *Chicago Defender*, May 24, 1924, 6.

16. Sterling A. Brown, "Our Literary Audience," *Opportunity* 8, no. 2 (1930): 43, 44; Brown, "Concerning Negro Drama," *Opportunity* 9, no. 9 (1931): 284.

17. Paul Robeson, "Reflections on O'Neill's Plays," *Opportunity* 2, no. 24 (1924): 368–70; W. E. B. Du Bois, "The Negro and Our Stage," *Sunday World*, May 4, 1924. Du Bois's essay "The Negro and Our Stage" is reproduced on page 2 of the playbill. The playbill is available at the Beinecke Rare Book and Manuscript Library, Yale University in clippings file of the James Weldon Johnson Memorial Collection, box 149, folder Robeson 1922–25. Another prominent Black supporter of the play was Alain Locke, who in reference to the play, wrote of "the fine craftsmanship and clairvoyant genius of O'Neill." See Alain Locke, "The Negro and the American Stage," *Theatre Arts Monthly*, February 1926, 112–13.

18. E. A. Carter, "All God's Chillun Got Wings," *Opportunity* 2, no. 16 (1924): 113; Eric D. Walrond, "All God's Chillun Got Wings," *Opportunity* 2, no. 19 (1924): 220–21; "The Negro on Stage," *The Crisis* 28, no. 1 (1924): 34–35.

19. W. E. B. Du Bois, "The Criteria of Negro Art," *The Crisis* 32, no. 6 (1926): 296; Sterling A. Brown, "Our Literary Audience," *Opportunity* 8, no. 2 (1930): 44.

20. Du Bois, "The Criteria of Negro Art," 296–97.

21. Brown, "Our Literary Audience," 45–46.

22. Lillian Krieger, "Theater," *The Reflex* 1, no. 3 (1927): 120.

23. For period reviews that linked the plays based on their shared theme of miscegenation, see Laurence Stallings, quoted in Heywood Broun, "Broun Calls in Great Critic to Rap His Stand on *All God's Chillun Got Wings*," *Wisconsin State Journal*, June 22, 1924, 61; George Jean Nathan, "The Theatre," *American Mercury* 2, no. 5 (1924): 113; and *All Colors: A Study Outline on Women's Part in Race Relations* (New York: The Woman's Press and Association Press, 1926), 93–94.

24. Given the efforts of Rose Mary to impersonate a Jew, it is interesting to note that at least one reviewer linked the play to minstrelsy through his reference to act 1 as the "burnt-cork first part." Donaghey Frederick, "Two of the New Plays Are Bids for Laughter," *Chicago Daily Tribune*, December 24, 1923, 13.

25. "Most Universally 'Panned' Play Breaks All Stage Records," *The Mixer and Server*, December 15, 1926, 29; Robert Benchley, "Confidential Guide," *Life*, August 10, 1922, 18; Benchley, "Confidential Guide," *Life*, August 17, 1922, 18.

26. Patterson James, "*Abie's Irish Rose*," *Billboard*, June 10, 1922, 19; George Jean Nathan, "The Bard and Some Others," *The Smart Set*, March 1923, 137.

27. The Professor, "Limitations of Intellectuals," *New Yorker*, April 11, 1925, 19; "Eight Years to Go: A Statistician Examines the Future of *Abie's Irish Rose*," *New Yorker*, April 3, 1926, 53; Robert L. Duffus, "The Play That May Make $5,000,000," *Collier's*, July 26, 1924, 5.

28. "Antiquity, Abie and O'Neill," *New York Times*, May 13, 1923, X1; "*Abie's Irish Rose*," *Variety*, July 7, 1926, 40.

29. "How a Million-Dollar Play Is Made," *Current Opinion*, August 1924, 201; "The End of *Abie's Irish Rose*," *The Nation*, November 2, 1927, 467; "*Abie's Irish Rose* at Castle Square: Joyously Amusing Comedy Arrives," *Boston Daily Globe*, October 6, 1925, 24A; "Personality and Comment," *The Spur*, February 1, 1927, 44; Duffus, "The Play That May Make $5,000,000," 30; Chandler Owen, "New Ideas on Art," *The Messenger* 7, no. 1 (1925): 23.

30. M. A. B., "Going to the Play with the Editor: *Abie's Irish Rose* and *Kosher Kitty Kelly*," *American Monthly*, July 1, 1925, 148; Arthur Hobson Quinn, *A History of the American Drama: From the Civil War to the Present Day* (New York: Harper & Brothers, 1927), 2:121–22. For reference to the play as a vehicle for softening the attitudes of the Ku Klux Klan, see Louis Weitzenkorn, "For Ann a Rose on Broadway Grows, When It Will Wither No One Knows," *New York World*, February 17, 1924, 3M.

31. Stark Young, "The Play of the Month: *Abie's Irish* Rose," *McCall's Magazine*, November 1926, 24; M. A. B., "Going to the Play with the Editor," 148; Lorenzo Jones Jr., "Theatre Talk: Atlanta Theatre Week June 1," *Atlanta Constitution*, May 24, 1925, F6; Walter D. Hickman, "There Are Many Reasons Why *Abie* Is a Big Success," *Indianapolis Times*, June 10, 1924, 3; Benjamin de Casseres, "In the Kingdom of Fol-de-Rol," *Art and Decoration* 21 (June 1924): 66.

32. Percy Hammond, "Oddments and Remainders," *New-York Tribune*, August 3, 1923, 10; J. Brooks Atkinson, "Comedies for All," *New York Times*, August 29, 1926, X1; "Says Big Bill," *Monthly Journal of Insurance Economics*, May 27, 1927, 19.

33. "The End of *Abie's Irish Rose*," *The Nation*, November 2, 1927, 467–68.

34. "*Abie's Irish Rose* A Winner," *American Israelite*, March 27, 1924, 7; "Plays: *Abie's Irish Rose*," *Medical Critic and Guide*, July 1924, 257.

35. Benjamin de Casseres, "A Non-Slush Probe into *Abie's Irish Rose*," *Theatre Magazine*, July 1927, 7–8.

36. Duffus, "The Play That May Make $5,000,000," 5; Young, "The Play of the Month," 24.

37. Gilbert Seldes, "The Theatre," *The Dial*, May 1925, 432; Robert Stone, "Broadway Falls for the Jewish 'Spirit,'" *Jewish Exponent*, March 12, 1926, 8.

38. William Z. Spiegelman, "New York Topics," *Jewish Advocate*, November 24, 1927, A1. In Peter Schuyler, "Footlight Flashes on Manhattan Stages," *Dearborn Independent*, August 8, 1925, 30, one critic claimed that the play "reeks with pro-Jewish propaganda." In "Century Crowd Likes *Abie's Irish Rose*," *Daily News*, July 3, 1922, 3, another noted its "pro-Jewish . . . arguments." For references to "stage Jews" and "imitation Jews," see Gilbert Seldes, "Jewish Plays and Jew-Plays in New York," *Menorah Journal* 8, no. 4 (1922): 236; and M. L., "Between the Book-Ends," *Menorah Journal* 10, no. 2 (1924): 196.

39. E. H., "Concerning an Epidemic," letter to the editor, *American Hebrew*, December 17, 1926, 239.

40. For reference to an anti-miscegenation sermon prompted by the play, see "Cong. B'nai Jeshurun. 257 West 88th St. Israel Goldstein, Rabbi. Friday, 'Intermarriage' (The Tragedy of *Abie's Irish Rose*)," *American Hebrew*, January 16, 1925, 328.

41. Seldes, "Jewish Plays and Jew-Plays in New York," 236.

42. "Nichols and Dimes," *Time*, January 24, 1927, 9; Zelda F. Popkin, "The Jew on the Stage and Screen," *National Jewish Monthly*, October 1927, 548.

43. Anne Nichols, *Abie's Irish Rose: A Comedy in Three Acts* (New York: Samuel French, 1952), 56.

44. Ibid., 18. Nichols had evidently absorbed the era's stereotypes on Jewish physiognomy, as her description of Solomon's face corresponds with Madison

Grant's discussion of the "round skull Jew" from Europe. Madison Grant, *The Passing of the Great Race* (New York: Charles Scribner's Sons, 1918), 17. For more on the acoustical difference in the dialects of stereotypes, see Sander L. Gilman, *Jewish Self-Hatred: Anti-Semitism and the Hidden Language of the Jews* (Baltimore: Johns Hopkins University Press, 1986), 71–80, 209–19; Gilman, *The Jews' Body* (New York: Routledge, 1991), 10–37.

45. "*Abie's Irish Rose* at Castle Square," *Boston Daily Globe*, October 6, 1925, 24A.

46. de Casseres, "A Non-Slushy Probe into *Abie's Irish Rose*," 8; "*Abie's Irish Rose* A Winner," 7.

47. Matthew Frye Jacobson, *Whiteness of a Different Color: European Immigrants and the Alchemy of Race* (Cambridge, MA: Harvard University Press, 1998), 41–73. Sander Gilman notes that the Shoah fundamentally changed how people of Jewish heritage understood their identities, writing: "Neither the high cultural attainments of the society in which one lived nor the acculturation or even assimilation of the Jew into society precluded the possibility of individuals being identified as Jews." Ironically, during the decades in which references to "Jewish blood" and the "Jewish race" declined, partly because of the Shoah, many people only tangentially connected to Judaism came to believe that their Jewishness was less of a choice than they had previously believed. Gilman, *Jewish Self-Hatred*, 319.

48. Grant, *The Passing of the Great Race*, 17–18; Francis P. Gaines, "The Racial Bar Sinister in American Romance," *South Atlantic Quarterly* 25, no. 4 (1926): 396, 402.

49. "*Abie's Irish Rose*," *Jewish Advocate*, December 17, 1925, 2. The passage quoted in the *Jewish Advocate* was taken from M. L. Malevinsky, "Anne Nichols as Creator; *Abie's Irish Rose* as a Play," *Variety*, May 20, 1925, 9.

50. Samuel P. Sharron, "Is the Jew Coming into His Own?," *Jewish Exponent*, April 29, 1927, 8.

51. "The Annual Appeal," *Jewish Advocate*, December 17, 1925, 2; "Amusement," *American Israelite*, February 14, 1924, 6. There is some ambiguity in the original script as to whether or not the Jewish characters were scripted to eat ham, but it's clear that in at least some of the stage productions the actor playing Solomon ad-libbed a line asking for "a large slice of ham, with rye bread of [*sic*] plenty of mustard." Quoted in "*Abie's Irish* Rose," *Music News*, September 5, 1924, 20. For a slightly different description of the ending, which also has Solomon eating ham, see Louis Weitzenkorn, "For Ann a Rose on Broadway Grows, When It Will Wither No One Knows," *New York World*, February 17, 1924, 3M. For additional supportive reviews in the Jewish press, see "Amusements,"

American Israelite, February 14, 1924, 6; "Amusements," *American Israelite*, March 6, 1924, 6; "Amusements," *American Israelite*, March 13, 1924, 6; "Amusements," *American Israelite*, December 7, 1928, 3; "*Abie's Irish Rose* Seats Now on Sale," *Jewish Advocate*, September 17, 1925, A6; "*Abie's Irish Rose* at the Adelphi," *Jewish Exponent*, September 3, 1926, 29; Charles H. Joseph, "Random Thoughts," *American Israelite*, December 17, 1931, 1; "*Abie's Irish Rose* Commences Its Fourth Week at Garden Pier Theatre, at Atlantic City, Monday," *Jewish Exponent*, August 10, 1923, 13; "*Abie's Irish Rose*," *Jewish Exponent*, January 7, 1927, 22; "*Abie's Irish Rose*," *Jewish Advocate*, December 3, 1925, 2; "*Abie's Irish Rose*," *Jewish Advocate*, March 11, 1926, 2; Elma Ehrlich Levinger, "The New Jew in Fiction," *American Hebrew*, January 2, 1925, 247; E. E. C., "Notes for a Modern History of the Jews," *Menorah Journal* 10, no. 1 (1924): 297. A number of these periodicals also published negative reviews of the play, sometimes in the same issues in which positive reviews appeared. The Jewish response to the play was nothing if not complex.

52. Sharron, "Is the Jew Coming into His Own?," 8.

53. For reviews that focus on the Jewish actors in productions of *Abie's Irish Rose*, see "*Abie's Irish Rose* at Garden Pier," *Jewish Exponent*, August 24, 1923, 15; "*Abie's Irish Rose* A Winner," 7; "*Abie's Irish Rose* at the Garden Pier Theatre, Atlantic City," *Jewish Exponent*, August 17, 1923, 15.

54. Paul Antonie Distler, "Exit the Racial Comics," *Educational Theatre Journal*, October 1966, 249; see also 247–54; Harley Erdman, *Staging the Jew: The Performance of an American Ethnicity, 1860–1929* (New Brunswick: Rutgers University Press, 1997), 149–52.

55. M. M. Z., "*Abie's Irish Rose*," *Jewish Forum* 5 (1922): 473. One Gentile reviewer deemed Rabbi Samuels "not Jewish-looking, and far from Jewish-spoken." Robert Littell, *Read America First* (New York: Harcourt, Brace and World, 1926), 241.

56. Stella Heilbrunn, "A Belated Critique," *The Reflex* 1, no. 5 (1927): 33.

57. Jeffrey S. Gurock, "American Judaism Between the Two World Wars," in *The Columbia History of Jews and Judaism in America*, ed. Marc Lee Raphael (New York: Columbia University Press, 2008), 93–96. Jonathan D. Sarna, *American Judaism: A History* (New Haven: Yale University Press, 2004), 223–27.

58. The review from *The Waterbury Democrat* is quoted in "Americana," *American Mercury* 10, no. 40 (1927): 428.

59. George Jean Nathan, "The Various New Plays," *The Smart Set*, November 1922, 131. Robert Littell's *New Republic* editorial was reprinted in his *Read America First*, 243. "*Abie's Irish* Rose," *Music News*, September 5, 1924, 20. The final line of the play was recounted slightly differently by the *New York World*:

"And the curtain comes down on Solomon Levy's utterly immortal line: 'Ham? Ham? I want a lot of mustard on mine.'" Weitzenkorn, "For Ann a Rose on Broadway Grows, When It Will Wither No One Knows," 3M.

60. M. M. Z., "*Abie's Irish Rose*," 473.

61. Zelda F. Popkin, "The Jew on the Stage and Screen," *National Jewish Monthly*, October 1927, 548; E. H., "Concerning an Epidemic," 239.

62. "*Abie's Irish Rose*," *Jewish Advocate*, January 21, 1926, 2.

63. Beth-Seva Hillman, "I Am a Jewess," *American Hebrew*, August 7, 1925, 385. The anarchist parade description is quoted in Aaron Antonovsky, *The Early Jewish Labor Movement in the United States* (New York: Yivo Institute for Jewish Research, 1961), 260; for more on the anarchists' efforts to wean Jewish immigrants from religion, see Antonovsky, chap. 13, "Racial Assaults on Religion," 246–71. For the symbolic importance of kashrut, see Sarna, *American Judaism*, 169–70.

64. J. Brooks Atkinson, "Comedies for All," *New York Times*, August 29, 1926, X1. For additional mainstream reviews that see the progression of the plot and ending as formulaic, see "Some Thoughts on *Abie's Irish* Rose; Some of Them Serious," *The Villager*, June 28, 1924, 156; Donaghey Frederick, "Two of the New Plays Are Bids for Laughter," *Chicago Daily Tribune*, December 24, 1923, 13; Kenneth Macgowan, "The Play of the Month," *Motion Picture Classic* 20, no. 2 (1924): 46; "*Abie's Irish Rose*," *Jewish Advocate*, January 21, 1926, 2.

65. For the development of the Jewish press in the US, see Arthur A. Goren, "The Jewish Press," in *The Ethnic Press in the United States*, ed. Sally M. Miller (New York: Greenwood Press, 1987), 203–28.

66. Eric L. Goldstein, "The Great Wave: Eastern European Jewish Immigration to the United States, 1880–1924," in Raphael, *The Columbia History of Jews and Judaism in America*, 70, 82–83.

67. Walter Lippmann, "Public Opinion and the American Jew," *American Hebrew*, April 14, 1922, 575.

CHAPTER 4

1. In a 1925 article, William McKnight Farrow noted that the Art Institute of Chicago "has the distinction of being one of the few art schools that has never closed its doors against us." W. M. Farrow, "Art and the Home," *Chicago Defender*, January 24, 1925, 4. After graduating from the School of the Art Institute of Chicago in 1917, Farrow joined the faculty, where he remained until 1945. He was the school's first Black faculty member.

2. Paul Richard, "The Black Painter's Cast of Caricatures," *Washington Post*, October 18, 1992, G1, G4. The catalogue essays that Richard criticizes appear in

Jontyle Theresa Robinson and Wendy Greenhouse, *The Art of Archibald Motley*, exhibition catalogue (Chicago: Chicago Historical Society, 1991). The art critic for *The New York Times* puzzled over the same features of Motley's art that troubled Richards when the retrospective arrived in New York City, questioning if the artist, in depicting Black figures with "large round lips and round eyes," was "aware of the extent to which those devices occasionally mimicked black stereotypes?" Michael Kimmelman, "A Black Painting Blacks with an Enigmatic Hand," *New York Times*, April 17, 1992, C22. As I will argue at greater length in this chapter, late twentieth- and twenty-first-century assessments of stereotypes in Motley's paintings are complicated by the fact that Motley consistently denied the use of stereotypes, arguing that his works sought to counterbalance older, stereotyped depictions with his "truthful" portrayals. Critics and historians tend to be more accepting of stereotypical representations when they are consciously used by members of the represented group to refute or complicate stereotypes. See Glenda R. Carpio, *Laughing Fit to Kill: Black Humor in the Fictions of Slavery* (Oxford: Oxford University Press, 2008); and Richard J. Powell, *Going There: Black Visual Satire* (New Haven: Yale University Press, 2020).

3. For contemporary analyses of race and stereotypes in Motley's art, see Cecile Whiting, "More Than Meets the Eye: Archibald Motley and Debates on Race in Art," *Prospects*, July 30, 2009, 449–76; Phoebe Wolfskill, "Caricature and the New Negro in the Work of Archibald Motley Jr. and Palmer Hayden," *Art Bulletin* 91, no. 3 (2009): 343–65; Phoebe Wolfskill, *Archibald Motley Jr. and Racial Reinvention: The Old Negro in New Negro Art* (Urbana: University of Illinois Press, 2017); Amy M. Mooney, *Archibald J. Motley Jr.* (San Francisco: Pomegranate, 2004); Richard J. Powell, ed., *Archibald Motley: Jazz Age Modernist*, exhibition catalogue (Durham, NC: Nasher Museum of Art, 2014); Jontyle Theresa and Wendy Greenhouse, *The Art of Archibald Motley*, exhibition catalogue (Chicago: Chicago Historical Society, 1991); Michael D. Harris, *Colored Pictures: Race and Visual Representation* (Chapel Hill: University of North Carolina Press, 2003), 150–78. While Motley consistently denied his use of Black stereotypes, Richard Powell produced a novel argument for why the artist may have consciously deployed stereotypes in his artwork. See Richard J. Powell, *Going There: Black Visual Satire* (New Haven: Yale University Press, 2020), 2–4, 10–11, 29, 25–36, 50, 113–14.

4. Helen Appleton Read, "Paintings by Negro Artist, Shown at the New Gallery, Attracting Much Attention," *Brooklyn Daily Eagle*, March 4, 1928, 66. Read, quoted in "News of the Artists and Galleries," *Chicago Daily News*, April 4, 1928, 19; and "The Independents," *Arts Digest* 11, no. 2 (1928): 22.

5. Marguerite B. Williams, "Negro Wins Prizes in Art Exhibition," *Chicago Daily News*, February 3, 1925, 22. Edward Alden Jewell, "A Negro Artist Plumbs

the Negro Soul," *New York Times Magazine*, March 25, 1925, 88; Carlyle Burrows, "News and Exhibitions of the Week," *New York Herald Tribune*, March 4, 1928, F11.

6. W. E. B. Du Bois, "Debit and Credit: The American Negro in Account with the Year of Grace, 1925," *The Crisis* 31, no. 3 (1926): 111; James Weldon Johnson quoted in "Negroes Here Honor to Race, Poet Declares," *Chicago Daily News*, February 25, 1931, 8.

7. "Persons and Achievements to Be Remembered in April," *Negro History Bulletin*, April 1939, 62; Albert G. Barnett, "Tanner and Motley Listed in Pair Art Exhibit," *Chicago Defender*, September 2, 1933, 10; "Race Actors Quit Imitating," *Chicago Defender*, February 23, 1929, 6; William M. Farrow, "Art and the Home," *Chicago Defender* [Chicago ed.], February 14, 1925, 10.

8. Geraldyn Dismond, "The Motley Exhibition," *Chicago Bee*, March 17, 1928, sec. 2, 1; Alain Locke, "The American Negro as Artist," *American Magazine of Art*, September 1931, 217; Charles S. Johnson, *A Preface to Racial Understanding* (New York: Friendship Press, 1936), 112.

9. Motley's 1932 artist statement was published in J. Z. Jacobson, *Art of Today: Chicago 1933* (Chicago: L. M. Stein, 1932), 93; Archibald Motley, "How I Solve My Painting Problems," 1947, 5–6, box 78, file folder 26, Harmon Foundation, Inc., Records, Manuscript Division, Library of Congress; Archibald Motley Jr., "Autobiography," n.p., 1920–1990, box 2, folder 15, Archibald Motley, Jr. Papers and Photographs Collection, Chicago Historical Society; Archibald Motley, oral history interview, January 23, 1978, and March 1, 1979, Archives of American Art, Smithsonian Institution. I write that Motley thought this way "for much of his career" because an early opinion piece he published after receiving his BFA argued for Black artists being free to choose the subject matter of their choice, unencumbered by racial considerations. Archibald Motley, "The Negro in Art," *Chicago Defender*, July 6, 1918, 16.

10. W. E. B. Du Bois, "The Contribution of the Negro to American Life and Culture," *Pacific Review*, June 1921, 129; Jessie Fauset, "Henry Ossawa Tanner," *The Crisis* 27, no. 6 (1924): 258.

11. Langston Hughes, "The Negro Artist and the Racial Mountain," *The Nation*, June 23, 1926, 693–94.

12. Locke, "The American Negro as Artist," 213–17; see also 218–20; Locke, "Foreword," *Contemporary Negro Art*, exhibition catalogue (Baltimore: Baltimore Museum of Art, 1939), n.p.; Locke, *The New Negro*, 266. Locke exerted a powerful influence within art and literary circles and did more than anyone to define how the "new Negro" would be understood. His definition was readily embraced by the influential professor of literature Benjamin Brawley. Writing in 1937, Benjamin Brawley seconded Locke's observation that America has long had

"Negro artists but not Negro art" and celebrated the "rapid" development of Negro art since 1920. Brawley noted a welcome trend toward "self-expression" and "racial subjects" among Black visual artists. Benjamin Brawley, *The Negro Genius: A New Appraisal of the Achievement of the American Negro in Literature and the Fine Arts* (New York: Dodd, Mead, 1937), 317.

13. James A. Porter, "The Negro Artist and Racial Bias," *Art Front*, June/July 1937, 8.

14. Sterling A. Brown, *The Negro in American Fiction* (Washington, DC: The Associates in Negro Folk Education, 1937), 77; Marcus Garvey, quoted in Raymond Wolters, *Du Bois and His Rivals* (Columbia: University of Missouri Press, 2002), 155; Alain Locke, *Negro Art: Past and Present* (Washington, DC: Associates in Negro Folk Education, 1936), 12.

15. Locke, *Negro Art*, 69.

16. "American Paintings on the Road to Fame," *The Museum* 1, no. 10 (1927): 152. In addition to the exhibition at the Newark Museum, *Mending Socks* was shown in 1925 in the *Twenty-Ninth Annual Exhibition by Artists of Chicago and Vicinity* at the Art Institute of Chicago; in 1928 in the *Exhibition of Paintings by Archibald John Motley, Jr.* at the New Gallery; in 1929 at the *Exhibition of Paintings and Sculpture by American Negro Artists* at the National Gallery of Art; in 1929 in the *Exhibit of Fine Arts by American Negro Artists* for the Harmon Foundation at International House, New York; in 1932 in the *John Simon Guggenheim Fellows* exhibition at Grand Central Galleries, New York; and in 1932 in the auction preview sale "Selection from the Collection of George S. Hellman" at the Anderson Galleries, New York. The Harmon exhibition had additional venues in Louisville, Nashville, Atlanta, Cleveland, and Washington, DC. At the New Gallery, the canvas was purchased by the collector Carl W. Hamilton. *Mending Socks* is also the artist's most analyzed painting by contemporary art historians. For a sampling, see Mooney, *Archibald Motley Jr.*, 13, 23–26; Kymberly N. Pinder, "'Our Father, God; Our Brother, Christ: or Are We Bastard Kin?': Images of Christ in African American Painting," *African American Review* 31, no. 2 (1997): 223–33; Powell, *Archibald Motley*, 22–24; Phoebe Wolfskill, *Archibald Motley Jr. and Racial Reinvention: The Old Negro in New Negro Art* (Urbana: University of Illinois Press, 2017), 37–38, 78–81, 85–96; Jennifer Van Horn, *Portraits of Resistance: Activating Art During Slavery* (New Haven: Yale University Press, 2022), 262–76.

17. Motley, "How I Solve My Painting Problems."

18. Motley, oral history interview, January 23, 1978, and March 1, 1979, Archives of American Art, Smithsonian Institution.

19. "Information on Artists Exhibiting at Second Annual Exhibit of Fine Arts, International House, 500 Riverside Drive, NY," box 25, file folder 2, Harmon Foundation, Inc., Records, Manuscript Division, Library of Congress.

20. Marguerite B. Williams, "Negro Wins Prizes in Art Exhibition," *Chicago Daily News*, February 3, 1925, 22.

21. Marguerite B. Williams, "Young Negro Artist Winning Recognition in the West and Also Many Prizes," *New York Amsterdam News*, February 11, 1925, 5.

22. "Chicago Artist Wins Two Prizes During Art Exhibition," *Afro-American*, February 14, 1925, B4. A fourth review describes "an old family portrait" on the back wall, leaving it unclear as to whether or not the reviewer connected the oil portrait to the sitter's "mistress." A fifth review describes the framed picture on the back wall as "a portrait of a very old Negress." The various interpretations contained in the reviews suggest the degree to which audiences were less likely to engage in a careful examination of the painting than interpret it through their preexisting mental frames. For the additional reviews, see "American Paintings on the Road to Fame," *The Museum* 1, no. 10 (1927): 152; and *Selections from the Collection of George S. Hellman*, exhibition catalogue (New York: American Art Association, Anderson Galleries Inc., 1932), 36. Amy M. Mooney notes that the Motley Archive at the Chicago Historical Society contains an 1882 photograph of Mrs. Craighead, Emily Sims Motley's former owner, inscribed "To Mammie." Mooney, *Archibald J. Motley Jr.*, 25.

23. Paul Buck, *The Road to Reunion, 1865–1900* (New York: Vintage Books, 1959), 215, 217, 213.

24. Ibid., 220–21.

25. Locke, *Negro Art*, 9–10.

26. William Howe Downes, *The Life and Works of Winslow Homer* (Boston: Houghton Mifflin, 1911), 86–87.

27. Thomas Nelson Page, *Social Life in Old Virginia: Before the War* (New York: Charles Scribner's Sons, 1897), 41, 60.

28. Buck, *The Road to Reunion*, 216; Thomas Nelson Page, *The Negro: The Southerner's Problem* (New York: Scribner's Sons, 1904), 164. For a sophisticated historical analysis of the postbellum reconciliation of North and South, see David W. Blight, *Race and Reunion: The Civil War in American Memory* (Cambridge, MA: Belknap Press of Harvard University Press, 2002). For an analysis of the social and cultural functions of the "mammy" in the twentieth-century US, see Micki McElya, *Clinging to Mammy: The Faithful Slave in Twentieth-Century America* (Cambridge, MA: Harvard University Press, 2007).

29. Brown, *The Negro in American Fiction*, 62, 84, 88.

30. Sterling A. Brown, "Negro Character as Seen by White Authors," *Journal of Negro Higher Education* 2, no. 2 (1933): 183–84, 186.

31. Charles M. Stedman, representative from North Carolina, speech on H.R. 13672, January 9, 1923 (Washington, DC: Government Printing Office, 1923),

2. For a thorough analysis of the debate over the mammy monument proposal, see McElya, *Clinging to Mammy*, 72–73, 117–18, 140–205.

32. For a detailed analysis of the development, aims, and achievements of the United Daughters of the Confederacy, with particular attention to its role in turning "a military defeat into a political and cultural victory," see Karen L. Cox, *Dixie's Daughters: The United Daughters of the Confederacy and the Preservation of Confederate Culture* (Gainesville: University Press of Florida, 2003).

33. Stedman, representative from North Carolina, speech on H.R. 13672, 3–4.

34. "'Black Mammies' Expressed by Contemporaries," *New York Amsterdam News*, March 21, 1923, 12.

35. It is noteworthy that Motley painted two canvases in 1924 that invoked a "mammy," *Mending Socks* and *Woman Peeling Apples* (*Mammy*) (*Nancy*). Both were displayed at his New Gallery exhibition in New York City in 1928. Taking for granted their readers' association of the "mammy" label with slavery, one Black newspaper described the sale of Motley's *Mammy* painting to a wealthy white collector in an article titled "Buys 'Mammy,'" *Pittsburgh Courier*, March 24, 1928, 3.

36. Despite my focus on a lack of recorded complaint regarding the visual links in *Mending Socks* to slavery, antebellum America, and mammies, I acknowledge the dangers in expecting all period sentiments to be printed and preserved. After describing the significance of the framed portrait he placed in the background of *Mending Socks* to an interviewer in 1972, Motley stated: "I've gotten this from various sources—from those artists out in New York— have criticized me for putting the . . . they say that I'm taking them back to slavery. Well, I'm not taking them back to slavery. This is the truth that exists. And the only thing I'm trying to do is tell the truth." From the context of the interview, it is not possible to determine the decade in which the criticism was expressed. Archibald Motley Jr., interview by Elaine D. Woodall, June 1972, sound recording, tape 2, side a, box 18, folder 3, Archibald J. Motley, Jr. Papers and Photographs Collection, Chicago Historical Society; the quote begins at minute 41:21.

37. Brown, "Negro Character as Seen by White Authors," 191, 201. See also Brown, *The Negro in American Fiction*, 3–4, 93–94.

38. See Frederick Douglass, *My Bondage and My Freedom* (New York: Miller, Orton, 1857), 129–32, 315–16; Harriet A. Jacobs, *Incidents in the Life of a Slave Girl* (Boston: Published for the author, 1861), 14–16.

39. "American Paintings on the Road to Fame," *The Museum* 1, no. 10 (1927): 152; Edward Alden Jewell, "Hellman Paintings on View," *New York Times*, December 11, 1932, 35; Edward G. Perry, "Ranks First Among American Artists,"

Pittsburgh Courier, March 24, 1928, 3; Archibald Motley Jr. to the John Simon Guggenheim Foundation, February 22, 1929, box 1, folder 2, Archibald Motley, Jr. Papers and Photographs Collection, 1920–1990, Chicago Historical Society. Motley was sufficiently committed to the title that he dutifully corrected the caption for a reproduction of the work in his personal copy of *The Crisis* when it erroneously labeled it *The Grandmother*. See Motley's personal copy of "The Horizon," *The Crisis* 3, no. 3 (1925): 134–35, box 8, folder 14, Archibald Motley, Jr. Papers and Photographs Collection, 1920–1990, Chicago Historical Society.

40. For more on US genre painting, see Elizabeth Johns, *American Genre Painting: The Politics of Everyday Life* (New Haven: Yale University Press, 1991); John Peter Brownlee, *American Encounters: Genre Painting and Everyday Life* (Chicago: Terra Foundation of American Art, 2012). For a study that argues against genre painting as a vehicle for reinforcing social hierarchies, see Lacey Baradel, *Mobility and Identity in US Genre Painting: Painting at the Threshold* (New York: Routledge, 2021).

41. Leila Mechlin, "Negro Artists Show Their Work in Interesting Exhibition at National Gallery," *Sunday Star*, May 19, 1929, part 2, 4; "In Native Colors," *The Survey*, August 1, 1927, 456.

42. Marguerite B. Williams, "Putting a Race in Pictures—Archibald Motley's Story," *Chicago Daily News*, July 31, 1929, 15. A number of Motley's portraits raised the specter of "types," including *Mulatress with Figurine and Dutch Seascape* (ca. 1920), *Octoroon* (1922), *Woman Peeling Apples* (*Mammy*) (*Nancy*) (1924), *The Octoroon Girl* (1925), and *Aline, an Octoroon* (ca. 1927). For a thoughtful discussion of "types" versus "portraits," see Brian Wallis, "Black Bodies, White Science: Louis Agassiz's Slave Daguerreotypes," *American Art* 9, no. 2 (1995): 54–59.

43. "Distinguished Painters Inspire Those of African Blood," *Negro History Bulletin* 2, no. 7 (1939): 58; Mechlin, "Negro Artists Show Their Work," 4.

44. Locke, *Negro Art*, 69; Locke, "The American Negro as Artist," 217; Williams, "Negro Wins Prizes in Art Exhibition," 22. Williams's uncredited review was also published in "Negro Wins Prizes Depicting His Race," *Arts News*, February 14, 1925, 6.

45. In a later review of Motley's work, Williams continued with her racialized reading, seeing his paintings as ones "swept by primitive moods that seemed born of the tropic jungles." Marguerite B. Williams, "Putting a Race in Pictures—Archibald Motley's Story," *Chicago Daily News*, July 31, 1929, 15. Locke described three "schools or trends" in Black art from the first third of the twentieth century—"Traditionists," "Modernists," and "Africanists or Neo-Primitives"—and assigned Motley's art to the "Modernists" camp. Locke, "The American Negro as Artist," 215, 217.

46. Buck, *The Road to Reunion*, 213; Brown, *The Negro in American Fiction*, 90, 88, 86, 85, 99.

47. Mechlin, "Negro Artists Show Their Work," 4; M. P., "The Art Galleries," *New Yorker*, March 10, 1928, 79.

48. "Rutherford Is 1928 Harmon Medal Winner," *Afro-American*, January 5, 1929, 1; "Harmon Awards Granted," *Pittsburgh Courier*, January 12, 1929, 12. For additional admiring Black reviews of *The Octoroon Girl*, see Perry, "Ranks First Among American Artists," 3; "New York Artists Predominate at International House Exhibit," *New York Amsterdam News*, January 9, 1929, 3. Amy M. Mooney notes the importance of the figure's light skin tone for signaling her social standing. Mooney, *Archibald J. Motley Jr.*, 41.

49. Motley, "How I Solve My Painting Problems." This particular discussion refers to Motley's *Aline, an Octoroon* (ca. 1927), but on the penultimate page of his essay, the painter writes under the heading for *The Octoroon Girl* "Same as #5," which refers readers back to his discussion of *Aline, an Octoroon*.

50. By the time *Mending Socks* was painted, Chicago homes were almost fully electrified, and the desire for "better lighting remained the primary reason." It is estimated that 92–95 percent of the city residences were hooked up to the electrical grid by 1925. Given that electrification came more slowly to Black neighborhoods, and considering that Motley lived in the almost wholly white Southwest-side neighborhood of Englewood, it is virtually certain that he had electricity at home when *Mending Socks* was painted. Harold L. Platt, *The Electric City: Energy and the Growth of the Chicago Area, 1880–1930* (Chicago: University of Chicago Press, 1991), 235, 241.

51. Paul Popenoe, *Modern Marriage: A Handbook* (New York: Macmillan, 1927), 117.

52. Sinclair Lewis, *Main Street: The Story of Carol Kennicott* (New York: Harcourt, Brace and Howe, 1920), 325.

53. Theodore Dreiser, *Free and Other Stories* (New York: Boni and Liveright, 1918), 324–25.

54. Motley, "How I Solve My Painting Problems."

55. Archibald Motley Jr., interview by his nephew Willard Motley, September 23 and 25, 1953, Chicago, transcribed by Craig Abbott, Department of English, Northern Illinois University, May 9, 2002, box 24, folder 28, The Willard Motley Collection, Rare Books and Special Collections, Northern Illinois University Libraries. In an interview with the art historian Elaine D. Woodall, Motley listed his jobs during this period as "dining car waiter on the railroad where his father was employed, as a steamfitter in the stockyard, as a coal heaver and as a plumber." Elaine D. Woodall, "Archibald J. Motley, Jr.: American Artist of the Afro-American People, 1891–1928" (master's thesis, Pennsylvania State

University, 1977), 29–30. For the interview with Motley in which he explains his job history, see Motley, interview by Woodall, June 1972, sound recording, tape 7, side b; the quote begins at minute 28:00. In a 1931 letter to the president of the New Gallery, Motley noted his continuing "lack of funds" as he sought additional gallery opportunities. Archibald J. Motley Jr. to Sidney Hellman, February 6, 1931, box 14, folder: Selected Correspondence—Motley, George Sidney Hellman Papers, Archives and Manuscripts, New York Public Library.

56. Amy M. Mooney notes the elevated social standing that Motley enjoyed by virtue of his light skin color, his and his parents' educational attainments, their Chicago neighborhood, and the family's New Orleans lineage. Mooney, *Archibald J. Motley Jr.*, 17–19. While Motley was doubtlessly more privileged than many in Chicago's Black population, it is also true that he and his family lived with significant financial uncertainty.

57. Sterling A. Brown, "Our Literary Audience," *Opportunity* 8, no. 2 (1930): 45–46.

58. Rose Henderson, "Exhibit of Painting and Sculpture by Negro Artists," *Southern Workman* 58, no. 4 (1929): 166; Carlyle Burrows, "News and Exhibitions of the Week in Art," *New York Herald Tribune*, March 4, 1928, F11.

59. Locke, *Negro Art*, 69.

60. Williams, "Putting a Race in Pictures," 15; Motley's detailed description of his painting was excerpted in "Archibald J. Motley, Jr.," *Opportunity* 6, no. 4 (1928): 115.

61. Motley's original inquiry is dated May 7, 1927; Hellman's reply is from May 9, 1927, and Motley's update on his progress is dated October 19, 1927; box 1, folder 4, Archibald Motley, Jr. Papers and Photographs Collection, 1920–1990, Chicago Historical Society. For a discussion of the research in which Motley engaged prior to producing the paintings, see Amy M. Mooney, "Representing Race: Disjunctures in the Work of Archibald J. Motley, Jr.," *Art Institute of Chicago Museum Studies* 24, no. 2 (1999): 173–74, 264n43, n44.

62. Edward Alden Jewell, "A Negro Artist Plumbs the Negro Soul," *New York Times Magazine*, March 25, 1928, 8. Despite Jewell's assertion, Motley was not the first Black artist to have had a one-person show in New York City. That distinction belongs to Henry O. Tanner, who staged a solo exhibition at the American Art Galleries in New York City in December 1908.

63. Jewell, "A Negro Artist Plumbs the Negro Soul," *New York Times Magazine*, March 25, 1928, 8.

64. Williams, "Putting a Race in Pictures," 15.

65. Worth Tuttle, "Negro Artists Are Developing True Racial Art," *New York Times*, September 9, 1928, 120.

66. "Advances in Negro Art," *The [Cincinnati] Enquirer*, May 19, 1929, 6; C. J. Bulliet, "Bulliet's Artless Comment," *Chicago Daily News*, February 11, 1933, 12; Williams, "Putting a Race in Pictures," 15.

67. While it was less common for Black publications to reference Motley's racial lineage, there are a few examples. See "Exhibit of Our Artist," *Cleveland Gazette*, March 1, 1928, 1; "Motley Stages One Man Art Exhibit," *Afro-American*, March 3, 1928, 8.

68. "Motley, Jr., Wins in Post Office Mural Contest," *Southtown Economist*, August 8, 1935, 2C.

69. Edward Alden Jewell, *Modern Art: Americans* (New York: Alfred A. Knopf, 1930), pls. 35 and 36.

70. Marguerite B. Williams, "No-Jury Exhibition Entertaining Show," *Chicago Daily News*, January 26, 1926, 7. For additional references to Motley's bloodlines in the white press, see "Negro Artist Recognized," *Decatur Herald*, February 27, 1928, 6; "One-Man Show of Art by Negro, First of Kind Here, Opens Today," *New York Times*, February 25, 1928, 1; Jewell, "A Negro Artist Plumbs the Negro Soul," 8. See also Williams, "Putting a Race in Pictures," 15.

71. Marya Mannes, "Gallery Notes," *Creative Art* 2, no. 4 (1928): xvi.

72. M. P., "The Art Galleries," 79. For a third negative white assessment, see *History of Englewood High School, 1874–1935* (Chicago: Students of Englewood High School, 1935), 157.

73. Burrows, "News and Exhibitions of the Week in Art," F11.

74. Brown, "Negro Character as Seen by White Authors," 197–98. For a discussion of Brown's aims in writing the essay, see Elizabeth Davey, "The Souths of Sterling A. Brown," *Southern Cultures* 5, no. 2 (1999): 21–23.

75. For an early, insightful analysis of the white coupling of Black Americans to the exotic primitive stereotype in the 1920s, and its decline toward the end of the 1930s, see George M. Frederickson, *The Black Image in the White Mind: The Debate on Afro-American Character and Destiny, 1817–1914* (New York: Harper & Row, 1971), 327–30.

76. "Archibald J. Motley, Jr.," *Opportunity* 6, no. 4 (1928): 114; Benjamin Brawley, *The Negro in Literature and Art in the United States* (New York: Duffield, 1929), 141. For reviews in Black publications that tout the "imaginative" nature of the paintings, see "Archibald J. Motley, Jr.," *Opportunity* 6, no. 4 (1928): 114; Dismond, "The Motley Exhibition," 1; "Exhibit of Our Artist," 1.

77. Dismond, "The Motley Exhibition," 1; "Archibald J. Motley, Jr.," *Opportunity* 6, no. 4 (1928): 114–15.

78. James A. Porter, *Modern Negro Art* (New York: The Dryden Press, 1943), 115. Alain Locke offered no assessment of the African paintings when he listed

them as one of Motley's three themes in *Negro Art: Past and Present* in 1936, but in 1940 appeared to express ambivalence, terming them "African phantasies." See Locke, *Negro Art,* 69; Locke, The *Negro in Art: A Pictorial Record of the Negro Artist and of the Negro Theme in Art* (Washington, DC: Associates in Negro Folk Education, 1940), 134.

79. W. E. B. Du Bois, *The Negro* (New York: H. Holt, 1915), 92, 93, 126, 175; Locke, *Negro Art,* 109; Brawley, *The Negro Genius,* 320–21. John Cullen Gruesser argues that prior to the Harlem Renaissance, most Black Americans saw Africa as a continent that required civilizing. For Gruesser's analysis of Locke's positions on Africa, see John Cullen Gruesser, *Black on Black: Twentieth-Century African American Writing About Africa* (Lexington: University of Kentucky Press, 2000), 50–53.

80. Alain Locke, "The Legacy of the Ancestral Arts," in Locke, *The New Negro,* 254–55. Locke's reversal of the traits traditionally ascribed to Africans and Europeans may be read as a lingering expression of "Ethiopianism," a religious strain of belief prominent among Black Americans stretching back to slavery that saw biblical evidence for the power and sophistication of peoples in Africa at a time when Europeans were barbarians. Gruesser, *Black on Black.*

81. Clare Corbould, *Becoming African Americans: Black Public Life in Harlem, 1919–1939* (Cambridge, MA: Harvard University Press, 2009), 3–12, 57–87.

82. Ibid., 58–59.

83. James Weldon Johnson, "The Larger Success," *Southern Workman* 52, no. 9 (1923): 429–30.

84. Amy M. Mooney argues that it was Motley's intent to use the African paintings to illustrate the distance between present-day Black Americans and their ancestors in Africa. Mooney, "Representing Race," 174. For a revisionist account of primitivism that sees it as a twentieth-century aesthetic employed by marginalized peoples to compensate for their loss of unalienated social worlds, see Ben Etherington, *Literary Primitivism* (Stanford: Stanford University Press, 2018).

85. Brawley, *The Negro Genius,* 320–21. Locke makes a similar, if less emphatic, point to Brawley's in *Negro Art,* 41. In a 1972 interview, Motley claimed to have been influenced by the permanent African sculpture installation at the Art Institute of Chicago while a student and after his graduation. Motley, interview by Woodall, June 1972, sound recording, tape 5, side a; the quote begins at minute 4:30.

86. Charles S. Johnson, "The Art of Winold Reiss," *Opportunity* 3, no. 25 (1925): 4–5.

87. Locke, "The Legacy of the Ancestral Arts," 266; Montgomery Gregory, "The Drama of Negro Life," in Locke, *The New Negro,* 154; "The Art of Winold Reiss," 4–5.

88. Porter, *Modern Negro Art*, 113.

89. Montgomery Gregory, "Native American Drama—A Review," *Opportunity* 3, no. 36 (1925): 382.

90. Alain Locke and Montgomery Gregory, eds., *Plays of Negro Life: A Source-Book of Native American Drama* (New York: Harper & Brothers, 1927), iii–iv, 421.

91. Sterling A. Brown, "Concerning Negro Drama," *Opportunity* 9, no. 9 (1931): 284; Brown, "Negro Character as Seen by White Authors," 203.

92. Locke, *Negro Art*, 47. For a sophisticated analysis of Locke's belief in the capacity of whites to create "Negro art," see Kobena Mercer, *Alain Locke and the Visual Arts* (New Haven: Yale University Press, 2022), 108–12. Such sentiments were also occasionally expressed by Jewish critics in their discussions of "Jewish art." In his analysis of the depiction of Jews in New York theatrical productions, Gilbert Seldes asserted: "It is obvious that no Jewish theme will be completely treated until it has been done by non-Jewish hands as well as Jewish." Gilbert Seldes, "Jewish Plays and Jew-Plays in New York," *Menorah Journal* 8, no. 4 (1922): 240.

93. Locke, *Negro Art*, 69.

94. "Archibald J. Motley, Jr.," *Arts Digest*, mid-March 1928, 22; Eleanor Jewett, "Many Commissions for Murals at Century of Progress Go to New York Artists," *Chicago Daily Tribune*, January 29, 1933, G4; "Artist and Count," *Arts Digest*, April 1, 1928, 7.

95. Locke, *The New Negro*, 266; James A. Porter, "Negro Art on Review," *American Magazine of Art* 27, no. 1 (1934): 38; Brawley, *The Negro Genius*, 317, 323.

96. "On View," *Time*, March 5, 1928, 30.

97. Read, "Paintings by Negro Artist, Shown at the New Gallery," 66; Jewell, "A Negro Artist Plumbs the Negro Soul," 22.

98. "Archibald J. Motley, Jr.," *Arts Digest*, 22; Edward Alden Jewell, "Further Comment on Exhibitions," *New York Times*, March 4, 1928, 129; Jewett, "Many Commissions for Murals," G4; Williams, "Negro Wins Prizes in Art Exhibition," 22; Williams, "The Passing of Davies—One of the Great Mysticists," *Chicago Daily News*, February 13, 1929, 15.

99. Locke, *Negro Art*, 69–70.

100. Burrows, "News and Exhibitions of the Week in Art," F11–12; Eleanor Jewett, "Many Commissions for Murals," G4; Williams, "Putting a Race in Pictures," 15.

101. For reviews in the Black press that reference the "modernity" of Motley's genre paintings, see "Negroes Show Work at Brooklyn Exhibit," *New York Amsterdam News*, June 29, 1932, 6; Edward G. Perry, "Art Devotees Purchase Paintings," *Pittsburgh Courier*, March 24, 1928, 3.

102. Hi Simons, "The 'Chicago Show' and Others," *The Arts* 2, no. 4 (1922): 213.

103. Gregory, "The Drama of Negro Life," 155.

104. Elise Johnson McDougald, "The Task of Negro Womanhood," in Locke, *The New Negro*, 370–71; Brown, *The Negro in American Fiction*, 179–80.

105. Locke, *Negro Art*, 87.

106. Ibid., 104–5.

107. Noah Webster, William Torrey Harris, and Noah Porter, eds., *Webster's International Dictionary of the English Language* (Springfield, MA: G. & C. Merriam, 1907), 653.

108. "Archibald J. Motley," *Negro History Bulletin*, April 1, 1939, 62.

109. Locke, *Negro Art*, 121–22.

110. Ibid., 52. In the spirit of my argument, I wish to make clear that my claim is that *The Banjo Lesson* looked this way to audiences in the 1920s and 1930s, not to Victorians when it was created in the nineteenth century. Motley did paint the occasional canvas depicting Black laborers or slaves, mainly for a series of WPA commissions in the 1930s focused on US history.

111. For the rise of Black support for communist prescriptions during the Great Depression, before its decline with the signing of the Molotov-Ribbentrop Pact in 1939, see Rod Bush, *We Are Not What We Seem: Black Nationalism and Class Struggle in the American Century* (New York: New York University Press, 1999), 121–29. For the ways in which the pact undermined the antifascist and anti-racist credentials of communism, see Glenda Elizabeth Gilmore, *Defying Dixie: The Radical Roots of Civil Rights, 1919–1950* (New York: W. W. Norton, 2008), 301–3.

112. Motley, interview by Woodall, June 1972, sound recording, tape 2, side a, and tape 4, side b. The references come at minute 23:30 on tape 2 and at minute 14:00 on tape 4; David C. Driskell, "Face to Face with Archibald Motley Jr.," in Powell, *Archibald Motley*, 17.

Index